YOU CAN SAY
THAT AGAIN

A word fitly spoken is like a boss of gold set in a filigree of silver.

PROVERBS 25:11, LITERAL TRANSLATION

Whatever is well said by another is mine.

SENECA

Though old the thought and oft exprest,
'Tis his at last who says it best.

JAMES RUSSELL LOWELL

Every thought which genius and piety throw into the world alters the world.

RALPH WALDO EMERSON

YOU CAN SAY THAT AGAIN

An Anthology of Words Fitly Spoken

Compiled and Arranged
by R. E. O. White

ZondervanPublishingHouse
Academic and Professional Books
Grand Rapids, Michigan

A Division of HarperCollins*Publishers*

Requests for information should be addressed to:
Zondervan Publishing House
Academic and Professional Books
1415 Lake Drive S.E.
Grand Rapids, Michigan 49506

Library of Congress Cataloging-in-Publication Data

You can say that again : an anthology of words fitly spoken / compiled and arranged by R.E.O. White.
      p.   cm.
    Includes bibliographical references and indexes.
    ISBN 0-310-53350-3 (alk. paper)
    1. Quotations. I. White, R. E. O. (Reginald Ernest Oscar), 1914– .
PN6081.Y68 1991
808.88'2–dc20   90-22587
                                                                CIP

Edited by Robert D. Wood
Designed by Rachel Hostetter

Printed in the United States of America

91 92 93 94 95 96 / AM / 10 9 8 7 6 5 4 3 2 1

This edition is printed on acid-free paper and meets the American National Standards Institute Z39.48 standard.

Contents
and Cross-references*

*Topics in parentheses are not separately illustrated.

Decision
    see: Conversion, Will
Dedication
    see: Devotion, Obedience,
        Vocation
Devotion
Discipleship
Discipline
    see: Self—Self-control
Doctrine
    see: Belief
Doubt
    see: Seasons of the Soul
(Drugs: *see* Addiction)
Duty
Earth
    see: Conservation, Nature,
        World
(Easter: *see* Jesus Christ—
    Resurrection)
Emotion
    see: Joy, Sorrow
Endurance
    see: Perseverance
Equality
Eternity
    see: Immortality, Time
Evil
    see: Sin
Evolution
Excellence
Experience
    see: Age
Faith
    see: Belief, Conviction, Patience
Family
    see: Parenthood
Fear
    see: Courage
Forgiveness
    see: Salvation

Freedom
Friendship
    see: Interdependence
Future
    see: Hope
(Gambling: *see* Addiction)
Gentleness
    see: Kindness
Giving
God
    Descriptions
    Seeking God
    Arguments
    Finding God
    Fellowship with God
Goodness
    see: Conscience, Love, Morality
Grace
    see: Salvation, Conversion
Gratitude
Greatness
Guidance
Happiness
    see: Joy
Harvest
    see: Earth, Nature, World
        Conservation
Heaven and Hell
    see: Immortality, Eternity
History
    see: Past, Future
Holiness
Holy Spirit
Hope
    see: Future, Death, Immortality
Hospitality
Humanism
    see: Man
Human Rights
    see: Justice

Humility
   see: Pride
Humour
Hypocrisy
   see: Sincerity
Idleness
   see: Work, Service
Idolatry
Ignorance
   see: Knowledge
Imagination
Imitation
Immortality
   see: Heaven, Hope, Eternity
(Incarnation: see Jesus Christ)
Independence
   see: Interdependence
Influence
Insight
   see: Wisdom
Interdependence
   see: Friendship, Independence
(Intolerance: see Tolerance)
Jesus Christ
   Tributes
   Birth, Incarnation
   Boyhood, Manhood
   Ministry, Teaching
   His Passion
   Resurrection, Ascension
   Historicity
   Assessments
   Testimony
   Response to Christ
Jews
   see: Racism
Joy
   see: Happiness
Judgement
   Divine
      see: Heaven and Hell, Reward
   Human

   see: Justice, Mercy
Justice
   see: Judgement, Mercy
Kindness
Kingdom of God
Knowledge
   see: Ignorance, Wisdom, Books
Law
(Liberty: see Freedom)
Life
Love
   God's Love
      see: God, Grace
   Love for God
      see: Devotion
   Love for Others
      see: Neighbour
Magnanimity
Man
   see: Humanism
Marriage
   see: Parenthood
Martyrdom
   see: Persecution
Mercy
   see: Justice, Kindness
Middle age
   see: Childhood, Youth, Age
Miracles
Missions
(Money: see Wealth)
Morality
Music
Nature
   see: Earth, World, Harvest
Neighbour
   see: Love—Love for Others
New Year
Oath
   see: Trust

Simplicity

Sin
  see: Evil, Salvation, Conversion

Sincerity
  see: Hypocrisy

Solitude
  see: Silence, Quietness

Sorrow
  see: Suffering, Affliction, Death

Soul
  see: Self

Strength
  see: Conflict, Courage, Power

Study
  see: Knowledge, Books

Suffering
  see: Affliction, Sorrow,
        Compassion

Suicide

Sunday

Superstition
  see: Faith, Religion, Atheism

Temptation
  see: Conflict, Self-control

Thought

Time
  see: Eternity

Tolerance

Tradition
  see: Belief, Past, History

Trifles

Trust
  see: Faith, Patience

Truth
  see: Belief, Doctrine

Unity
  see: Church

Universe
  see: Nature

Vice
  see: Virtue, Sin, Evil

Victory
  see: Conflict

Virtue
  see: Holiness, Vice, Character

Vocation
  see: Work, Idleness, Service

War

Wealth

Will
  see: Self-control

Wisdom
  see: Knowledge, Insight

Witness

Women

(Word of God: see Bible)

Words

Work
  see: Idleness, Service

World
  The Father's World
    see: Nature, Earth, Conservation

Worldliness

Worship

Youth

Zeal

INTRODUCTION

Beside providing an excellent—if unputdownable—book for browsing in, an anthology of other people's sayings, wise, beautiful, amusing, satisfying, or just memorable, is an invaluable resource for the enrichment of our own meditation and of our own public speaking. No substitute for original thought, of course, since we must already know what we are looking for, the collocation of minds here represented provides a store of illuminating, analysing, persuasive, often unarguable comment with which to adorn a discussion, clinch an argument, or "turn the tail of a paragraph" as C. E. Montague suggests.

Some well-phrased sayings are preserved to be admired, enjoyed, perhaps envied; some longer, and profound ones, to be considered and explored; many, so persuasive and unanswerable as to demand to be used again; a few, stimulating and provocative, not to be accepted without examination nor rejected without reason.

Like the general title, the citation of Scripture at the head of each subject (in the Revised Standard Version except where otherwise indicated) emphasises that such a collection of gems has very practical use for preachers, group leaders, class teachers, and others often called upon to prepare talks and addresses on Christian themes. Hence the arrangement under topics, which will often suggest new aspects or further applications, of familiar truths. But Christian ideas come in closely related families and some subjects will seem omitted which are in fact included under other headings—*Money* and *Poverty* under *Wealth*, for example; while *Conservation* invites reference also to *Earth*, *World*, and *Nature*. The *Contents and Cross-Reference* pages are intended to facilitate and reward such thoughtful use.

Attributing authorship presents problems in a few instances. Out of 2,696 quotations given, of very varying length, on 225 subjects from 998 different sources, some whose insight, aptness or beauty are well worth preserving have been so remoulded by use, distorted by memory, predilection, or changing vocabulary, or so often repeated in the process of oral (especially homiletic) transmission, that to attach one name as the "true, original source" would be hazardous, and often unfair. Various symbols, therefore, acknowledge different degrees of indebtedness for the thought, without attributing blame for inaccuracy of the form.

Thus, "indebted to" and "after . . . " mean what they say. Thirty or so of the quotations appear always to have been *deliberately* anonymous, and another thirty should be included with them, as from

the bravely dumb, that did their deed
And scorned to blot it with a name.

JAMES RUSSELL LOWELL

Another twenty-seven have long been preserved with authorship "Unknown," presumably by accident, or from earlier days when literary ethics were somewhat careless of indebtedness. Some fifty sayings or summaries undoubtedly derive in varying degrees from the wisdom, shrewdness, or teaching of others, who yet never gave their thought precisely its present form. In another twenty instances, the form but not the thought, is largely the compiler's. For all these, the symbol "X" is used to express gratitude for the content without venturing to cite any one authority for the expression.

The List of Sources is not meant to provide biographies, but only identification, by indicating a time, place, and status as background to the quotation. Occasionally, part of this information is given also with the quotation where such reminder might add emphasis or piquancy to the words. Dates are given, where known, up to 1930 or so. For later sources, courtesy suggests that "twentieth century" is sufficient; not all contemporaries wish their age or other personal details to be publicised. For similar reasons, English or American "divine" includes priests, clergy, ministers, pastors, and preachers of all types, ranks, and denominations; as "poet" includes minor poet, song writer, versifier, hymnist, and occasional verse-writer.

Two unexpected bonuses accrue from assembling perceptive reflections and striking remarks or verses on particular topics. One is the many-sidedness of Christian truth. The other is, quite frequently, an outline essay on what significant, articulate people have thought and felt, through decades, on great Christian themes, on Christian conversion, freedom, immortality, and much else. A rewarding example is the collection of quotations on *Seasons of the Soul*. And another, of course, under the general title *Jesus*.

Doubtless some would complain, with Robert Burton, of those who "lard their lean books with the fat of other works." And it might well be said that the compiler has "merely made up a bunch of other men's flowers and provided nothing of his own but the string" (Montaigne). That string, however, is twisted out of personal appreciation and gratitude. This compilation is a personal thank you for the wit, wisdom, and wealth of many scholars, poets, saints, and friends whose words have often enlightened, inspired, or nourished the soul in difficult times and varying moods. This is the only criterion of selection, a purely individual choice. May it be used, nevertheless, to preserve and share one grateful "reader's treasure-house and preacher's store."

At the very least, it must escape the criticism of T. Love Peacock, that "a book that furnishes no quotations is in my judgement no book—it is a plaything!"

A

ABBA

When we cry, "Abba! Father!" it is the Spirit himself bearing witness with our spirit that we are children of God.

PAUL: ROMANS 8:15–16

The word that Jesus used to address God . . . while the common form of address for children, was not limited to children. The childish character receded, and "Abba" acquired the warm, familiar ring we may feel in . . . "dear father."

T. E. MCCOMISKEY

In us "Abba, Father," cry,
    Earnest of the bliss on high,
Seal of immortality,
    Comforter Divine.

GEORGE RAWSON

If Joseph had not driven
Straight nails through honest wood;
If Joseph had not cherished
His Mary as he should;
Would Christ have prayed "Our Father,"
Or cried that name in death,
Unless he first had honoured
Joseph of Nazareth?

UNKNOWN

The recurrence of the sweet and deep name, Father, unveils the secret of Christ's being. His heart is at rest in God.

HUGH ROSS MACKINTOSH

Since Jesus lived, God has been another, and nearer, Being to man.

A. M. FAIRBAIRN

ADDICTION

"All things are lawful for me," but I will not be enslaved by anything.

PAUL: 1 CORINTHIANS 6:12

O God! that men should put an enemy in their mouths to steal away their brains.

WILLIAM SHAKESPEARE

At the first cup man drinks wine; at the second, wine drinks wine; at the third, wine drinks man.

JAPANESE PROVERB

The vine bears three kinds of fruit: the first pleasure, the second intoxication, the third disgust.

DIOGENES LAERTIUS

Drunkenness is nothing but voluntary madness.

SENECA

Since the creation of the world there has been no tyrant like Intemperance, and no slave so cruelly treated as his.

WILLIAM LLOYD GARRISON
(anti-slavery crusader)

Gambling is the child of avarice, the brother of iniquity, the father of mischief.

GEORGE WASHINGTON

The best throw of the dice is to throw them away.

ENGLISH PROVERB

There are two times in a man's life when he should not speculate: when he can't afford it and when he can.

MARK TWAIN

Opiate: an unlocked door in the prison of Identity. It leads into the jail yard.

AMBROSE BIERCE

What is dangerous about the tranquillizers is that . . . where you buy a pill and buy peace with it, you get conditioned to cheap solutions instead of deep ones.

MAX LERNER

It takes a deep influence in a life to enable it to stand against its only, but distorted, source of pleasure. It must be a *displacing* influence, a *filling* influence. . . . An empty life (needs) to be filled with Christ.

D. W. VERE

ADMIRATION

Remember your leaders, those who spoke to you the word of God; consider the outcome of their life, and imitate their faith.

HEBREWS 13:7

Man does not live by bread alone, but by faith, by admiration, by sympathy.

RALPH WALDO EMERSON

> We live by admiration, hope, and love;
> And even as these are well and wisely fixed,
> In dignity of being we ascend.

WILLIAM WORDSWORTH

No sadder proof can be given by a man of his own littleness, than disbelief in great men.

THOMAS CARLYLE

ADVENT

As often as you eat this bread and drink the cup, you proclaim the Lord's death until he comes.

PAUL: 1 CORINTHIANS 11:26

Away with gloom, away with doubt!
　　With all the morning stars we sing;
With all the sons of God we shout
　　The praises of a King!
　　　Hallelujah!
　　Of our returning King.

Then welcome beauty, He is fair;
　　And welcome youth, for He is young;
And welcome Spring; and everywhere
　　Let merry songs be sung!
　　　Hallelujah!
　　For such a King be sung!

　　　　　　　　EDWARD SHILLITO

The best way to prepare for the coming of Christ is never to forget the presence of Christ.

　　　　　　　　WILLIAM BARCLAY

O the crowning day is coming,
　　Is coming by and by,
When our Lord shall come in power
　　And glory from on high.
O the glorious sight will gladden
　　Each waiting, watchful eye,
In the crowning day that's coming
　　By and by.

　　　　　　　　DAVID W. WHITTLE

All men shall dwell in His marvellous light,
Races long severed His love shall unite,
Justice and truth from His sceptre shall spring,
Wrong shall be ended when Jesus is King.

Kingdom of Christ, for thy coming we pray,
Hasten, O Father, the dawn of the day
When this new song Thy creation shall sing:
Satan is vanquished and Jesus is King.

　　　　　　　　C. SILVESTER HORNE

Lo, as some ship, outworn and overladen,
   Strains for the harbour where her sails are furled:
Lo, as some innocent and eager maiden
   Leans o'er the wistful summit of the world . . .

So even I, and with a heart more burning,
   So even I, and with a hope more sweet,
Groan for the hour, O Christ, of Thy returning,
   Faint for the flaming of Thine advent feet.

F. W. H. MYERS' "ST. PAUL"

And now, eternal Jesus, Thou dost heave
Thy blessed hands to bless these Thou dost leave;
The cloud doth now receive Thee, and their sight
Having lost Thee, behold! two men in white
Two and no more: "What two attest is 'true"
Was thine own answer to the stubborn Jew.
Come then, Thou faithful Witness, come dear Lord,
Upon the clouds again, to judge this world.

HENRY VAUGHAN

I cannot tell how all the lands shall worship
   When, at His bidding, every storm is stilled;
Or who can say how great the jubilation
   When all the hearts of men with love are filled?
But this I know, the skies will thrill with rapture,
   And myriad, myriad human voices sing,
And earth to heaven, and heaven to earth will answer,
   At last the Saviour, Saviour of the world, is King.

W. Y. FULLERTON

ADVENTURE

By faith Abraham obeyed when he was called to go out . . . and he
went out, not knowing where he was to go.

HEBREWS 11:8

   I do not fear the road,
   The great adventure into tracts unknown;

My questing spirit wanders not alone
· Where other feet have trod.

ELIZABETH F. HOWARD

I go to prove my soul!
I see my way as birds their trackless way.
I shall arrive! What time, what circuit first,
I ask not . . .
In some time, His good time, I shall arrive:
He guides me and the bird. In His good time.

ROBERT BROWNING

He ne'er is crowned
With immortality, who fears to follow
Where airy voices lead.

JOHN KEATS

ADVOCATE

If any one does sin, we have an advocate with the Father, Jesus Christ the righteous.

JOHN: 1 JOHN 2:1

The Advocate of the old jurisprudence, in the best times of antiquity, was no hired pleader . . . ; he was his client's patron and standing counsel, the head of the order or of the clan to which both belonged, bound by the claims of honour and family association to stand by his humble dependent, and to see him through when his legal standing was imperilled. He was the client's natural protector, the appointed captain of his salvation.

G. G. FINDLAY

For there Christ is the King's attorney,
Who pleads for all without degrees . . .
And when the twelve grand million jury
Of our sins with direful fury
'Gainst our souls black verdicts give,
Christ pleads His death, and then we live.

WALTER RALEIGH (Sixteenth Century)

Even now, behold, my witness is in heaven,
and he that vouches for me is on high.

JOB: JOB 16:19

Good and great God! How should I fear
To come to Thee, if Christ not there!
Could I but think, He would not be
Present, to plead my cause for me;
To Hell I'd rather run, than I
Would see Thy face, and He not by.

ROBERT HERRICK

O Thou, the contrite sinner's Friend,
    Who, loving, lovest to the end,
On this alone my hopes depend,
    That Thou wilt plead for me.

When I have erred and gone astray,
    Afar from Thee and wisdom's way,
And see no glimmering, guiding ray,
    Still, Saviour, plead for me.

When the full light of heavenly day
    Reveals my sins in dread array,
Say Thou hast washed them all away;
    Dear Saviour, plead for me.

CHARLOTTE ELLIOTT

AFFLICTION

. . . despise not the chastening of the Almighty.
    For he wounds, but he binds up;
he smites, but his hands heal.

JOB 5:17–18

Then welcome each rebuff
That turns earth's smoothness rough,
Each sting that bids nor sit nor stand—but Go!

ROBERT BROWNING

Calamity is man's true touchstone.

FRANCIS BEAUMONT AND JOHN FLETCHER

Let us be patient! These severe afflictions
Not from the ground arise,
But oftentimes celestial benedictions
Assume this dark disguise.

HENRY WADSWORTH LONGFELLOW

He knows not his own strength that hath not met adversity.

BEN JONSON

The Lord gets his best soldiers out of the highlands of affliction.

CHARLES H. SPURGEON

Unto a broken heart
No other one may go
Without the high prerogative
Itself hath suffered too.

EMILY DICKINSON

If afflictions refine some, they consume others.

THOMAS FULLER

I ask Thee for a thoughtful love,
Through constant watching wise
To meet the glad with joyful smiles,
To wipe the weeping eyes;
A heart at leisure from itself,
To soothe and sympathise.

ANNE L. WARING

In all their affliction he was afflicted,
and the angel of his presence saved them.

ISAIAH 63:9

Blessed be the God and Father of our Lord Jesus Christ, the Father of
mercies and God of all comfort, who comforts us in all our affliction, so

that we may be able to comfort those who are in any affliction, with the comfort with which we ourselves are comforted by God.

PAUL: 2 CORINTHIANS 1:3–4

AGE

[Israel] who have been borne by me from your birth,
    carried from the womb;
even to your old age I am He,
    and to gray hairs I will carry you.
I have made, and I will bear;
    I will carry and will save.

ISAIAH 46:3–4

Abide with me, fast falls the eventide;
The darkness deepens—Lord, with me abide.

HENRY FRANCIS LYTE

It is too late! Ah, nothing is too late
Till the tired heart shall cease to palpitate.
Cato learned Greek at eighty; Sophocles
Wrote his grand Oedipus, and Simonides
Bore off the prize of verse from his compeers,
When each had numbered more than fourscore years . . .
Chaucer, at Woodstock with the nightingales,
At sixty wrote the Canterbury Tales;
Goethe at Weimar, toiling to the last,
Completed Faust when eighty years were past.
These are indeed exceptions, but they show
How far the gulf-stream of our youth may flow
Into the Arctic regions of our lives . . .
For age is opportunity no less
Than youth itself, though in another dress;
And as the evening twilight fades away
The sky is filled with stars invisible by day.

HENRY WADSWORTH LONGFELLOW

For old age is not honored for length of time,
    nor measured by number of years;

but understanding is gray hair for men,
and a blameless life is ripe old age.

WISDOM OF SOLOMON 4:8–9

It is always the case that when the Christian looks back, he is looking at the forgiveness of sins.

KARL BARTH

Grow old along with me!
    The best is yet to be,
The last of life, for which the first was made:
    Our times are in His hand
    Who saith "A whole I planned,
Youth shows but half; trust God, see all, nor be afraid."

ROBERT BROWNING

To know how to grow old is the master work of wisdom, and one of the most difficult chapters in the great art of living.

HENRI F. AMIEL

To keep the heart unwrinkled, to be hopeful, kindly, cheerful, reverent— that is to triumph over old age (T. B. ALDRICH); The true way to render age vigorous is to prolong the youth of the mind (MORTIMER COLLINS).

Nobody loves life like an old man.

SOPHOCLES

Old age hath yet his honour and his toil;
Death closes all: but something ere the end,
Some work of noble note may yet be done . . .
Though much is taken, much abides; and though
We are not now that strength which in old days
Moved earth and heaven, that which we are, we are;
One equal temper of heroic hearts,
Made weak by time and fate, but strong in will
To strive, to seek, to find, and not to yield.

ALFRED TENNYSON

The older I grow, and the more I abandon myself to God's will, the less I value intelligence that wants to know, and the will that wants to do; as the only element of salvation I recognise faith, which can wait patiently without asking too many questions.

UMBERTO ECO

O Lord, support us all the day long of this troublous life,
until the shadows lengthen, and the evening comes,
and the busy world is hushed,
the fever of life is over,
and our work is done.
Then, Lord, in Thy mercy, grant us safe lodging, a holy rest,
and peace at the last, through Jesus Christ our Lord.

UNKNOWN

ANGER

Be angry but do not sin; do not let the sun go down on your anger, and give no opportunity to the devil.

PAUL: EPHESIANS 4:26–27

Anger is one of the sinews of the soul; he that lacks it hath a maimed mind. . . . Act nothing in furious passion: it is putting to sea in a storm.

THOMAS FULLER

To be angry with the right person, to the right extent, at the right time, with the right object and in the right way—it is not everyone who can do it.

ARISTOTLE

I would that to the world would come again
That indignation, that anger of the Lord,
Which once was known among us.

LASCELLES ABERCROMBIE

Chain anger, lest it chain thee.

HINDU PROVERB

Renan even represented [Christ's] righteous anger at Jerusalem as a mere nervous breakdown after the idyllic expectations of Galilee. As if there were any inconsistency between having a love for humanity and having a hatred for inhumanity!

G. K. CHESTERTON

Beware the fury of a patient man!

JOHN DRYDEN

ART

"See, the Lord has called by name Bezalel . . . and he has filled him with the Spirit of God, with ability, with intelligence, with knowledge, and with all craftsmanship, to devise artistic designs, to work in gold and silver and bronze, in cutting stones for setting, and in carving wood, for work in every skilled craft."

EXODUS 35:30–33

He never took his pencil up without a prayer, and could not paint a Crucifixion without tears running down his cheeks.

GIORGO VASARI, OF FRA ANGELICO

Neither painting nor sculpture can any longer bring peace to the soul that seeks the divine love, which opened its arms on the cross to receive us.

MICHELANGELO

Fine art is that in which the hand, the head and the heart of man go together.

JOHN RUSKIN

Religious poetry . . . touches the love of beauty inherent in man's soul, and the thirst for God which, however unrecognised, lurks in every human heart.

G. LACEY MAY

Nature is the art of God.

DANTE

A faithful study of the liberal arts humanizes character.

OVID

Give honour unto Luke Evangelist;
    For he it was (the aged legends say)
Who first taught Art to fold her hands and pray.

DANTE GABRIEL ROSSETTI

ASPIRATION

Set your minds on things that are above.

PAUL: COLOSSIANS 3:2

A lover of Jesus and of truth . . . can lift himself above himself in spirit.

THOMAS À KEMPIS

Raise thy head—take stars for money (GEORGE HERBERT); Not failure, but low aim, is crime (JAMES RUSSELL LOWELL); Live unto the dignity of thy nature (THOMAS BROWNE); God give me hills to climb, and strength for climbing (ARTHUR GUITERMAN).

Ah, but a man's reach should exceed his grasp,
Or what's a heaven for?

ROBERT BROWNING

Let each man think himself an act of God,
His mind a thought, his life a breath of God;
And let each try, by great thoughts and good deeds,
To show the most of heaven he hath in him.

P. J. BAILEY

The thing we long for, that we are
For one transcendent moment.

JAMES RUSSELL LOWELL

I had Ambition, by which sin
The angels fell;
I climbed, and step by step, O Lord,

Ascended into Hell.
Returning now to peace and quiet,
And made more wise,
Let my descent and fall, O Lord,
Be into Paradise.

W. H. DAVIES

Slight not what's near through aiming at what's far (EURIPIDES); He who stands on tiptoe does not stand firm (LAO TSE); He that strives to touch the stars oft stumbles at a straw (EDMUND SPENSER).

Nor strive to wind ourselves too high
For sinful man beneath the sky.

JOHN KEBLE

I would be true, for there are those who trust me;
I would be pure, for there are those that care.
I would be strong, for there is much to suffer;
I would be brave, for there is much to dare.
I would be friend to all—the foe, the friendless;
I would be giving, and forget the gift.
I would be humble, for I know my weakness;
I would look up—and laugh—and love—and lift.

HOWARD A. WALTER

All we have willed or hoped or dreamed
Of good shall exist . . .
The high that proved too high, the heroic for earth too hard,
The passion that left the ground to lose itself in the sky,
Are music sent up to God by the lover and the bard;
Enough that He heard it once: we shall hear it by and by.

ROBERT BROWNING

ATHEISM

The fool says in his heart, "There is no God."

PSALM 14:1

"There is no God" the foolish saith,
But none, "There is no sorrow";
And nature oft the cry of faith
In bitter need will borrow.
Eyes, which the preacher could not school,
By wayside graves are raisèd;
And lips say "God be pitiful"
Who ne'er said "God be praisèd."

ELIZABETH BARRETT BROWNING

No rational man, with sensitive conscience and warm affections, can be content to live in a world whose origin is accident, in which reason, sanity, love, and moral purpose have no home. An idiot world frightens us, frustrates, infuriates, offends us.

ANONYMOUS

There is no unbelief:
Whoever plants a seed beneath the sod
And waits to see it push away the clod—
    He trusts in God.

LIZZIE YORK CASE

It is the melancholy fact that all characteristically human values, which foster science, art, morality, civilisation, confer no advantage for survival in the struggle for existence. The intellectual brilliance of Euclid or Einstein, the imagination of Shakespeare, the genius of Mozart, the selfless sensitivity of the saint, are useless by-products of a mechanistic process of development. On the chance-evolutionary theory of origins, all that civilisation prizes ought to have been weeded out long ago, in the relentless competition of the ruthlessly selfish for survival in a morally indifferent world.

X

The life-force, afflicted with doubt
As to what it was bringing about,
Cried, "Alas, I am blind,
But I'm making a mind
Which may possibly puzzle it out."

THOMAS THORNELY

Forth from his dark and lonely hiding-place
(Portentous sight!) the owlet Atheism,
Sailing on obscene wings athwart the Noon,
Drops his blue-fringed lids, and holds them close,
And hooting at the glorious sun in heaven,
Cries out, "Where is it?"

SAMUEL TAYLOR COLERIDGE

A little philosophy inclineth man's mind to atheism, but depth in philosophy bringeth men's minds about to religion.

FRANCIS BACON

AUTHORITY

"It is no longer because of your words that we believe, for we have heard for ourselves, and we know that this is indeed the Savior of the world."

SAMARITAN VILLAGERS: JOHN 4:42

The ultimate authority, which alone is infallible, is the eternal and living truth (WILLIAM R. INGE) . . . is truth as it reveals itself in experience and compels assent (C. H. DODD); Scripture is imperishable treasure, yet our authority is not in the words but in the Word (X).

But man, proud man,
Dressed in a little brief authority
Most ignorant of what he's most assured,
His glassy essence, like an angry ape
Plays such fantastic tricks before high heaven
As make the angels weep.

WILLIAM SHAKESPEARE

Superior knowledge has the authority of truth, against which it is folly to revolt; greater experience has the authority of wisdom, against which slick cleverness sounds silly; the majority has the authority of justice, forbidding the few to injure the many—and vice versa; deeper insight has the authority of valid discovery, which only equal insight may question; intrinsic right has the authority of God. All so-called "authorities" derive their right to speak from one or other of these sources—or they lie.

ANONYMOUS

New faces
Have more authority than accustomed ones.

EURIPIDES

The reliance on authority measures the decline of religion.

RALPH WALDO EMERSON

The tension between authority and freedom, between tradition and inspiration, cannot safely be resolved either by the repudiation of authority, or by the repression of inspiration. The church fares best when apostle and prophet stand together as the firm foundation of its life.

C. H. DODD

The man who says to one "Go" and he goeth, and to another "Come" and he cometh, has in most cases more sense of restraint and difficulty than the man who obeys him.

JOHN RUSKIN

Authority intoxicates.

SAMUEL BUTLER I

When Euclid says, "The angles at the base of an isosceles triangle are equal," *it stays said.*

ALISTAIR COOKE

BEAUTY

He has made everything beautiful in its time.

ECCLESIASTES 3:11

Beauty is a form of divine speech (F. J. GILLMAN) . . . God's handwriting (ANONYMOUS). . . . The gift of God (ARISTOTLE). . . . The smile of God (ROBERT UNDERWOOD JOHNSON); The good is the beautiful (PLATO); "She has done a beautiful thing" (JESUS: MATTHEW 26:10).

> If you get simple beauty and naught else,
> You get about the best thing God invents.

ROBERT BROWNING

There's a lump of greasy pigment at the end of Michael Angelo's hog-bristle brush, and by the time it has been laid on the stucco there is something there that all men with eyes recognise as divine.

EDWARD BURNE-JONES

> Tell them, dear, that if eyes were made for seeing,
> Then beauty is its own excuse for being.

RALPH WALDO EMERSON

Everything, from a dew-drop to a mountain, is the bearer of beauty. And yet beauty has no function, no utility. . . . It is its own excuse for being. It greases no wheels, it bakes no puddings. It is a gift of sheer grace. . . . It must imply behind things a Spirit that enjoys beauty.

RUFUS M. JONES

> Look thy last on all things lovely
> Every hour.

WALTER DE LA MARE

Nothing in human life, least of all in religion, is ever right until it is beautiful.

HARRY EMERSON FOSDICK

BELIEF

"Blessed are those who have not seen and yet believe."

JESUS: JOHN 20:29

Christian belief is no mere intellectual persuasion, but the capitulation of the mind to Christ's teaching, of the heart to Christ's love, of the will to Christ's lordship; it is the outgoing of the whole self in trust and allegiance towards Christ as Master, Redeemer, Son of God.

ANONYMOUS

I will not call it my philosophy, for I did not make it. God and humanity made it, and it made me.

G. K. CHESTERTON

> I lived on borrowings of belief,
>   Only the arguments were mine—
> An unremunerative brief,
>   And hard, defending the divine.
> Then Jesus stood before my mind;
>   I was arrested, held by Him:
> And in astonishment I find
>   Belief in God no longer dim.

"A MODERN SCHOLAR"

Belief gives the trend to politics, constitutes the rule of business, composes the atmosphere of home, creates the horizon of the soul, becomes the arbiter of our destinies. For character itself is the precipitate of belief.

JOHN WATSON

Having creeds without faith is like hugging a timetable without making a journey.

JOHN HENRY JOWETT

He *does not believe*, that does not live according to his "belief."

THOMAS FULLER

> So he died for his faith: that was fine;
>   More than most of us do.
> But say this, can you add to this line
>   That he lived for it too?
> But to live, every day, to live out
>   All the truth that he meant,
> While his friends met his conduct with doubt,
>   And the world—with contempt?

UNKNOWN

It is natural for the mind to believe, for the will to love; for want of true objects, they must attach themselves to false.

BLAISE PASCAL

Man prefers to believe what he prefers to be true.

FRANCIS BACON

A man must not swallow more beliefs than he can digest.

H. HAVELOCK ELLIS

If we begin by believing absurdities we shall end by committing atrocities.

WILLIAM R. INGE

> Light half-believers in our casual creeds,
>   Who never deeply felt, or clearly will'd;
> Whose insight never has borne fruit in deeds,
>   Whose vague resolves never have been fulfilled—
> We hesitate and falter life away,
> And lose tomorrow the ground won today.

MATTHEW ARNOLD

There is no justification without sanctification, no forgiveness without renewal of life, no real faith from which the fruits of new obedience do not grow.

MARTIN LUTHER

BIBLE

"You study the scriptures diligently, supposing that in having them you have eternal life; yet, although their testimony points to me, you refuse to come to me for that life."

JESUS: JOHN 5:39–40, NEB

The Bible is "history preaching" (P. T. FORSYTH). . . . The cradle wherein Christ is laid (MARTIN LUTHER). . . . Literature, not dogma (GEORGE SANTAYANA). . . . The word that works (COMPARE 1 THESSALONIANS 2:13). . . . One book wherein, for several thousands of years, the spirit of man has found light, and nourishment, and an interpreting response to whatever is deepest in him (THOMAS CARLYLE).

> Most wondrous book! The only star
> By which the bark of man could navigate
> The sea of life, and gain the coast of bliss
> Securely.

ROBERT POLLOK

The Bible is like an old Cremona; it has been played upon by the devotion of thousands of years until every word and particle is public and tunable.

RALPH WALDO EMERSON

Not a book dropped down from heaven, untouched with a feeling of our infirmities, but a book wrought out through the struggles, hopes, trials, victories, of the soul of man in his quest after God.

JOHN WATSON

We present you with this Book, the most valuable thing that this world affords; here is wisdom; this is the royal law; these are the lively oracles of God.

BRITISH CORONATION SERVICE

The Bible, alone, is the religion of Protestants (WILLIAM CHILLINGWORTH, EPITAPH). . . . Not the Bible alone, but belief in the inspiration of the individual, is the religion of Protestants (WILLIAM R. INGE).

We may not contrast scripture and tradition; the primary tradition is scripture, and scripture is the primary tradition.

STEPHEN WINWARD

There are times when one wishes he had never read the New Testament, that he might some day open St. Luke's Gospel, and the most beautiful book in the world might come upon his soul like sunrise.

JOHN WATSON

It is most wonderful to read the Bible at such a time! How alive it suddenly becomes, and how real! It really gives you the impression of having been written especially for prisoners and for prison.

GERMAN PASTOR, IN PRISON 1933–1937

Of all history-makers, none equal those who give men in their mother tongue the word of God.

LONDON REVIEW 1859

I wish that even the weakest woman might read the Gospels and the Epistles of St. Paul. I wish that they were translated into all languages . . . I long that the husbandman should say them to himself as he follows the plough, that the weaver should hum them to the tune of his shuttle, that the traveller should beguile with them the weariness of his journey.

ERASMUS

The church did not at first regard these writings as specially authoritative because they were canonical; they became canonical because they had already made good their authority (C. H. DODD); [In canonising certain writings] the church was not conferring authority on the books; rather, it was acknowledging them to possess authority (ARTHUR MICHAEL RAMSEY).

The meaning of a passage is never ours to decide, but only ours to discover.

ANONYMOUS

The analysis of sources [of scripture] sets oft-quoted verses against the background of their time, and the purpose of the original writers, providing a control for exegesis by insisting that every passage *means* what it was intended by the writer to convey to the original readers, in their terms, for their immediate need, as the Spirit led.

X

Be sure that you go to the author to get at *his* meaning, not to find yours.

JOHN RUSKIN (not said of Scripture only)

We pick out a text here and there to make it serve our turn; whereas if we took it all together, and considered what went before and what followed after, we should find it meant no such thing.

JOHN SELDEN, IN 1689

The allegorical method [of interpretation] neutralised the social contents of the Bible by spiritualising everything. It was an ingenious way of getting ready-made doctrinal results. . . . But it never took anything out of the Bible that was not already in the mind of the interpreter, and it learned nothing new from the Bible.

WALTER RAUSCHENBUSCH

Five short narratives, a few letters, a handful of tracts and an underground pamphlet—nothing could look less like a textbook on religion than our New Testament. It is hardly a treatise on doctrine, certainly not a blueprint for heaven; it most resembles a driver's handbook designed to keep the working Christian on the road. We might call it a do-it-yourself manual for pilgrims, if it did not constantly warn that you cannot do-it-yourself. But it is a "How to . . . " book, a guide to actually living the Christian life.

ANONYMOUS

Although St. John saw many strange monsters in his vision, he saw no creature so wild as one of his own commentators.

G. K. CHESTERTON

The devil can cite scripture for his purpose.

WILLIAM SHAKESPEARE

Learn to read slow: all other graces
Will follow in their proper places.

WILLIAM WALKER

He who would fulfill the scriptures must see to it that he does not miss God in his own soul.

MEISTER ECKHART

BIGOTRY

He is puffed up with conceit, he knows nothing; he has a morbid craving for controversy and for disputes about words, which produce envy, dissension, slander, base suspicions, and wrangling among men who are depraved in mind and bereft of the truth.

1 TIMOTHY 6:4–5

Bigotry may be roughly defined as the anger of men who have no opinions.

G. K. CHESTERTON

Bigotry: to be positive; to be mistaken at the top of one's voice.

AMBROSE BIERCE

The man who never alters his opinion is like standing water, and breeds reptiles of the mind.

WILLIAM BLAKE

For modes of faith let graceless zealots fight:
His can't be wrong whose life is in the right.

ALEXANDER POPE

Bigotry tries to keep truth safe in its hand
With a grip that kills it.

TAGORE

The implacable stand is directed more against the doubt within than the assailant without.

ERIC HOFFER

Be calm in arguing; for fierceness makes
Error a fault, and truth discourtesy.

GEORGE HERBERT

A bigot delights in public ridicule, for he begins to think he is a martyr.

SYDNEY SMITH

Ah, snug lie those that slumber
Beneath Conviction's roof;
Their floors are sturdy lumber,
Their windows weather-proof.
But I sleep cold forever,
And cold sleep all my kind:
For I was born to shiver
In the draught from an open mind.

PHYLLIS MCGINLEY

BLESSING

Blessed be the God and Father of our Lord Jesus Christ, who has blessed us in Christ with every spiritual blessing.

PAUL: EPHESIANS 1:3

But O! Thou bounteous Giver of all good,
Thou art of all Thy gifts Thyself the crown!
Give what Thou canst, without Thee we are poor;
And with Thee rich, take what Thou wilt away.

WILLIAM COWPER

The world had its own idea of blessedness. Blessed is the man who is always right . . . who is satisfied with himself . . . who is strong . . . who rules . . . who is rich . . . who is popular . . . who enjoys life. It comes with a shock, that not one of these men entered Jesus' mind when [in the Beatitudes] He treated of blessedness.

JOHN WATSON

Bless me in this life with but peace of my conscience, command of my affections, the love of Thyself, and of my dearest friends, and I shall be happy enough to pity Caesar.

THOMAS BROWNE

BOOKS

Of making many books there is no end.

ECCLESIASTES 12:12 (perhaps 200 B.C.)

A good book is the precious life-blood of a master-spirit, embalmed and treasured up on purpose to a life beyond life.

JOHN MILTON

Thank God for books! And yet thank God that the great realm of truth lies yet outside of books, too vast to be mastered by types, or imprisoned in libraries.

HENRY WARD BEECHER

Richard Sibbes, the old Puritan, wrote *The Bruised Reed,* which fell into the hands of a tin-pedlar who gave it to a boy. Through it, that boy became saintly Richard Baxter, who wrote *A Call to the Unconverted* so kindling the flame in the heart of Philip Doddridge, who in turn wrote *The Rise and Progress of Religion in the Soul.* This changed the life of William Wilberforce, and indirectly that of thousands of slaves. Wilberforce wrote *A Practical View of Christianity,* which deeply affected Leigh Richmond, leading him to write *The Dairyman's Daughter,* a most powerful influence in the life of Queen Victoria, and a major factor in transforming Thomas Chalmers, one of Scotland's greatest preachers and social reformers.

AFTER RITA SNOWDEN

This books can do—nor this alone: they give
New views to life, and teach us how to live;
They soothe the grieved, the stubborn they chastise;
Fools they admonish, and confirm the wise.
Their aid they yield to all: they never shun
The man of sorrow, nor the wretch undone . . .
Nor tell to various people various things,
But show to subjects what they show to kings.

GEORGE CRABBE

A book is a mirror: if an ass peers into it, you cannot expect an apostle to look out.

GEORG C. LICHTENBERG

The richest minds need not large libraries.

AMOS B. ALCOTT

A man is known by the company his mind keeps.

THOMAS BAILEY ALDRICH

There is a great deal of difference between the eager man who wants to read a book and the tired man who wants a book to read.

G. K. CHESTERTON

How many a man has dated a new era in his life from the reading of a book.

HENRY DAVID THOREAU

BROTHERHOOD

Have we not all one father? Has not one God created us?

MALACHI 2:10

The Fatherhood of God is the only source of the brotherhood . . . Brothers are born, not made.

G. S. BARRETT

Modern progress has made the world a neighbourhood: God has given us the task of making it a brotherhood.

PHILIP GIBBS

A low capacity for getting along with those near us often goes hand in hand with a high receptivity to the idea of the brotherhood of man.

ERIC HOFFER

There is a destiny which makes us brothers;
None goes his way alone.

EDWIN MARKHAM

Either men will learn to live as brothers or they will die like beasts.

MAX LERNER

> Yes, you'd know him for a heathen
> If you judged him by the hide;
> But bless you, he's my brother,
> For he's just like me inside.

ROBERT FREEMAN

A shape loomed ahead in the heavy morning mist; I thought it was a tree, and then a farm beast; but as I approached I saw it was a man, and when we drew near I recognised my brother.

X

CHARACTER

He was . . . a good and righteous man, who had not consented to their purpose and deed, and he was looking for the kingdom of God.

LUKE 23:50–51

Character is the unification of personality through a dominant purpose.

UNKNOWN

Character is much easier kept than recovered (THOMAS PAINE) . . . is higher than intellect (RALPH WALDO EMERSON). . . . Can do without success (RALPH WALDO EMERSON) . . . is destiny (HERACLITUS) . . . is what you are in the dark (DWIGHT L. MOODY) . . . is to count as naught in world, or church, or State, but inwardly in secret to be great (JAMES RUSSELL LOWELL).

But all, that the world's coarse thumb
   And finger failed to plumb,
So passed in making up the main account:
   All instincts immature,
   All purposes unsure,
That weighed not as his work, yet swelled the man's amount:

Thoughts hardly to be packed
Into a narrow act,
Fancies that broke through language and escaped;
   All I could never be,
   All men ignored in me,
This I was worth to God, whose wheel the pitcher shaped. . . .

He fixed thee mid this dance
   Of plastic circumstance,
This present thou forsooth wouldst fain arrest:
   Machinery just meant
   To give thy soul its bent,
Try thee and turn thee forth, sufficiently impressed.

ROBERT BROWNING

By nothing do men show their character more than by the things they laugh at (GOETHE). . . . A man never shows his own character so plainly as by the way he portrays another's (J. PAUL F. RICHTER).

Sow a thought and you reap an act; sow an act and you reap a habit; sow a habit and you reap a character; sow a character and you reap a destiny.

CHARLES A. HALL/CHARLES READE

Genius develops in quiet places,
Character out in the full current of human life.

GOETHE

Our deeds still travel with us from afar,
And what we have been makes us what we are.

GEORGE ELIOT

His magic was not far to seek,
He was so human! Whether strong or weak,
Far from his kind he neither sank nor soared,
But sat an equal guest at every board.
No beggar ever felt him condescend,
No prince presume; for still himself he bare
At manhood's simple level, and where'er
He met a stranger, there he left a friend.

JAMES RUSSELL LOWELL

A life founded upon faith, informed with truth, directed by goodwill, upheld by honour, preserved in purity, dedicated to service, nerved by obedience, nourished by prayer, graced with humility, irradiated by charity, fruitful of social impulses, cheered with abounding hopefulness, strong to defend others and oppose wrong, motivated by steadfast love for Christ, is the noblest life a man can know—and never wholly impossible so long as life still lasts.

X

He is truly good who hath great charity, truly great who is little in his own estimation . . . truly wise who counts all earthly things but dross that he may win Christ, truly learned who has learned to abandon his own will and do the will of God.

THOMAS À KEMPIS

Stiff-necked Glasgow beggar!
I've heard he's prayed for my soul,
    But he couldn't lie if you paid him,
And he'd starve before he stole.

RUDYARD KIPLING

[It is worth while to look at] . . . the type of character which Jesus admires. . . . The parable of the talents turns on energetic thinking and decisive action; and these are the things that Jesus admires in the virgins who thought ahead and brought extra oil, in the vigorous man who found the treasure and made sure of it, in the friend at midnight who hammered, hammered, hammered till he got his loaves, in the man who will hack off his hand to enter into life. . . . It is energy of mind that he calls for—"either with me or against me."

T. R. GLOVER

And character counts: more than any other factor it determines our reaction to adversity, temptation, sorrow, and approaching death. In every worthwhile aim it determines our success. It limits our influence over others; it decides our destiny; it—and not happiness—is the true end of life. It is the only possession truly our own, the only form of riches immune from the acids of misfortune; the only treasure that cannot corrupt the owner; the only wealth we take with us when we die as capital for a new life's investment.

ANONYMOUS

CHARITY

Now abideth faith, hope, charity, these three; but the greatest of these *is* charity.

PAUL: 1 CORINTHIANS 13:13, AV/KJV

In Faith and Hope the world will disagree,
But all mankind's concern is charity.

ALEXANDER POPE

Charity is the power of defending that which we know to be indefensible.

G. K. CHESTERTON

He that has no charity deserves no mercy.

ENGLISH PROVERB

In necessary things unity; in doubtful things liberty; in all things charity.

PHILIPP MELANCHTHON(?)

Charity is indeed a noble and beautiful virtue, grateful to man, approved by God. But charity must be built on justice—it cannot supersede justice.

HENRY GEORGE

Charity begins at home: justice begins next door.

CHARLES DICKENS

This I think charity, to love God for himself and our neighbours for God.

THOMAS BROWNE

CHILDHOOD

Children ought not to lay up for their parents, but parents for their children.

PAUL: 2 CORINTHIANS 12:14

> In praise of little children I will say
> God first made man, then found a better way
> For woman, but his third way was the best:
> Of all created things the loveliest
> And most divine are children. Nothing here
> Can be to us more precious or more dear.
> And though, when God saw all his works were good,
> There was no rosy flower of babyhood,
> 'Twas said of children in a later day
> That none could enter heaven save such as they.

W. CANTON

Children, after being limbs of Satan in traditional theology, and mystically illuminated angels in the minds of educational reformers, have reverted to being little devils—not theological demons inspired by the Evil One, but scientific Freudian abominations inspired by the Unconscious.

BERTRAND RUSSELL

We strangle mad dogs, slaughter a fierce ox, plunge the knife into sickly cattle lest they taint the herd; children also, if they are born weakly or deformed, we drown.

SENECA, EDUCATIONIST, B.C. 4?–65 A.D.

If God gives us children . . . we shall need them to help us and to support us in our old age (XENOPHON); No father would cast off his son and thereby rob himself of his assistance in old age (ARISTOTLE); "At one time I . . . had many hopes that you would feed me in my old age" (MEDEA, ABOUT TO SLAY HER CHILDREN).

Your children are not your children; they are the sons and daughters of Life's longing for itself.

KAHLIL GIBRAN

Children need models rather than critics (JOSEPH JOUBERT); Give a little love to a child and you get a great deal back (JOHN RUSKIN); That energy which makes a child hard to manage is the energy which afterward makes him a manager of life (HENRY WARD BEECHER); The best of all opportunities belongs to those parents who will confess their faults to their children; there is no way so straight and sure to their hearts (JEREMY TAYLOR).

He who takes the child by the hand takes the mother by the heart.

DANISH PROVERB

I remember, I remember
The fir trees dark and high:
I used to think their slender tops
Were close against the sky.
It was a childish ignorance,
But now 'tis little joy
To know I'm farther off from heaven
Than when I was a boy.

THOMAS HOOD

They look up with their pale and sunken faces,
    And their look is dread to see;
For they mind you of their angels in high places,
    With eyes turned on Deity.
"How long," they say, "How long, O cruel nation,
    Will you stand, to move the world, on a child's heart,
Stifle down with a mailed heel its palpitation,
    And tread onward to your throne amid the mart?
Our blood splashes upward, O gold-heaper,
    And your purple shows your path!
But the child's sob in the silence curses deeper
    Than the strong man in his wrath."

                  ELIZABETH BARRETT BROWNING

Present your religion to a little child, set him in the midst of those who profess it. If it frightens him, and freezes the smiles on his lips, then whatever sort of religion it is, it is not Christianity.

                  UNKNOWN

They are idols of hearts and of households;
    They are angels of God in disguise;
The sunlight still sleeps in their tresses,
    His glory still gleams in their eyes.
These truants from home and from heaven,
    They have made me more manly and mild;
And I know now how Jesus could liken
    The kingdom of God to a child.

                  CHARLES M. DICKINSON

Little Jesus, wast thou shy
Once, and just so small as I? . . . .
Didst thou kneel at night to pray,
And didst thou join thy hands this way? . . . .
Thou canst not have forgotten all
That it feels like to be small:
And thou know'st I cannot pray
To thee in my father's way—
When thou wast so little, say,

Couldst thou talk thy Father's way?
So, a little child, come down
And hear a child's tongue like thine own;
Take me by the hand and walk,
And listen to my baby-talk.
To thy Father show my prayer
(He will look, thou art so fair),
And say: "O Father, I thy Son
Bring the prayer of a little one."

And He will smile, that children's tongue
Has not changed since thou wast young!

FRANCIS THOMPSON

Children were more to Jesus than helpless, gentle creatures to be loved and protected; they were His chief parable of the kingdom of heaven.

JOHN WATSON

CHRISTIANITY

In Antioch the disciples were for the first time called Christians.

ACTS 11:26

A Christian is the highest style of man.

EDWARD YOUNG

There was never law, or sect, or opinion did so much magnify goodness as the Christian religion doth.

FRANCIS BACON

He who begins by loving Christianity better than truth will proceed by loving his own sect or church better than Christianity, and end in loving himself better than all.

SAMUEL TAYLOR COLERIDGE

Instead of making Christianity a vehicle of truth, you make truth only a horse for Christianity.

RALPH WALDO EMERSON

Almost every sect of Christianity is a perversion of its essence, to accommodate it to the prejudices of the world.

WILLIAM HAZLITT

We live in a post-Christian era because Christianity has sunk into religiosity.

GABRIEL VAHANIAN

CHURCH

Christ loved the church and gave himself up for her.

PAUL: EPHESIANS 5:25

I believe in the beloved community and the spirit that makes it beloved, and in the communion of all who are, in will and in deed, its members.

JOSIAH ROYCE

Those children of God to whom it has been granted to see each other face to face . . . and to feel the same spirit working in both, can never more be sundered, though the hills may lie between. For their souls are enlarged for evermore by that union, and they bear one another about in their thoughts continually, as it were a new strength.

GEORGE ELIOT

If I look at myself I am nothing. But if I look at us all I am hopeful.

JULIAN OF NORWICH

Every heresy has been an effort to narrow the church.

G. K. CHESTERTON

O blest communion, fellowship divine!
We feebly struggle, they in glory shine;
Yet all are one in Thee, for all are thine,
Hallelujah.

WILLIAM W. HOW

Faith founded the church; hope has sustained it; I cannot help thinking that it is reserved for love to reform it.

ARTHUR PENRHYN STANLEY

For the might of Thine arm we bless Thee,
    our God, our fathers' God.
Thou hast kept Thy pilgrim people by the strength
    of Thy staff and rod;
Thou hast called us to the journey which faithless feet ne'er trod;
For the might of Thine arm we bless Thee, our God,
    our fathers' God.

C. SILVESTER HORNE

Thy hand, O God, has guided
    Thy flock from age to age;
The wondrous tale is written
    Full clear, on every page;
Our fathers owned Thy goodness,
    And we their deeds record;
And both of these bear witness—
    One Church, one faith, one Lord.

EDWARD H. PLUMPTRE

Not throned above the skies,
    Nor golden-walled afar,
But where Christ's two or three
    In His Name gathered are;
He in the midst of them
God's own Jerusalem!

FRANCIS T. PALGRAVE

While God waits for His temple to be built of love,
Men bring stones.

TAGORE

COMPASSION

He that hath pity upon the poor lendeth unto the Lord.

PROVERBS 19:17, AV/KJV

Compassion will cure more sins than condemnation.

HENRY WARD BEECHER

O Brother man, fold to thy heart thy brother;
Where pity dwells, the peace of God is there.

JOHN GREENLEAF WHITTIER

More helpful than all wisdom is one draught of simple human pity that
will not forsake us.

GEORGE ELIOT

CONFLICT

Take the whole armor of God, that you may be able to withstand in the
evil day, and having done all, to stand.

PAUL: EPHESIANS 6:13

Christianity is essentially, centrally, a heroism.

VICTOR HUGO

He has no enemy, you say;
My friend, your boast is poor.
He who has mingled in the fray
Of duty that the brave endure,
Must have made foes.

ANASTASIUS GRÜN

Glory to God, who thus to men has given,
Best of His gifts, the call to share His strife;
Glory to God, who bids us fight for heaven,
Here, in the dust and joy of human life.

G. H.

No, when the fight begins within himself,
A man's worth something. God stoops o'er his head,
Satan looks up between his feet—both tug—
He's left, himself, in the middle: the soul wakes
And grows. Prolong that battle through his life!
Never leave growing till the life to come!

ROBERT BROWNING

With force of arms we nothing can,
　　Full soon were we down-ridden;
But for us fights the proper Man
　　Whom God himself hath bidden.
　　　　Ask ye, Who is this same?
　　　　Christ Jesus is His name
　　　　The Lord Sabaoth's Son;
　　　　He, and no other one
　　Shall conquer in the battle.

And were this world all devils o'er,
　　And watching to devour us,
We lay it not to heart so sore;
　　Not they can overpower us.
　　　　And let the prince of ill
　　　　Look grim as e'er he will,
　　　　He harms us not a whit;
　　　　For why? his doom is writ;
　　A word shall quickly slay him.

　　　　　　MARTIN LUTHER, TRANS. THOMAS CARLYLE

Believe not those who say
　　The upward path is smooth,
Lest thou shouldst stumble in the way
　　And faint before the truth.

Arm, arm thee for the fight!
　　Cast useless loads away;
Watch through the darkest hours of night,
　　Toil through the hottest day.

　　　　　ANNE BRONTË

O great Lord Christ, my Saviour,
　　Thou goest forth to war!
Against Thee surge the foemen—
　　They muster from afar!
I hear Thy clear voice ringing
　　Above the eager fight,

"Come hither, son, and serve Me,
    And wield the arms of light."

But I am all unstable
    As a wind-shaken reed;
Forgotten vow, and failure,
    And sins, my way impede . . .
My Captain, O my Captain,
    Stretch forth Thy nail-pierced hand,
And claim me by that token
    One of Thy soldier band!

A. H. VINE

CONSCIENCE

I always take pains to have a clear conscience toward God and toward men.

PAUL: ACTS 24:16

Conscience—(i) the *voice* of God within, mysterious, authoritative, inarguable (TRADITIONAL VIEW); the voice of the repressed good (HARRY EMERSON FOSDICK);

(ii) a *feeling* of shame, guilt, fear, or of self-satisfaction, kindled upon self-examination (TRADITIONAL); the agenbite of inwit (JOHN WYCLIFFE);

(iii) the mind making moral *judgements* (THOMAS AQUINAS); a principle of reflection by which men distinguish between approved and disapproved actions, thoughts, desires (AFTER JOSEPH BUTLER); the exercise of moral judgement upon options presented to the mind and will, accompanied by feelings of attraction, repugnance, obligation, or inhibition (ANONYMOUS); a judgement of value exercised upon the foreseen, or actual, consequences of actions and attitudes (AFTER HASTINGS RASHDALL);

(iv) the repressive "super-ego," that is, the total self moving to censor and suppress disapproved feelings and desires (AFTER SIGMUND FREUD); the emotional deposit within the subconscious of ancient custom, tabu, and fears, or of contemporary society's assumed level of tolerance, or of both (ANONYMOUS).

There is another man within that is angry with me.

THOMAS BROWNE

My conscience hath a thousand several tongues,
And every tongue brings in a several tale,
And every tale condemns me for a villain.

WILLIAM SHAKESPEARE

Conscience is the frame of character, and love is the covering for it.

HENRY WARD BEECHER

You cannot form a notion of this faculty, conscience, without taking in judgement, direction, superintendency; to preside and govern belongs to it. Had it strength as it has right, had it power as it has manifest authority, it would absolutely govern the world.

JOSEPH BUTLER (abbreviated)

An approving conscience is a foretaste of heaven; an accusing conscience is a "hell-worm" which shooteth like a stitch in a man's side, a kind of private judgement-day before the public day of judgement.

A PURITAN

I give you the end of a golden string:
Only wind it into a ball,
It will lead you in at heaven's gate,
Built in Jerusalem's wall.

WILLIAM BLAKE

There is a dangerous error . . . that a man is bound to do everything which his conscience telleth him is the will of God; and that every man must obey his conscience as if it were the lawgiver of the world; whereas indeed it is not ourselves but God that is our Lawgiver. Conscience is not authorised to make us any duty which God hath not made us, only to discern the law of God and call upon us to observe it. An erring conscience is not to be obeyed, but to be better informed.

RICHARD BAXTER

"My conscience is not so," said Queen Mary of Scotland to John Knox. "Conscience, Madam," Knox replied, "requires knowledge, and I fear that right knowledge ye have none."

SOURCE UNKNOWN

Thus conscience does make cowards of us all.

SHAKESPEARE

CONSERVATION

The earth is the LORD's and all that is in it, the world and those who dwell therein.

PSALM 24:1, NEB

> His are the mountains, and the valleys His,
> And the resplendent rivers. His to enjoy
> With a propriety that none can feel
> But who, with filial countenance inspired,
> Can lift to heaven an unpresumptuous eye
> And smiling say, "My Father made them all."

WILLIAM COWPER

Hurt not the earth, neither the sea, nor the trees.

JOHN THE SEER: REVELATION 7:3, AV/KJV

> Detested sport,
> That owes its pleasures to another's pain.

WILLIAM COWPER

Man is the only one to whom the torture and death of his fellow creatures is amusing in itself (JAMES A. FROUDE); The strongest motive for the care of natural things is not self-interest, but reverence (X).

> A Robin Redbreast in a cage
> Puts all heaven in a rage . . .
> A dog starved at his master's gate
> Predicts the ruin of the State . . .
> Each outcry of the hunted hare
> A fibre from the brain does tear;
> A skylark wounded in the wing
> Doth make a cherub cease to sing.
> He who shall hurt the little wren
> Shall never be beloved by men;
> He who the ox to wrath has moved
> Shall never be by women loved.

Kill not the moth nor butterfly,
For the last judgement draweth nigh.

WILLIAM BLAKE

I brought you into a plentiful land
  to enjoy its fruit and its good things.
But when you came in you defiled my land,
  and made my heritage an abomination.

JEREMIAH: JEREMIAH 2:7

CONSISTENCY

Was I vacillating . . . ? Do I make my plans like a worldly man, ready to say Yes and No at once?

PAUL: 2 CORINTHIANS 1:17

It is simplicity of intention that gives consistency to life.

WILLIAM C. BRAITHWAITE

It is not best to swap horses while crossing the river.

ABRAHAM LINCOLN

A foolish consistency is the hobgoblin of little minds, adored by little statesmen, philosophers, and divines.

RALPH WALDO EMERSON

There are those who would misteach us that to stick in a rut is consistency and a virtue, and that to climb out of the rut is inconsistency and a vice.

MARK TWAIN

I could never divide myself from any man upon the difference of an opinion, or be angry with his judgement for not agreeing with me in that, from which perhaps in a few days I myself should dissent.

THOMAS BROWNE

CONTENTMENT

I have learned to be content whatever the circumstances.

PAUL: PHILIPPIANS 4:11, NIV

Content is happiness (THOMAS FULLER) . . . a kingdom (THOMAS HEYWOOD) . . . the philosopher's stone that turns all it touches into gold (BENJAMIN FRANKLIN) . . . is all (JOHN CLARKE); He is poor that does not feel content (JAPANESE PROVERB); He that's content hath enough (BENJAMIN FRANKLIN).

True contentment is a thing as active as agriculture. It is the power of getting out of any situation all that there is in it. It is arduous, and it is rare.

G. K. CHESTERTON

Contented with your lot, you will act wisely.

HORACE

Let not thy thoughts run on what thou lackest, as much as on what thou already hast.

MARCUS AURELIUS

All good fortune belongs to a contented mind, as the world is leather-covered for him who walks in shoes.

PANCHATANTRA

> Contentment is a sleepy thing
> If it in death alone must die;
> A quiet mind is worse than poverty,
> Unless it from enjoyment spring
> That's blessedness, alone, that makes a king!

THOMAS TRAHERNE

CONVERSION

"Saul, Saul, why do you persecute me?" . . . "Who are you, Lord?" . . . "I am Jesus of Nazareth whom you are persecuting" . . . "What shall I do, Lord?"

ACTS 22:7–10

It is a depressing exercise to examine the widely held belief that "psychological treatment" would solve all the many forms of anti-social violence with which criminologists have to deal . . . The crux of the problem is that we know little about how to change human beings, or to touch them at the level where the spring of action lies.

G. HAWKINS, PRISON SERVICE COLLEGE

The Moving Finger writes; and, having writ,
Moves on: nor all thy Piety nor Wit
Shall lure it back to cancel half a Line,
Nor all thy Tears wash out a Word of it.

EDWARD FITZGERALD/OMAR KHAYYÁM

Man is made, not by the past alone but by the sought-for future, the ideal ahead, the spiritual forces within, the accessible God above, and by all these as focussed in the Saviour of men. In the forgiveness He speaks, the love He kindles, the faith He imparts, the gratitude He evokes, even the past is changed from burden to incentive, through the new freedom and hope awakened by "if any man be in Christ he is a new creature . . . all things are become new."

ANONYMOUS

Love bade me welcome; yet my soul drew back,
    Guilty of dust and sin.
But quick-ey'd Love, observing me grow slack
    From my first entrance in,
Drew nearer to me, sweetly questioning,
    If I lacked anything.
"A guest," I answered, "worthy to be here":
    Love said, "You shall be he."
"I, the unkind, ungrateful? Ah, my dear,
    I cannot look on Thee."
Love took my hand, and smiling did reply,
    "Who made the eyes but I?"
"Truth, Lord, but I have marred them; let my shame
    Go where it doth deserve."
"And know you not," says Love, "who bore the blame?"
    "My dear, then I will serve."

"You must sit down," says Love, "and taste My meat."
So I did sit and eat.

GEORGE HERBERT

The essential religious experience is marked first by wonder at the utter
dependence of all things, including our human limitations, upon God as the
sole dependable resource. Secondly, it is associated with immediate needs—
danger, migration, failure, poverty, fear, guilt; or with immediate
contentment, relief, happiness. Thirdly, it is marked by a bating of breath,
a stillness of mind, by illumination, understanding, relief of tension, and
joy. With this arises desire for fellowship with others of similar experience.
Fourthly, it awakens alertness of mind, a heightened perceptiveness and
sensitivity to beauty, with new perspectives, a new sense of proportion, and
new, more selective, interests. Fifthly, the experience of God engenders a
wholly new concern for truth, for sincerity, for integrity of mind and
honesty of attitude, and for all ethical considerations. Sixthly, new
emotional energy is released, and channeled into fresh creative and costly
activity, of both individual and social value. All these characteristics,
infolded within the initial experience of God, are increasingly unfolded as
religious experience matures.

AFTER H. D. LEWIS

The moment we set our face in the same direction as His, we are walking
with God.

HELEN WODEHOUSE

"There is more joy in heaven over one sinner that repenteth than over
ninety and nine that need no repentance." That, when all is said and
done, was the most wonderful declaration of the nature of God . . . ever
made.

MIDDLETON MURRY

Of all conversions—of the coarsely vicious (John Newton), or the refined
vicious (Augustine), of the intellectual (Henry Drummond), the dishonest
(Zaccheus), the sexually undisciplined ("the woman of the city"), the
religious pilgrim (Cornelius), the habitually sceptical (Thomas), the
emotional and weak (Peter), the scholarly (Nicodemus)—probably the
rarest, because most difficult, is the conversion of the religious mind, to
whom spiritual matters are familiar, professional, and passionately held, like
that of Saul of Tarsus.

ANONYMOUS

I put my conversion as a lad into the polish on my father's shoes.

SAMUEL CHADWICK

(Advised to turn from philosophy to Jesus, and to pray "that before all things the gates of light may be opened to thee")—"At this point a fire was kindled in my soul, a love of the prophets and the friends of Christ . . . I found this philosophy alone to be safe and profitable. Thus, and for this reason, I am a philosopher."

JUSTIN MARTYR

I floated on the stormy sea, a stranger to the light and uncertain where to plant my feet. How can a man be born again? The very idea seemed hard and impossible. But suddenly I breathed the breath of heaven. That lay open which before was shut, that was light which before was darkness, that became easy which before was impracticable.

CYPRIAN

A cauldron of unholy loves bubbled up all around me . . . I bore about me a rent and polluted soul . . . my back was to the light . . . By marvellous ways didst thou deal with me. [Feeling desperate, and hearing a cry, "Take up and read," he picked up a Testament and read, "Not in rioting and drunkenness, not in chambering and wantonness . . . but put ye on the Lord Jesus Christ, and make no provision for the flesh. . . ."] Instantly, as the sentence ended, it was as if the light of peace was poured into my heart, and all the gloom of doubt vanished away.

AUGUSTINE

Late have I loved Thee, O Beauty so ancient and so new, late have I loved Thee! And behold, Thou wert within and I was without. I was looking for Thee out there, and I threw myself, deformed as I was, upon those well-formed things which Thou hast made. These things held me from Thee. . . . Thou didst call and cry out and burst in upon my deafness; Thou didst shine forth and glow and drive away my blindness; Thou didst send forth Thy fragrance and I drew in my breath, and now I pant for Thee; I have tasted and now I hunger and thirst; Thou didst touch me, and I was inflamed with desire for Thy peace. When I shall cleave to Thee with all my being . . . my life will be alive, wholly filled with Thee.

AUGUSTINE, CONFESSIONS
(Book X section 38)

Bear with my foolishness for a little, for I want to tell you how these things took place in me. . . . You will ask how, since His track is traceless, I could know that He is present. Because He quickened my sleeping soul, and aroused, softened, and goaded my heart, which was torpid and hard as stone. . . . In the reformation and renewal of the spirit of my mind, that is, my inward man, I have seen something of the loveliness of His beauty; and meditating on these things I have been filled with wonder at the multitude of His greatness.

BERNARD OF CLAIRVAUX

(To his wife) "Go, read where I cast my first anchor." (She read, "This is life eternal, that they should know Thee, the only true God, and Him whom thou didst send, even Jesus Christ.") He repeated, "Ah, it was *there* I cast my first anchor."

JOHN KNOX

I went very unwillingly to a society in Aldersgate Street, where one was reading Luther's Preface to the Epistle to the Romans. About a quarter before nine, while he was describing the change God works in the heart through faith in Christ, I felt my heart strangely warmed. I felt I did trust in Christ, Christ alone, for salvation; and an assurance was given me that He had taken away *my* sins, even mine and saved *me* from the law of sin and death.

JOHN WESLEY

God was pleased to remove my heavy load and to enable me, by a living faith, to lay hold on His dear Son . . . I know the exact place . . . Whenever I go to Oxford, I cannot help running to the spot where Jesus Christ first revealed himself to me and gave me a new birth.

GEORGE WHITEFIELD

[At the ship's pumps in a storm] If this will not do, the Lord have mercy! I thought I saw the hand of God. I began to pray. I could not utter the prayer of faith. I could not draw near to a reconciled God and call him Father . . . On that day the Lord came from on high and delivered me out of deep waters.

JOHN NEWTON, once Libertine, Infidel, servant of slaves, by the mercy of our Lord and Saviour preserved, restored, pardoned and appointed to preach . . . self-composed epitaph

I was a stricken deer, that left the herd
Long since. With many an arrow deep infixt
My panting side was charged, when I withdrew
To seek a tranquil death in distant shades.
There I was found by One who had Himself
Been hurt by th' archers. In his side He bore,
And in his hands and feet, the cruel scars.
With gentle force soliciting the darts,
He drew them forth, and healed, and bade me live.

WILLIAM COWPER

I had pride sufficient for a thousand times my knowledge. . . . But I was often afterwards convinced that, though I had the last word, my fellow-apprentice had the better of the argument, and I felt a growing uneasiness and stings of conscience. . . . He became importunate with me, lending me books . . . which gradually wrought a change in my thinking. . . . I also determined to leave off lying, swearing, and other sins, to which I was addicted, and sometimes when alone I tried to pray. I had a counterfeit shilling . . . told the falsehood, and was detected . . . overwhelmed with shame . . . [so learned my] deep need of a Saviour.

WILLIAM CAREY

[A friend's letter] led to my conversion. I sprang out of bed and leaped about the room, rejoicing and praising God that Jesus died for me. From that day to this I have lived under the shadow of His wings.

JAMES HANNINGTON, AFRICAN BISHOP

[After long insisting upon her freedom] He, the King of Heaven, was stronger than my wayward heart. God Himself took me into His school. My eyes were opened to the misery of the world. . . . There was work for me to do in the world. Jesus had sought me and found me. I broke down every bridge behind me; I could never leave Him again.

SISTER EVA OF FRIEDENSHORT

[Confucian scholar, lawyer, drug addict, bereaved, but received with great kindness by Christian friends]—All sense of fear was gone; my mind was at rest. Pride broke with tears that flowed and could not cease. He loved me and gave himself for me. He has redeemed me. I am for ever His.

PASTOR HSI

CONVICTION

Let every one be fully convinced in his own mind.

PAUL: ROMANS 14:5

One in whom persuasion and belief
Had ripened into faith, and faith become
A passionate intuition.

WILLIAM WORDSWORTH

Too fond of the right to pursue the expedient.

OLIVER GOLDSMITH OF EDMUND BURKE

Unless I am convicted of error by the testimony of Scripture . . . or . . .
by manifest reasoning I stand convicted by the Scriptures . . . and my
conscience is taken captive by God's word, I cannot and will not
recant. . . . On this I take my stand. I can do no other—God help me!

MARTIN LUTHER

COUNSEL

The way of a fool is right in his own eyes,
but a wise man listens to advice.

PROVERBS 12:15

Every counselor praises counsel,
    but some give counsel in their own interest.
Be wary of a counselor. . . .
Do not consult with one who looks at you suspiciously;
    hide your counsel from those who are jealous of you.
Do not consult with a woman about her rival
    or with a coward about war,
with a merchant about barter
    or with a buyer about selling,
with a grudging man about gratitude
    or with a merciless man about kindness;
with an idler about any work
    or with a man hired for a year about completing his work,

with a lazy servant about a big task. . . .
But . . . establish the counsel of your own heart,
    for no one is more faithful to you than it is. . . .
And besides all this pray to the Most High
    that he may direct your way in truth.

                SIRACH 37:7–15

He who builds to every man's advice will have a crooked house.

                DANISH PROVERB

Whoso comes to thee, ask him meekly what he will; hear him gladly,
and suffer him to say what he will, for the ease of his own heart; and
when he hath done, comfort him if thou canst, goodly and charitably, and
soon break off.

                JULIAN OF NORWICH

To help a brother up the mountain while you yourself are only just able
to keep your foothold, to struggle through the mist together—that surely is
better than to stand at the summit and beckon.

                FORBES ROBINSON

      Canst thou not minister to a mind diseased,
      Pluck from the memory a rooted sorrow,
      Raze out the written troubles of the brain,
      And with some sweet oblivious antidote
      Cleanse the stuff'd bosom of that perilous stuff
      Which weighs upon the heart?

                WILLIAM SHAKESPEARE

Beware lest clamour be taken for counsel.

                ERASMUS

      Good counsel *failing* men may give—for why?
      He that's aground knows where the shoal doth lie. . . .
      Thus, like the whetstone, many men are wont
      To sharpen others while themselves are blunt.

                BENJAMIN FRANKLIN

Extremely foolish advice is likely to be uttered by those who are looking at the labouring vessel from the land.

ARTHUR HELPS

COURAGE

"Take heart, it is I; have no fear."

JESUS: MATTHEW 14:27

Jesus, as much as pagan teachers, insists on courage as the primary virtue . . . not a matter of physical constitution, or a purely moral quality, but the expression of faith in God. Thus [courage was] a vital element not only in the ethic of Jesus but in his religion.

E. F. SCOTT

Courage is resistance to fear, mastery of fear, not absence of fear.

MARK TWAIN

> Great is the facile conqueror;
> Yet haply he, who, wounded sore,
> Breathless, unhorsed, all covered o'er
>   With blood and sweat,
> Sinks foiled, but fighting evermore,
>   Is greater yet.

WILLIAM WATSON

God grant me the courage to change the things I can change; the serenity to accept those I cannot change; the wisdom to know the difference—but God grant me the courage not to give up what I think is right even though I think it hopeless.

CHESTER W. NIMITZ, AFTER R. W. WOODS

> One who never turned his back
>   But strode breast forward,
> Never doubted clouds would break,
> Held, we fall to rise,
> Are baffled to fight better,
>   Sleep to wake.

ROBERT BROWNING

Fools, when their roof-tree
Falls, think it doomsday:
Firm stands the sky!

JAMES RUSSELL LOWELL

The brave man is not he who feels no fear,
For that were stupid and irrational;
But he whose noble soul its fear subdues,
And bravely dares the danger nature shrinks from.

JOANNA BAILLIE

The man so bravely played the man
He made the fiend to fly.

JOHN BUNYAN

Why, courage then! what cannot be avoided
'Twere childish weakness to lament, or fear.

WILLIAM SHAKESPEARE

COURTESY

Finally, *be ye* all of one mind . . . *be* pitiful, *be* courteous.

1 PETER 3:8, AV/KJV

Know, dear Brother, that courtesy is one of the qualities of God Himself,
who of his courtesy giveth his sun and his rain to the just and the unjust;
and courtesy is the sister of charity. . . .

FRANCIS OF ASSISI

Of courtesy, it is much less
Than courage of heart, or holiness;
Yet in my walks it seems to me
That the grace of God is in courtesy.

HILAIRE BELLOC

The first point of courtesy must always be truth.

RALPH WALDO EMERSON

Courtesy will often ask of us some exercise of self-withdrawal, self-denial; some promptness to take the lower or less pleasant part; some carelessness about our own comfort; some perseverance when we are tired, and perhaps when others are ungracious; some resoluteness not to let ourselves off easily.

FRANCIS PAGET

Politeness is to do and say
The kindest thing in the kindest way.

LUDWIG LEWISOHN

DEATH

Precious in the sight of the LORD
is the death of his saints.

PSALM 116:15

Death is a gate on the sky-line (MARY WEBB) . . . finally runs the robustest of us down (WILLIAM JAMES) . . . shall have no dominion (DYLAN THOMAS). . . . Only a larger kind of going abroad (SAMUEL BUTLER II); "One of our pilots is safe" (WAR-PILOT'S DEATH-ANNOUNCEMENT); Death's but a path that must be trod if man would ever pass to God (THOMAS PARNELL); So he passed over, and all the trumpets sounded for him on the other side (JOHN WILLIAM BUNYAN); After life's fitful fever he sleeps well (WILLIAM SHAKESPEARE).

There is no death: what seems so is transition (HENRY WADSWORTH LONGFELLOW); There is no death—that I am absolutely sure of (GERMAN WOMAN, 23, AWAITING EXECUTION); Life is a great surprise: I do not see why death should not be an even greater one (VLADIMIR NABOKOV).

> The door of death is made of gold,
> That mortal eyes cannot behold;
> But, when the mortal eyes are closed,
> And cold and pale the limbs reposed,
> The soul awakes; and wondering sees
> In her mild hand the golden keys.

WILLIAM BLAKE

Jesus, who . . . changed the accursed tree into the cross, and made chief sinners into saints, hath put a fair face on death, so that it becometh only His dark disguise as He returns to receive us home.

JOHN WATSON

Death, be not proud, though some have called thee
Mighty and dreadful, for thou art not so;
For those whom thou thinkest thou dost overthrow
Die not, poor death, nor yet canst thou kill me. . . .
One short sleep past, we wake eternally,
And death shall be no more; death, thou shalt die.

JOHN DONNE

There is not room for death,
Nor atom that his might could render void:
Thou—Thou art Being, and Breath,
And what Thou art may never be destroyed.

EMILY BRONTË

"Let the dead bury the dead": there is not a single word of Christ to
which the so-called Christian religion has paid less attention.

ANDRÉ GIDE

Fear death?—to feel the fog in my throat,
The mist in my face,
When the snows begin, and the blasts denote
I am nearing the place. . . .
For the journey is done and the summit attained,
And the barriers fall.
Though a battle's to fight ere the guerdon be gained,
The reward of it all,
I was ever a fighter, so—one fight more,
The best and the last!
I would hate that death bandaged my eyes and forbore
And bade me creep past. . . .
For sudden the worst turns the best, to the brave,
The black minute's at end,
And the elements' rage, the fiend-voices that rave,
Shall dwindle, shall blend,
Shall change, shall become first a peace, then a joy,
Then a light, then thy breast,
O thou soul of my soul! I shall clasp thee again,
And with God be the rest!

ROBERT BROWNING

When he was come at the river, where was no bridge, there again Mr. Fearing was in a heavy case. Now, now, he said, he should be drowned for ever. . . . And here, also, I took notice of what was very remarkable: the water of that river was lower at this time than ever I saw it in all my life. So he went over at last, not much above wet-shod.

JOHN BUNYAN

Be near me when my light is low,
    When the blood creeps, and the nerves prick
    And tingle, and the heart is sick,
And all the wheels of being slow.

Be near me when the sensuous frame
    Is rack'd with pangs that conquer trust,
    And Time, a maniac scattering dust,
And Life, a fury slinging flame.

Be near me when I fade away,
    To point the term of human strife,
    And on the low dark verge of life
The twilight of eternal day.

ALFRED TENNYSON

Life, we've been long together,
Through pleasant and through cloudy weather; . . . .
Then steal away, give little warning;
    Choose thine own time;
Say not "Good night": but in some brighter clime
    Bid me "Good morning!"

ANNA L. BARBAULD

Under the wide and starry sky
Dig the grave and let me lie.
Glad did I live and gladly die,
    And I laid me down with a will.
This be the verse you grave for me:
"Here he lies where he longed to be;
Home is the sailor, home from the sea,
    And the hunter home from the hill."

ROBERT LOUIS STEVENSON

Any man's death diminishes me, because I am involved in mankind; therefore never send to know for whom the bell tolls; it tolls for thee.

JOHN DONNE

> Sunset, and evening star,
> And one clear call for me!
> And may there be no moaning of the bar
> When I put out to sea. . . .
> For though from out our bourne of Time and Place
> The flood may bear me far,
> I hope to see my Pilot face to face
> When I have crost the bar.

ALFRED TENNYSON

Death had replaced sex as the great unmentionable, to be denied in prospect, endured in a decent privacy, preferably behind the drawn curtains of a hospital bed, and followed by discreet, embarrassed, uncomforted mourning.

P. D. JAMES

> When John prepared the way before Thy face,
> O Christ, 'twas no small grace
> Unto the Baptist then;
> Much greater dost Thou now bestow on men,
> In that Thou goest before to make us room
> In heaven against we come.

THOMAS WASHBOURNE

> Carry me over the long, last mile,
> Man of Nazareth, Christ for me!
> Weary I wait by death's dark stile
> In the wild and the waste where the wind blows free. . . .
> Lord, is it long that my spirit must wait?
> Man of Nazareth, Christ for me!
> Deep is the stream, and the night is late;
> And grief blinds my soul, for I cannot see.
> Speak to me out of the silences, Lord,
> That my spirit may know as forward I go
> That Thy pierced hands are lifting me over the ford.

LAUCHLAN MACLEAN WATT

Not spilt like water on the ground,
Not wrapt in dreamless sleep profound,
Not wandering in unknown despair,
Beyond Thy voice, Thine arm, Thy care;
Not left to lie like fallen tree:
Not dead—but living unto Thee.

JOHN ELLERTON

DECISION

"No one who puts his hand to the plow and looks back is fit for the kingdom of God."

JESUS: LUKE 9:62

One person we cannot avoid—the inevitable Christ; one dilemma we must face—"What shall I do with Jesus, which is called Christ?"

JOHN WATSON

Either be hot or cold: God doth despise
Abhor, and spew out all neutralities.

ROBERT HERRICK

. . . that gleaming flash of resolve which lifts the heart of men and nations, and springs from the spiritual foundations of human life itself.

WINSTON SPENCER CHURCHILL

Whoso has felt the Spirit of the Highest
Cannot confound nor doubt Him, nor deny;
Yea, with one voice, O world, though thou deniest,
Stand thou on that side, for on this am I.

F. W. H. MYERS

There is no more miserable human being than one in whom nothing is habitual but indecision.

WILLIAM JAMES

Then to side with truth is noble when we share her wretched crust,
Ere her cause bring fame and profit, and 'tis prosperous to be just;

Then it is the brave man chooses, while the coward stands aside,
Doubting in his abject spirit, till his Lord is crucified.

JAMES RUSSELL LOWELL

He who considers too much will perform little.

J. C. FRIEDRICH VON SCHILLER

On the Plains of Hesitation bleach the bones of countless millions who, at
the dawn of victory, sat down to wait, and waiting died.

G. W. CECIL/ADLAI STEVENSON

DEDICATION

But one thing I do. . . . I press on toward the goal for the prize of the
upward call of God in Christ Jesus.

PAUL: PHILIPPIANS 3:13–14

A good archer is not known by his arrows but his aim.

THOMAS FULLER

> In a small chamber, friendless and alone,
>   Toiled o'er his types one poor unlearned young man.
> The place was dark, unfurnitured, and mean,
>   Yet there the freedom of a race began.
>
> Help came but slowly—surely no man yet
>   Put lever to the heavy world with less!
> What need of help? He knew how types were set,
>   He had a dauntless spirit, and a press.

UNKNOWN, ON WILLIAM LLOYD GARRISON

Oh, if only there were something worth dedicating oneself to, utterly and
for ever!

WINIFRED HOLTBY

> Greatly begin! Though thou have time
> But for a line, be that sublime:
> Not failure, but low aim is crime.

JAMES RUSSELL LOWELL

What makes life dreary is the want of motive.

GEORGE ELIOT

When a man does not know what harbour he is making for, no wind is the right wind.

SENECA

> I made no vows, but vows
> Were then made for me; bond unknown to me
> Was given, that I should be, else sinning greatly,
> A dedicated spirit.

WILLIAM WORDSWORTH

DEVOTION

Cornelius . . . a devout man who feared God with all his household, gave alms liberally to the people, and prayed constantly to God.

ACTS 10:1–2

Devotion, mother of obedience (SAMUEL DANIEL). . . . Daughter of astronomy—an undevout astronomer is mad (EDWARD YOUNG).

At my devotion, I love to use the civility of my knee, my hat, my hand.

THOMAS BROWNE

> The waves for ever move,
> The hills for ever rest,
> Yet each the heavens approve;
> So love alike hath blessed
> A Martha's household care,
> A Mary's cloistered prayer.

JOHN BANNISTER TABB

One can always measure a man's devotion to the cause of Christ by his readiness to be called to responsibility, by his diligence in it, by the personal risks he runs through his involvement in it, or by the ease with which he lays it down.

X

This sanctuary of my soul
Unwitting I keep white and whole,
Unlatched and lit, if Thou shouldst care
To enter or to tarry there.
With parted lips and outstretched hands,
And listening ears Thy servant stands:
Call Thou early, call Thou late,
To Thy great service dedicate.

CHARLES H. SORLEY

DISCIPLESHIP

"If any one comes to me and does not hate ... even his own life ... does not bear his own cross ... does not renounce all that he has ... [he] cannot be my disciple."

JESUS: LUKE 14:26–27, 33

In the ancient world every teacher had his company of disciples or *learners*—the Greek philosophers, the Jewish rabbis, John the Baptist, and the Pharisees.

DAVID SMITH

Comes faint and far Thy voice,
From vales of Galilee;
Thy vision fades in ancient shades
How should we follow Thee?

Within our heart of hearts
In nearest nearness be:
Set up Thy throne within Thine own:
Go, Lord, we follow Thee.

FRANCIS T. PALGRAVE

What makes a man a Christian is neither his intellectual acceptance of certain ideas, nor his conformity to a certain rule, but his possession of a certain Spirit, and his participation in a certain Life.

JOHN BAILLIE

Some idle day, when least we look for grace,
Shall we see stand upon the shore indeed
The visible Master, and the Lord of us,
And leave our nets, nor question of his creed,
Following the Christ within a young man's face?

EDWARD DOWDEN

[For "a mere Christian"] the Ten Commandments, the creed, and the Lord's Prayer were all that were required: a rule under which to live, a faith in which to believe, a hope in which to pray.

F. HIGHAM ON RICHARD BAXTER

The Christian must do a great many things that others do, but he does them with a difference. When a man is in Christ, all the meanings deepen and all the values rise. . . . The authentic Christian, however, has some things to do that others do not . . . divergences from conventional conduct: a habit of being alone, dependence on fellowship, care in his use of time, a peculiar attitude towards money; he will not retaliate, bear grudges, or assert himself; he thinks himself debtor to all the world. . . . A blithe creature, he makes no suburban groans and excuses.

W. R. MALTBY

O let me hear Thee speaking
    In accents clear and still,
Above the storms of passion,
    The murmurs of self-will;
O speak to reassure me,
    To hasten or control—
O speak, and make me listen,
    Thou Guardian of my soul.

O let me see Thy footmarks
    And in them plant mine own.
My hope to follow duly
    Is in Thy strength alone.

O guide me, call me, draw me,
Uphold me to the end;
And then in heaven receive me,
My Master, and my Friend.

JOHN E. BODE

DISCIPLINE

Every athlete exercises self-control. . . . Well, I do not run aimlessly, I do not box as one beating the air; but I pommel my body and subdue it, lest after preaching to others I myself should be disqualified.

PAUL: 1 CORINTHIANS 9:25–27

This is the true athlete, he who in the great stadium, the fair world, is crowned for the true victory over all the passions. He who obtains the mastery wins immortality.

CLEMENT OF ALEXANDRIA

Christ is the bridle of colts untamed.

CLEMENT OF ALEXANDRIA

I cannot praise a fugitive and cloistered virtue, unexercised and unbreathed, that never sallies out and sees her adversary, but slinks out of the race where that immortal garland is to be run for, not without dust and heat.

JOHN MILTON

You cannot run away from a weakness: you must some time fight it out or perish; and if that be so, why not now, and where you stand?

ROBERT LOUIS STEVENSON

Renunciation is necessary if one wants to be or to become something. To be everything at once is impossible.

SPRANGER

In life's small things be resolute and great
To keep thy muscle trained: know'st thou when Fate
Thy measure takes, or when she'll say to thee,
"I find thee worthy; do this deed for me"?

JAMES RUSSELL LOWELL

Religion is bound to exclude some areas of experience and some experiments in thought and conduct, as morally wrong, religiously unholy, socially injurious, intellectually false. Only a generation slipshod in thinking and spineless in morality would find fault with a church that knows what it teaches and is loyal to what it knows.

X

Prune thou thy words, the thoughts control
That o'er thee swell and throng;
They will condense within thy soul
And change to purpose strong.

JOHN HENRY NEWMAN

Combat and concentration, hardness and asceticism, are an absolutely essential constituent of the Christian outlook. Where this element is absent, there is not authentic Christianity, but some sentimental humanitarianism, or some other weakening inadequacy.

FRIEDRICH VON HÜGEL

DOCTRINE

Bid slaves ... to show entire and true fidelity, so that in everything they may adorn the doctrine of God our Savior.

TITUS 2:9–10

Doctrine is nothing but the skin of truth set up and stuffed.

HENRY WARD BEECHER

Erasmus' patron saint was ever the penitent thief, because he was saved with so little theology.

ROLAND H. BAINTON

One can hardly imagine a greater sin against light, within the church, than indifference, or enmity, towards theology.

JOHN WATSON

The best interpreter of Christian doctrine is Christian work.

G. A. SELWYN

It is growing clearer that many doctrines of Christian men are not lasting, but that every word of Jesus is eternal. . . . To correct the results of theological science by the actual teaching of Jesus—surely nothing could be more hopeful.

AFTER JOHN WATSON

Churches and sects which begin by fighting for their creeds are apt to end by fighting for their own importance.

L. P. JACKS

Live to explain thy doctrine by thy life.

MATTHEW PRIOR

Terms like grace, new birth, justification . . . terms, in short, which with St. Paul are literary terms, theologians have employed as if they were scientific terms.

MATTHEW ARNOLD

There is no expeditious road
To pack and label men for God,
And save them by the barrel-load.

FRANCIS THOMPSON

In discourse more sweet
(For eloquence the soul, song charms the sense)
Others apart sat on a hill retired,
In thoughts more elevate, and reasoned high
Of providence, foreknowledge, will, and fate,
Fixed fate, free will, foreknowledge absolute,
And found no end, in wandering mazes lost.

JOHN MILTON

It is in the uncompromisingness with which dogma is held, and not in the dogma or want of dogma, that the danger lies.

SAMUEL BUTLER II

I have always found, myself, that the unconscious dogmatists were by far the most dogmatic.

G. K. CHESTERTON

Any stigma will do to beat a dogma.
PHILIP GUEDELLA

The more dogmas there are, the more fruitful is the ground in producing heresies. Never was the Christian faith purer or more undefiled than when the world was content with a single creed, and that the shortest creed we have.
ERASMUS

The mark of heresy is pride.
UMBERTO ECO

A modernist married a fundamentalist wife
And she led him a catechism and dogma life.
KEITH PRESTON

DOUBT

Lord, I believe; help thou mine unbelief.
MARK 9:24, AV/KJV

The man that feareth, Lord, to doubt,
In that fear doubteth Thee.
GEORGE MACDONALD

An honest man can never surrender an honest doubt.
WALTER MALONE

The centipede was happy quite,
    Until the toad in fun
Said, "Pray which leg goes after which?"
And worked her mind to such a pitch
She lay distracted in the ditch
    Considering how to run.
MRS. EDMUND CRASTER

Ten thousand difficulties do not make one doubt.
JOHN HENRY NEWMAN

Faith which does not doubt is dead faith.

MIGUEL DE UNAMUNO

> . . . one indeed I knew
>> In many a subtle question versed,
>> Who touched a jarring lyre at first,
> But ever strove to make it true:
>
> Perplexed in faith, but pure in deeds,
>> At last he beat his music out;
>> There lives more faith in honest doubt,
> Believe me, than in half the creeds.
>
> He fought his doubts, and gathered strength;
>> He would not make his judgement blind;
>> He faced the spectres of the mind,
> And laid them, thus he came at length
>
> To find a stronger faith his own;
>> And Power was with him in the night,
>> Which makes the darkness and the light,
> And dwells not in the light alone.

ALFRED TENNYSON

Materialists and madmen never have doubts.

G. K. CHESTERTON

> John Grubby, who was short and stout,
> And troubled with religious doubt,
> Refused, about the age of three,
> To sit upon the curate's knee.

G. K. CHESTERTON

> Our doubts are traitors,
> And make us lose the good we oft might win
> By fearing to attempt.

WILLIAM SHAKESPEARE

Scepticism is slow suicide (RALPH WALDO EMERSON). . . . Doubt makes the mountain which faith removes (UNKNOWN). . . . Doubt indulged soon becomes doubt realized (FRANCES RIDLEY HAVERGAL). . . . Doubt is brother devil to despair (J. B. O'REILLY). . . . There is a vulgar incredulity which finds it easier to doubt than to examine (WALTER SCOTT).

> And in the twilight, looking back
> In lapses on my frontier track,
> I almost could conceive
> That to blaspheme with tears is to believe.
>
> JACK CLEMO

DUTY

Fear God, and keep his commandments; for this is the whole duty of man [margin: the duty of all men].

ECCLESIASTES 12:13

"When you have done all that is commanded you, say, 'We are unworthy servants; we have only done what was our duty.' "

JESUS: LUKE 17:10

It is not given to the cleverest and most calculating of mortals to know with certainty what is their interest. Yet it is given to quite a lot of simple folk to know every day what is their duty.

WINSTON SPENCER CHURCHILL

> The trivial round, the common task,
> Would furnish all we ought to ask—
> Room to deny ourselves, a road
> To bring us, daily, nearer God.
>
> JOHN KEBLE (against exaggerated asceticism)

Do the duty which lies nearest thee, which thou knowest to be a duty. Thy second duty will already have become clearer.

THOMAS CARLYLE

There is no duty we so much underrate as the duty of being happy.

ROBERT LOUIS STEVENSON

So nigh is grandeur to our dust,
So near is God to man,
When Duty whispers low, "Thou must,"
The youth replies, "I can!"

RALPH WALDO EMERSON

Well, when you are doing your duty, and you are sure of that, you need not worry too much about the dangers or the consequences.

WINSTON SPENCER CHURCHILL

EARTH

For "the earth is the Lord's, and everything in it."

PAUL: 1 CORINTHIANS 10:26

He findeth God who finds the earth he made.

JOHN BUCHAN

> Earth's crammed with heaven,
> And every common bush afire with God,
> But only he who sees takes off his shoes—
> The rest sit round it and pluck blackberries.

ELIZABETH BARRETT BROWNING

Earth! though mother of numberless children, the nurse and the mother,
Sister thou of the stars, and beloved by the sun, the rejoicer!
Guardian and friend of the moon, O Earth, whom the comets
    forget not,
Yea, in the measureless distance wheel round, and again they
    behold thee!

SAMUEL TAYLOR COLERIDGE

> Man makes a great fuss
> About this planet,
> Which is only a ball-bearing
> In the hub of the Universe.

CHRISTOPHER MORLEY

EMOTION

I will take out of your flesh the heart of stone and give you a heart of
flesh.

EZEKIEL 36:26

Intellect enlightens and guides, will focusses effort, emotion alone, as its name implies, moves to action.

UNKNOWN

All evidence goes to show that there can be no new Protestant revival while the policy continues of appealing mainly to adult intelligence and reason, and until church leaders consent to take more advantage of the normal person's emotional mechanism for disrupting old behaviour patterns and implanting new.

W. A. SARGANT

The true meaning of religion is thus not simply morality, but morality touched by emotion.

MATTHEW ARNOLD

Trust not to thy feeling, for whatever it be now, it will quickly be changed.

THOMAS À KEMPIS

Sentiment is intellectualised emotion, emotion precipitated, as it were, in pretty crystals by the fancy.

JAMES RUSSELL LOWELL

> Mary her buried Lord (she thought) had lost;
> Yet see how dear this small adventure cost
> Her tender heart; mark how she wept and prayed . . .
> But thou, my senseless soul—Oh dreadful word!—
> Canst lose the presence of thy glorious Lord
> Days without number, yet find scarce a tear
> To witness that thou once didst hold Him dear.
> Ah, my vile heart, if thou thy Christ didst prize
> As Mary did, thou wouldst have Mary's eyes.
>
> NATHANIEL EATON

ENDURANCE

"He who endures to the end will be saved."

JESUS: MATTHEW 24:13

"What I do thou knowest not now, but thou shalt know hereafter": that saying has always been a perfect treasure to me. I have never been able to get along without it.

EDWARD WILSON, OF THE ANTARCTIC:
JOHN 13:7

God hath called you to Christ's side, and the wind is now in Christ's face in this land; and seeing ye are with him, ye cannot expect the lee side or the sunny side of the brae.

SAMUEL RUTHERFORD

The kingdom of God is not spread by people in armchairs (J. S. STANSFIELD). . . . To bear is to conquer our fate (THOMAS CAMPBELL). . . . It is the end that crowns us, not the fight (ROBERT HERRICK).

> Endurance is the crowning quality,
> And patience all the passion, of great hearts.

JAMES RUSSELL LOWELL

EQUALITY

"They love the place of honor . . . and the best seats in the synagogues, and salutations in the market places, and being called rabbi. . . . But you are not to be called rabbi, for you have one teacher, and you are all brethren . . . you have one Father . . . one master."

JESUS: MATTHEW 23:6–10

Did not he who made me in the womb make them?

JOB, ON HIS SLAVES: JOB 31:15, NEB

> One place there is—beneath the burial sod,
> Where all mankind are equalised by death;
> Another place there is—the fane of God,
> Where all are equal who draw living breath.

THOMAS HOOD

We hold these truths to be self-evident: that all men are created equal. . . .

THOMAS JEFFERSON (The Declaration of
Independence, the United States of America)

Men are made by nature unequal. It is vain, therefore, to treat them as if
they were equal.

JAMES A. FROUDE

ETERNITY

He has put eternity into man's mind.

ECCLESIASTES 3:11

The sand of the sea, the drops of rain,
    and the days of eternity—who can count them?

SIRACH 1:2

He lived in eternity, which is a manner of living, not a length of life.

PROFESSOR WALTER A. RALEIGH

        The One remains, the many change and pass;
        Heaven's light forever shines, Earth's shadows fly;
        Life, like a dome of many-coloured glass,
        Stains the white radiance of Eternity,
        Until Death tramples it to fragments.

PERCY BYSSHE SHELLEY

In the presence of eternity, the mountains are as transient as the clouds.

ROBERT G. INGERSOLL

        Those spacious regions where our fancies roam . . .
        Shall pass away, nor leave a rack behind;
        And Time's revolving wheels shall lose at last
        The speed that spins the future and the past:
        And, sovereign of an undisputed throne,
        Awful eternity shall reign alone.

PETRARCH

Eternity for bubbles proves at last
A senseless bargain.

WILLIAM COWPER

EVIL

Deliver us from evil.

MATTHEW 6:13

Evil is a fact not to be explained away, but to be accepted; and accepted not to be endured, but to be conquered. It is a challenge neither to our reason nor to our patience, but to our courage.

JOHN H. HOLMES

Evil, like the rolling stone upon a mountain-top,
A child may first impel, a giant cannot stop.

RICHARD C. TRENCH

Man creates the evil he endures (ROBERT SOUTHEY); Destroy the seed of evil, or it will grow up to your ruin (AESOP); To liberal thinkers Evil was right in the wrong place: it only needed shuffling (WILLIAM R. INGE); Evil is wrought by want of thought as well as by want of heart (THOMAS HOOD); Evil often triumphs, but never conquers (JOSEPH ROUX).

God had written . . . a play he had planned as perfect, but which had necessarily been left to human actors and stage-managers, who had since made a great mess of it.

G. K. CHESTERTON

When you choose the lesser of two evils, always remember that it is still an evil (MAX LERNER): Of two evils choose neither (CHARLES H. SPURGEON).

It is among people who think no evil that Evil can flourish without fear.

LOGAN PEARSALL SMITH

Evil shall have that evil well deserves.

GEOFFREY CHAUCER

EVOLUTION

"The earth produces of itself, first the blade, then the ear, then the full grain in the ear."

JESUS: MARK 4:28

All descriptions of the creating or sustaining principle in things must be metaphorical. . . . Thus the pantheist is forced to speak of God *in* all things, as if He were in a box. Thus the evolutionist has, in his very name, the idea of being unrolled like a carpet. . . . The root phrase for all Christian theism was this, that God was a creator, as an artist is a creator.

G. K. CHESTERTON

A fire-mist and a planet,
A crystal and a cell,
A jellyfish and a saurian,
And caves where the cave-men dwell;
Then a sense of law and beauty,
And a face turned from the clod—
Some call it Evolution,
And others call it God.

W. H. CARRUTH

Men were first produced in fishes, and when they were grown and able to help themselves, were thrown up, and so lived upon the land.

ANAXIMANDER, C. SIXTH CENTURY B.C.

The evolutionists seem to know everything about the missing link except the fact that it is missing.

G. K. CHESTERTON

"The unfit die, the fit both live and thrive."
Alas, who says so? They who do survive.

SARAH N. CLEGHORN

EXCELLENCE

Forgetting what lies behind and straining forward to what lies ahead. . . .

PAUL: PHILIPPIANS 3:13

If a man write a better book, preach a better sermon, or make a better mousetrap than his neighbour, though he build his house in the woods, the world will make a beaten path to his door.

RALPH WALDO EMERSON

Who aimeth at the sky
Shoots higher much than he that means a tree.

GEORGE HERBERT

So slow
The growth of what is excellent; so hard
T' attain perfection in this nether world.

WILLIAM COWPER

What is excellent, as God lives, is permanent.

ROBERT LOUIS STEVENSON

EXPERIENCE

Tribulation worketh patience; And patience, experience; and experience, hope.

PAUL: ROMANS 5:3–4, AV/KJV

To St. Paul, stripes, stones, shipwrecks, and thorns in the flesh were religious experiences; to Judas Iscariot, the daily companionship of Jesus of Nazareth was not.

LEONARD HODGSON

I am a part of all that I have met;
Yet all experience is an arch wherethro'
Gleams that untravelled world whose margin fades
For ever and for ever when I move.

ALFRED TENNYSON, ON ULYSSES

Experience is a comb which Nature gives us when we are bald (CHINESE PROVERB); The years teach much which the days never know (RALPH WALDO EMERSON); It is far better to borrow experience than to buy it (C. C. COLTON); It is costly wisdom that is bought by experience (ROGER ASCHAM);

He who has once burnt his mouth always blows his soup (GERMAN PROVERB); A shipwrecked man fears every sea (OVID).

Till old experience do attain
To something like prophetic strain.

JOHN MILTON

Experience is not what happens to you; it is what you do with what happens to you.

ALDOUS HUXLEY

We spend our lives in learning pilotage,
And grow good steersmen when the vessel's crank!

GEORGE MEREDITH

A failure is a man who has blundered, but is not able to cash in the experience.

ELBERT HUBBARD

FAITH

Faith is being sure of what we hope for and certain of what we do not see.

HEBREWS 11:1, NIV

Faith is . . . believing what you do not yet see: its reward is to see what you believe (AUGUSTINE); . . . an indivisible totality of beliefs that inspire . . . it reinvigorates the will, enriches the affections, awakens creativeness (HELEN KELLER); . . . the force of life (LEO N. TOLSTOI); . . . an act of self-consecration in which the will, the intellect, and the affections all have their place (WILLIAM R. INGE); . . . a kind of winged intellect: the great workmen of history have been men who believed like giants (C. H. PARKHURST); . . . the subtle chain which binds us to the infinite, the voice of a deep life within that will remain until we crowd it hence (ELIZABETH OAKES SMITH); . . . simply betting your life that Christ was right and finding in experience how right He was (X); . . . the grand venture, in which we commit our whole soul and future to the conviction that Christ was not an illusion, but the very reality of God (P. T. FORSYTH); Godliness is faith made visible: faith is godliness of mind and heart (X).

Cleave ever to the sunnier side of doubt,
And cling to faith, beyond the forms of faith.

ALFRED TENNYSON

The steps of faith
Fall on the seeming void, and find
The Rock beneath.

UNKNOWN

What is this faith? In the Gospels it consists of reaching out a hand to touch the hem of Christ's robe; muttering, alone, "God be merciful!"; it is shame washing Christ's feet with penitent tears, and insisting, in spite of admitted failure, "Lord, thou knowest that I love thee!"

X

Faith is the cliff on which the weak wave breaks;
   The tree around whose might frail tendrils twine;
   In cloudy skies it sets a starry sign,
And in the sorrowing soul an altar makes.

T. S. JONES

It is essential to choose carefully the faith one lives by. Intellectually, a sound faith should throw light on all the salient facts of experience, not only upon a prejudiced selection; morally, it should work out well, enriching personality and not impoverishing it, purifying the common life and not corrupting it, sustaining justice, protecting the weak, defending the oppressed, redeeming the wayward; emotionally, it should endow life with courage, contentment, joy and hope; and it should rob death of its finality.

X

Shipwreck was ours if Thou didst sleep uncaring;
   We did not wait to see that God was near.
We could not understand a faith so daring,
   Calmly to slumber 'till the storm should clear.
It was our faith, not He, that needed waking!

HOWARD USSHER

In no case can true reason and right faith contradict each other (SAMUEL TAYLOR COLERIDGE); Reason is itself a matter of faith—it is an act of faith to assert that our thoughts have any relation to reality at all (G. K. CHESTERTON); The heart has its reasons which Reason does not know (BLAISE PASCAL); It is always right that a man should be "able to render a *reason* for the *faith* that is within him" (SYDNEY SMITH); It is not reason which makes faith hard, but life (JEAN INGELOW).

We live by faith; but faith is not the slave
Of text and legend. Reason's voice, and God's,
Nature's and Duty's, never are at odds.

JOHN GREENLEAF WHITTIER

Faith is a bulb that needs darkness to root well (X); I would rather walk with God in the dark than go alone in the light (MARY G. BRAINARD); If a thing is right it should be done, and if it should it can (MOTTO OF THE RATHBONE FAMILY); Hundreds may believe, but each has to believe by himself (W. H. AUDEN); No faith is our own that we have not arduously won (H. HAVELOCK ELLIS).

> Though vine nor fig-tree neither
>   Their wonted fruit shall bear;
> Though all the field should wither
>   Nor flocks nor herds be there:
> Yet God the same abiding,
>   His praise shall tune my voice;
> For while in Him confiding
>   I cannot but rejoice.
>
> WILLIAM COWPER, ON HABAKKUK 3:17–18

> But give me, Lord, eyes to behold the truth;
>   A seeing sense that knows the eternal right;
> A heart with pity filled, and gentlest ruth,
>   A manly faith, that makes all darkness light.
>
> THEODORE PARKER

My deepest conviction is that love is the one thing to cling to in all the darkness. I too . . . have been disappointed and disillusioned a hundred times. But nothing and no-one has been able to undermine my very simple faith that God is as Jesus Christ.

> H. R. L. SHEPPARD

> It fortifies my soul to know
> That, though I perish, Truth is so:
> That, howsoe'er I stray and range,
> Whate'er I do, Thou dost not change.
> I steadier step when I recall
> That, if I slip, Thou dost not fall.
>
> ARTHUR H. CLOUGH

Expect great things from God; attempt great things for God.

> WILLIAM CAREY

> Columbus found a world, and had no chart
> Save one that faith deciphered in the skies;
> To trust the soul's invincible surmise
> Was all his science, and his only art.
>
> GEORGE SANTAYANA

Faith, mighty faith, the promise sees,
And looks to that alone,
Laughs at impossibilities
And cries "it shall be done!"

CHARLES WESLEY

Just as there is a lower carelessness which means death to the soul, so there is a higher carelessness which is the supreme gift of religion. We must all at length rest back upon God.

W. E. ORCHARD

Faith is a fine invention
For gentlemen who see;
But microscopes are prudent
In an emergency.

EMILY DICKINSON

But all comes out right at the end of the day . . . all will come out yet more right at the end of all the days.

WINSTON SPENCER CHURCHILL

FAMILY

I bow my knees before the Father, from whom every family in heaven and on earth is named.

PAUL: EPHESIANS 3:14–15

By associating the family with his central religious ideas, Jesus gave it a new consecration. . . . Jesus at the same time clearly perceived that loyalty to the family is wont to conflict with larger loyalties, and did not hesitate to affirm that in such cases it must yield.

E. F. SCOTT

Strength of character may be acquired at work, but beauty of character is learned at home. . . . The family is the supreme conductor of Christianity.

HENRY DRUMMOND

Christ's love rebukes no home-love, breaks no tie of kin apart;
    Better heresy in doctrine than heresy of heart.
Tell me not the church must censure: she who wept
      the cross beside
    Never made her own flesh strangers, nor the claims
      of blood denied.

JOHN GREENLEAF WHITTIER

FEAR

    The Lord is my light and my salvation;
      whom shall I fear?
    The Lord is the stronghold of my life:
      of whom shall I be afraid?

PSALM 27:1

There is no fear in love—except the fear of hurting one another and affronting the love of God.

AFTER C. H. DODD

The history of the soul: without fear or love; with fear, without love; with fear and love; without fear, with love.

JOHANN ALBRECHT BENGEL

    No coward soul is mine,
    No trembler in the world's storm-troubled sphere:
      I see heaven's glories shine,
    And faith shines equal, arming me from fear.

EMILY BRONTË

While the best men are well guided by love, most men are still goaded by fear.

AUGUSTINE

The only thing we have to fear is fear itself.

FRANKLIN DELANO ROOSEVELT
(echoing Thoreau, Bacon)

Were the diver to think on the jaws of the shark, he would never lay hands on the pearl.

SA'DI, C. 1258

Early and provident fear is the mother of safety (EDMUND BURKE); Keep your fears to yourself: share your courage (ROBERT LOUIS STEVENSON).

FORGIVENESS

> "Forgive us our debts,
> As we also *have forgiven* our debtors."

JESUS: MATTHEW 6:12 (emphasis added)

Forgiveness does not mean the cancellation of all the consequences of wrongdoing. It means the refusal on God's part to let our guilty past affect His relationship with us.

UNKNOWN

We believe in the forgiveness of sin, not by convincing ourselves that our sins were excusable, or remediable, or that we meant well, or that "we won't do it again." It is because the principle of forgiveness is built into the structure of a moral order created and determined by the character of a just and faithful God.

C. H. DODD

Though the soul's wounds heal, the scars remain. God sees them not as blemishes but as honours (JULIAN OF NORWICH); A man that studieth revenge keeps his own wounds green, which otherwise would heal and do well (FRANCIS BACON); Certainly, in taking revenge, a man is but even with his enemy; in passing it over he is superior (FRANCIS BACON).

> Can it be true, the grace he is declaring?
>   Oh let us trust him, for his words are fair!
> Man, what is this, and why art thou despairing?
>   God shall forgive thee all, but thy despair.

F. W. H. MYERS

We live by forgiveness (KARL BARTH); The worst of men are those who will not forgive (THOMAS FULLER); The glory of Christianity is to conquer by forgiveness (WILLIAM BLAKE); Not to relent is beastly, savage, devilish (WILLIAM SHAKESPEARE).

"I can forgive but I cannot forget" is only another way of saying "I cannot forgive."

HENRY WARD BEECHER

FREEDOM

It is for freedom that Christ has set us free. Stand firm, then, and do not let yourselves by burdened again by a yoke of slavery.

PAUL: GALATIANS 5:1, NIV

Onesimus, a slave, ran away seeking freedom. He found himself in prison, a slave to fears. There he discovered a free man of Rome, now a bondslave of Jesus Christ and a prisoner for the gospel. This man led Onesimus through bondage to Christ into perfect freedom.

X, ON PHILEMON PASSIM

Remember that to change your mind and follow him who sets you right is to be none the less free than you were before.

MARCUS AURELIUS

Gospel freedom from the past, moral freedom from the law, psychological freedom from the flesh, social freedom from the fear of man, political freedom from idolatry of the State, spiritual freedom from the demons and from fate—it is hard to believe that we are listening to assurances from a Pharisee, an authoritarian to the ends of his phylacteries, until we remember that this is a Pharisee's testimony to the freedom he has found in Christ.

ANONYMOUS

I love, I love my Master,
I will not go out free!
For He is my Redeemer,
He paid the price for me . . .
Rejoicing and adoring

Henceforth my song shall be
"I love, I love my Master,
And will not go out free!"

FRANCES RIDLEY HAVERGAL,
ON EXODUS 21:5

The sweetest freedom is an honest heart (JOHN FORD); Liberty is freedom to do what one's conscience says is right (LORD ACTON); Liberty means responsibility: that is why most men dread it (GEORGE BERNARD SHAW).

Freedom and slavery are mental states (MAHATMA GANDHI); There can be no real freedom without the freedom to fail (ERICH FROMM); Freedom cannot be bestowed, bought, or claimed: it must be deserved, achieved, exercised and guarded, or it dies (X); Emancipation from the bondage of the soil is no freedom for the tree (TAGORE); Liberty exists in proportion to wholesome restraint (DANIEL WEBSTER); None can love freedom heartily but good men: the rest love license (JOHN MILTON).

To those the truth makes free,
Sacred as truth itself is lawful liberty.

AUBREY DE VERE

True freedom is to share
All the chains our brothers wear,
And with heart and hand to be
Earnest to make others free.

JAMES RUSSELL LOWELL

Give me the liberty to know, to utter, and to argue freely, according to conscience, above all liberties.

JOHN MILTON

If but the least and frailest, let me be
Evermore numbered with the truly free,
Who find Thy service perfect liberty!

JOHN GREENLEAF WHITTIER

Make me a captive, Lord,
And then I shall be free.

Force me to render up my sword
And I shall conqueror be . . .

My will is not my own
Till Thou hast made it Thine:
If it would reach a monarch's throne
It must its crown resign.

GEORGE MATHESON

A surfeit of freedom can be fatal. The Greeks saw the danger, and prized freedom with moderation, within citizenship; the Romans saw it, and prized freedom within order and discipline; the Jews saw it, and lost the notion of freedom in that of obedience to divine law. Christians prized freedom informed and inspired by the Spirit of Jesus.

X

If Thou hadst not
Been stern to me,
But left me free,
I had forgot
Myself, and Thee.

BEN JONSON

Freedom is not procured by a full enjoyment of what is desired, but by controlling the desire. . . . No man is free who is not master of himself (EPICTETUS); Among a people generally corrupt, liberty cannot long exist (EDMUND BURKE); Man's liberty ends, and it ought to end, when that liberty becomes the curse of his neighbours (FREDERIC W. FARRAR); Only in fetters is liberty: without its banks could a river be? (LOUIS GINSBERG); When everyone does exactly what he likes no one gets anything he wants (RABBINIC COUNSEL); To obey God is freedom (SENECA); Freedom is recreated year by year, in hearts wide open on the godward side (JAMES RUSSELL LOWELL); All spirits are enslaved which serve things evil (PERCY BYSSHE SHELLEY); The liberty of the individual must be thus far limited: he must not make himself a nuisance to other people (JOHN STUART MILL); We have confused the free with the free and easy (ADLAI STEVENSON).

In the beauty of the lilies Christ was born across the sea,
With a glory in His bosom that transfigures you and me;
As He died to make men holy, let us live to make men free,
While God is marching on.

JULIA WARD HOWE

Do not say, "Because of the Lord I left the right way";
    for he will not do what he hates . . .
It was he who created man in the beginning,
    and he left him in the power of his own inclination.
If you will, you can keep the commandments,
    and to act faithfully is a matter of your own choice.
He has placed before you fire and water:
    stretch out your hand for whichever you wish.
Before a man are life and death,
    and whichever he chooses will be given to him.
For great is the wisdom of the Lord . . .
He has not commanded any one to be ungodly,
    and he has not given any one permission to sin.

SIRACH 15:11, 14–18, 20

In giving freedom to the slave we assure freedom to the free—honourable
alike in what we give and what we preserve.

ABRAHAM LINCOLN

A lad grows up at a street intersection where a church, a drinking saloon,
a gaming club, and a gymnasium occupy the four corners. He may
become a devotee of any one, of two, of three, or of all four; or he
may violently reject any one, two, three, or all four. Only he will know
the lure, or the repulsion, exercised by each; how he will react—and
why. Clever observers will explain how his resultant character simply "had
to be," but only afterwards. The form, the area, and the strength of his
choices will largely be determined by his complicated environment: but
among the options open to him, he will "come of age" in authentic, self-
originating choices of his own. That is his freedom.

X

You may say, if you like, that the determinist is free to disbelieve in the
reality of the will. But it is a much more massive and important fact that
he is *not* free to praise, to curse, to thank, to justify, to urge, to punish,
to resist temptations, to incite mobs, to make New Year resolutions, to
pardon sinners, to rebuke tyrants, or even to say "thank you" for the
mustard.

G. K. CHESTERTON

"What did the first frog say?" . . . "Lord, how you made me jump!" . . . but the frog prefers jumping.

G. K. CHESTERTON

All we have of freedom, all we use, or know,
This our fathers bought for us, long and long ago.

RUDYARD KIPLING

The king is a mortal man and not God, and therefore hath no power over the immortal souls of his subjects, to make laws and ordinances for them and to set up lords over them. . . . Our lord the king is but an earthly king . . . if the king's people be obedient and true subjects, obeying all human laws made by the king, our lord the king can require no more; for men's religion to God is betwixt God and themselves; the king shall not answer for it, neither may the king be judge between God and man; let them be heretics, Turks, Jews or whatsoever, it appertains not to the earthly power to punish them in the least measure.

THOMAS HELWYS, C. 1612

Sir, as diverse times before, so now again I must tell you: there are two kings and two kingdoms in Scotland; there is Christ Jesus, and His kingdom the kirk, whose subject King James the Sixth is, and of Whose kingdom [he is] not a head nor a lord but a member.

ANDREW MELVILLE, SPEAKING TO JAMES VI

The magistrate is not by virtue of his office to meddle with religion. . . . For Christ only is the King and Lawgiver of the church and conscience.

JOHN SMYTH, C. 1612

The condition upon which God hath given liberty to man is eternal vigilance.

JOHN PHILPOT CURRAN

. . . A world founded upon four essential freedoms: The first is freedom of speech and expression, everywhere in the world; the second is freedom of every person to worship God in his own way. . . . The third is freedom from want . . . the fourth, freedom from fear.

FRANKLIN DELANO ROOSEVELT, 1941

FRIENDSHIP

Faithful are the wounds of a friend.

PROVERBS 27:6

A true friend unbosoms freely, advises justly, assists readily, adventures boldly, takes all patiently, defends courageously, and continues a friend unchangeably.

WILLIAM PENN

God help the soul that bars its own door (MICHAEL FAIRLESS); Friendship multiplies the good of life and divides the evil (BALTASAR GRACIAN); Between friends there is no need of justice (ARISTOTLE); A faithful friend is an elixir of life (SIRACH 6:16); There's nothing worth the wear of winning, but laughter and the love of friends (HILAIRE BELLOC).

When my friends are one-eyed, I look at them in profile (JOSEPH JOUBERT); The friends of my friend are my friends (FRENCH PROVERB); Keep your friendships in repair (RALPH WALDO EMERSON).

God gives us relatives; thank God we can choose our friends.

ADDISON MIZNER

FUTURE

"No eye has seen,
no ear has heard,
no mind has conceived
what God has prepared for those who love him."

PAUL: 1 CORINTHIANS 2:9, NIV

Yesterday is not ours to recover, but tomorrow is ours to win or lose.

LYNDON B. JOHNSON

God finds a way for what none foresaw.

EURIPIDES

I know not what the future hath
　　Of marvel or surprise,
Assured alone that life and death
　　His mercy underlies.

JOHN GREENLEAF WHITTIER

If a man carefully examine his thoughts he will be surprised to find how much he lives in the future. His well-being is always ahead. Such a creature is probably immortal.

RALPH WALDO EMERSON

Men, my brothers, men the workers, ever reaping something new:
That which they have done but earnest of the things that they
　　　shall do;
For I dipt into the future, far as human eye could see,
Saw the Vision of the world, and all the wonder that would be;
Saw the heavens fill with commerce, argosies of magic sails,
Pilots of the purple twilight, dropping down with costly bales;
Heard the heavens fill with shouting, and there rain'd a ghastly dew
From the nations' airy navies grappling in the central blue,
Far along the world-wide whisper of the south wind rushing warm
With the standards of the peoples plunging through the
　　　thunder storm.
Till the war drums throbbed no longer and the battle flags
　　　were furled
In the Parliament of man, the Federation of the world.
There the common sense of most shall hold a fretful realm in awe,
And the kindly earth shall slumber, lapt in universal law.

ALFRED TENNYSON, IN 1842

These things shall be: a loftier race
　　Than e'er the world hath known shall rise,
With flame of freedom in their souls
　　And light of knowledge in their eyes.

They shall be gentle, brave, and strong
　　To spill no drop of blood, but dare
All that may plant man's lordship firm
　　On earth, and fire, and sea, and air.

There shall be no more sin, nor shame,
    Though pain and passion may not die;
For man shall be at one with God
    In bonds of firm necessity.

J. ADDINGTON SYMONDS

We steal if we touch tomorrow. It is God's.

HENRY WARD BEECHER

GENTLENESS

The fruit of the Spirit is . . . gentleness.

PAUL: GALATIANS 5:22−23

Nothing is so strong as gentleness: nothing so gentle as real strength.

RALPH W. SOCKMAN

When a man is made up wholly of the dove, without the least grain of the serpent in his composition, he becomes ridiculous in many circumstances of his life, and very often discredits his best actions.

JOSEPH ADDISON

Power can do by gentleness what violence fails to accomplish (CLAUDIAN); "Gentleman"?—Gentle is as gentle does! (ENGLISH PROVERB); The cat in gloves catches no mice (ENGLISH PROVERB).

GIVING

" 'It is more blessed to give than to receive.' "

JESUS: ACTS 20:35

Give all thou canst; high heaven rejects the lore
Of nicely calculated less or more.

WILLIAM WORDSWORTH

"Sell all thou hast, and give it to the poor. and follow me": *but* sell not all thou hast except thou come and follow me—that is, except thou have a vocation wherein thou mayest do as much good with little means as with great. For otherwise, in feeding the streams, thou driest the fountain.

FRANCIS BACON

Whatever I have given I still possess (SENECA); All you can hold in your cold, dead hand is what you have given away (SANSKRIT PROVERB); The wise man does not lay up treasure, for the more he gives to others the more he has for his own (LAO TSE); Feel for others—in your pocket (CHARLES H. SPURGEON); He gives twice who gives promptly . . . a gift in season is double favour (PUBLILIUS SYRUS); He gives by halves who hesitates (WILLIAM BROOME); Generosity gives assistance rather than advice (VAUVENARGUES); It is better to give unasked, through understanding (KAHLIL GIBRAN).

> A man there was, though some did count him mad,
> The more he cast away the more he had.

RALPH WALDO EMERSON

JOHN BUNYAN

If riches increase, let thy mind hold pace with them; think it not enough to be liberal, but munificent.

THOMAS BROWNE

The only gift is a portion of thyself. . . . Therefore the poet brings his poem, the shepherd his lamb. the farmer corn, the miner a gem, the sailor coral and shells, the painter his picture, the girl a handkerchief of her own sewing.

RALPH WALDO EMERSON

> Give unto all, lest he whom thou deniest
> May chance to be no other man but Christ.

ROBERT HERRICK

It is the very life, and character, of God—to give.

X

GOD

> "Can you fathom the mysteries of God?
> can you fathom the perfections of the Almighty? . . .
> If he passes by he may keep secret his passing;
> if he proclaims it, who can turn him back?"

JOB 11:7, 10, NEB

> The hunger in man's heart is infinite
>> And craves infinity for food:
> I dare not give man bread unless I give him more—
>> He must have God.

STUDDERT KENNEDY

Descriptions of God

God is truth, and light his shadow (PLATO); God is light that is never
darkened, an unwearied life that cannot die, a fountain always flowing, a
garden of life, a seminary of wisdom, a radical beginning of all goodness
(FRANCIS QUARLES); The shadow of a mighty right hand is cast over
Waterloo; on that day the perspective of the human race was changed . . .
and He to whom there is no reply undertook the task (VICTOR HUGO);
God is a circle whose centre is everywhere and whose circumference is
nowhere (EMPEDOCLES); God is an unutterable sigh, planted in the depths of
the soul (JEAN PAUL RICHTER); God, to be God, must transcend what is; He
must be the maker of what ought to be (RUFUS M. JONES); Man doth what
he can, and God what He will (JOHN RAY); God is Christlike, and in him
is no unChristlikeness at all (ARTHUR MICHAEL RAMSEY, ATTRIBUTED).

In the pre-Christian and non-Christian religions every quality, good and bad,
has been deified except self-sacrificing love. Power, beauty, fecundity,
warlike courage, knowledge, industry, art, wisdom, justice, benevolence and
mercy—the apotheosis of all these has been achieved by the human soul.
The one deity awanting to the world's pantheon is—the God who is
love.

ROBERT LAW

Jewish piety has laid the world under a hopeless debt by imagining the
austere holiness of God, and has doubled the obligation by adding His
tenderness.

JOHN WATSON

With moderns, Deity and virtue are synonymous; with the ancients, deities
and vice were inseparable.

JOHN WATSON

> I think this is the authentic sign and seal
> Of Godship, that it ever waxes glad,
> And more glad, until gladness blossoms, bursts

Into a rage to suffer for mankind,
And recommence at sorrow.

ROBERT BROWNING

From Thee, great God, we spring, to Thee we tend,
Path, motive, guide, original, and end.

SAMUEL JOHNSON

I have never understood why it should be considered derogatory to the Creator to suppose that He has a sense of humour.

WILLIAM R. INGE

Seeking God

We must know men to love them, but love God to know Him.

BLAISE PASCAL

Earth gets its price for what earth gives us;
 The beggar is taxed for a corner to die in,
The priest hath his fee who comes and shrives us,
 We bargain for the graves we lie in.
At the Devil's booth are all things sold:
Each ounce of dross costs its ounce of gold.
 For a cap and bells our lives we pay,
Bubbles we earn with a whole soul's tasking;
 'Tis heaven alone that is given away,
 'Tis only God may be had for the asking.

JAMES RUSSELL LOWELL

There is no great excellence in . . . running to Rome or Jerusalem with bare feet. . . . The divine treasure lies hidden in thine own soul. . . . The silver coin, the groat, is lost in thine own house. . . .

WALTER HILTON, BEFORE 1396

Two worlds are ours: 'tis only sin
 Forbids us to descry
The mystic heaven and earth *within*,
 Plain as the sea and sky.

Thou who hast given us eyes to see
 And love this sight so fair,

Give me a heart to find out Thee,
And read Thee everywhere.

JOHN KEBLE

Speak to Him, thou, for He hears, and Spirit with spirit can meet:
Closer is He than breathing, and nearer than hands and feet.

ALFRED TENNYSON

Just when we are safest, there's a sunset-touch,
A fancy from a flower-bell, some one's death,
A chorus-ending from Euripides—
And that's enough for fifty hopes and fears
As old and new at once as Nature's self,
To rap and knock and enter in our soul,
Take hands and dance there. . . .

ROBERT BROWNING

Be comforted. You would not be seeking Me if you had not found Me.

BLAISE PASCAL

Short arm needs man to reach to heaven,
So ready is heaven to stoop to him.

FRANCIS THOMPSON

To seek God is not difficult, for the earnest soul, for He has left us
countless clues to His presence—within us in conscience, behind us in
history, around us in the best people we know, in our hands in His
word, before us in the heart's resilient hopefulness, and plainest of all in
the ever-accessible Christ. God may not always be obvious: but He is
there, discernible, knowable, reachable, dependable, and ever welcoming.

ANONYMOUS

Arguments for God's Existence

Thus, anxious thoughts in endless circles roll,
Without a centre where to fix the soul:
In this wild maze their vain endeavours end:
How can the less the greater comprehend?
Or finite reason reach infinity?
For what could fathom God were more than He!

JOHN DRYDEN

God is to me that creative Force, behind and in the Universe, who manifests himself as energy, as life, as order, as beauty, as thought, as conscience, as love.

HENRY SLOANE COFFIN

I had rather believe all the fables in the Legend, and the Talmud, and the Alcoran, than that this universal frame is without a mind.

FRANCIS BACON

The very possibility of science depends on the fact that Nature answers to our thought about it, and that our thought answers to Nature. . . . We cannot help believing, therefore, that the system which thus responds to mind is itself the work of mind, a Mind which is infinite and universal . . . a Mind which cannot be contained within the Universe.

J. S. WHALE

We are all careering through space, clinging to a cannonball. . . . An invisible force holds us in our own armchairs while the earth hurtles like a boomerang; and men still go back to dusty records to prove the mercy of God.

G. K. CHESTERTON

"Tell them I AM," Jehovah said
To Moses; while earth heard in dread
    And smitten to the heart.
At once above, beneath, around,
All Nature without voice or sound
    Replied, "O Lord, THOU ART."

CHRISTOPHER SMART

Finding God

I sought the Lord, but afterward I knew
    He moved my soul to seek Him, seeking me.
It was not I that found, O Saviour true,
    No, I was found of Thee.

I find, *I* walk, *I* love, but oh, the whole
    Of love is but my answer, Lord, to Thee;

For Thou wert long beforehand with my soul,
   Always Thou lovest me.

               ANONYMOUS, *PLYMOUTH HYMNAL*

I found Him not in world or sun,
   Or eagle's wing, or insect's eye;
   Nor through the questions men may try,
The petty cobwebs we have spun . . .

A warmth within the breast would melt
   The freezing reason's colder part,
   And, like a man in wrath, the heart
Stood up and answered, "I have felt!"

               ALFRED TENNYSON

Does the fish soar to find the ocean,
   The eagle plunge to find the air,
That we ask of the stars in motion
   If they have rumour of Thee there?

The angels keep their ancient places;
   Turn but a stone, and start a wing!
'Tis ye, 'tis your estrangèd faces
   That miss the many-splendoured thing.

But (when so sad thou canst not sadder)
   Cry—and upon thy so sore loss
Shall shine the traffic of Jacob's ladder
   Pitched between Heaven and Charing Cross.

Yea, in the night, my soul, my daughter,
   Cry, clinging Heaven by the hems;
And lo, Christ walking on the water,
   Not of Gennesaret but Thames!

               FRANCIS THOMPSON

            I have felt
A presence that disturbs me with the joy
Of elevated thoughts, a sense sublime
Of something far more deeply interfused,
Whose dwelling is the light of setting suns,
And the round ocean, and the living air,
And in the mind of man;

A motion, and a spirit, that impels
All thinking things, all objects of all thought,
And rolls through all things.

WILLIAM WORDSWORTH

And I smiled to think God's greatness flowed around
our incompleteness,
Round our restlessness, His rest.

ELIZABETH BARRETT BROWNING

At times, in the lonely silence of the night, and in rare and lonely
moments, I come upon a sort of communion with myself, and with
something great that is not myself. It is perhaps a poverty of mind and
language which obliges me to say that this universal scheme takes on the
effect of a sympathetic person, and my communion a quality of fearless
worship.

H. G. WELLS

God often visits us, but most of the time we are not at home.

JOSEPH ROUX

Fellowship with God

God is Alpha and Omega in the great world; endeavour to make Him so
in your little world—make Him thy evening epilogue and thy morning
prologue. . . . So shall thy rest be peaceful, thy labours prosperous, thy life
pious, and thy death glorious.

FRANCIS QUARLES

Who walks with God in just and generous ways
With humble heart, His chief demand obeys.
For such the desert blooms, the way is clear;
The lame leap, and the dumb can raise a cheer.
From strength to strength they journey, minds content,
Their wings like eagles', and their hearts not faint.
With Christ they walk the waters through the storm
While yet within broods His unruffled calm.
The rod and staff still comfort, and the vale
Loses its shadow, for hope cannot fail.

Who walk with God in just and gentle ways
Walk on with Enoch to eternal days.

ANONYMOUS

There are in this loud stunning tide
    Of human care and crime,
With whom the melodies abide
    Of everlasting chime;
Who carry music in their heart
Through dusky lane and wrangling mart,
Plying their daily task with busier feet
Because their secret souls a holy strain repeat.

JOHN KEBLE

They say there is a hollow, safe and still,
    A point of coolness and repose
Within the centre of a flame, where life might dwell
    Unharmed and unconsumed . . .
    There is a point of rest
At the great centre of the cyclone's force
    A silence at its secret source—
A little child might slumber undistressed . . .
So in the centre of these thoughts of God,
    Cyclones of power, consuming glory-fire,
There, *there* we find a point of perfect rest,
    And glorious safety. . . .

FRANCES RIDLEY HAVERGAL

As the marsh hen secretly builds on the watery sod,
Behold, I will build me a nest on the greatness of God.
I will fly in the greatness of God as the marsh hen flies
In the freedom that fills all the space 'twixt the marsh
        and the skies.
By so many roots as the marsh-grass sends in the sod,
I will heartily lay me ahold of the greatness of God.

SIDNEY LANIER, NATURALIST, DYING AT 39

God be in my head,
And in my understanding;
God be in mine eyes,

And in my looking;
God be in my mouth,
And in my speaking;
God be in my heart,
And in my thinking;
God be at my end,
And at my departing.

UNKNOWN, "KNIGHT'S PRAYER"

GOODNESS

Do not be overcome by evil, but overcome evil with good.

PAUL: ROMANS 12:21

Goodness is easier to recognise than to define (W. H. AUDEN); He was so "good" he would pour rose-water on a toad (DOUGLAS JERROLD); So very good he was good for nothing (ITALIAN PROVERB); Experience makes us see an enormous difference between piety and goodness (BLAISE PASCAL); Goodness without wisdom always accomplishes evil (R. A. HEINLEIN).

Nothing can possibly be conceived in the world or out of it which can without qualification be called good except a Good Will. Intelligence, wit, judgement, courage, perseverance are undoubtedly good in many respects. But these may also become extremely bad if the will is not good. The same with fortune, power, riches, honour, health, happiness. . . . Even if this Good Will should wholly lack power to accomplish its purpose . . . then like a jewel it would still shine by its own light, as a thing which has its whole value in itself.

IMMANUEL KANT

Good will is the mightiest practical force in the universe.

C. F. DOLE

Good works are not all specifically religious. . . . A mother washing her baby, the miller's girl putting corn on the mule's back, the farmer ploughing, the cobbler at his last, the scholar with his students, the prince governing his people. . . . These are "good works". . . . God wants His people to do for one another, so that His world may continue in harmony.

J. ATKINSON, SUMMARISING LUTHER

Abashed the Devil stood,
And felt how awful goodness is.

JOHN MILTON

Every person is responsible for all the good within the range of his abilities—and for no more.

GAIL HAMILTON

The omission of good is no less reprehensible than the commission of evil.

PLUTARCH

"Good" critics who have stamped out poet's hope,
"Good" statesmen who pulled ruin on the State,
"Good" patriots who for a theory risked a cause,
"Good" kings who disembowelled for a tax,
"Good" popes who brought all good to jeopardy,
"Good" Christians who sat still in easy chairs
And damned the general world for standing up—
Now may the good God pardon all "good" men!

ELIZABETH BARRETT BROWNING

None deserves praise for being good who has not spirit enough to be bad.

LA ROCHEFOUCAULD

All the beautiful sentiments in the world weigh less than a single lovely action.

JAMES RUSSELL LOWELL

We know the good, we apprehend it clearly. But we cannot bring it to achievement.

EURIPIDES (fifth century B.C.)

It is good to be tired and wearied by the vain search after the true good, that we may stretch out our arms to the Redeemer.

BLAISE PASCAL

Knowledge we ask not—knowledge Thou hast lent,
But, Lord, the will—there lies our bitter need;
Give us to build above our deep intent
The deed, the deed.

JOHN DRINKWATER

The evil cannot brook delay,
  The good can well afford to wait.
Give ermined knaves their hour of crime—
  Ye have the future, grand and great,
  The safe appeal of Truth to Time!

ELIZABETH BARRETT BROWNING

The reward of a good deed is to have done it.

ELBERT HUBBARD

There shall never be one lost good! what was shall live as before.
The evil is null, is nought, is silence implying sound;
What was good shall be good. . . .

ROBERT BROWNING

GRACE

Grace be multiplied—Grace that was to be yours—Grace that is
coming—the grace of life—God's varied grace—Grace to the humble—
the God of all grace—the true grace of God.

PETER: 1 PETER PASSIM

The depths of religious experience are sounded when a man awakens to
the truth that, while he has nothing to hope for from himself, he may
dare to hope for everything from God; that the source of his confidence
does not lie in himself at all, but in the inexhaustible mercy and
unchanging love of God.

X

Amazing grace! how sweet the sound
That saved a wretch like me:

I once was lost, but now am found;
    Was blind, but now I see.

'Twas grace that taught my heart to fear,
    And grace my fears relieved;
How precious did that grace appear
    The hour I first believed!

Through many dangers, toils and snares
    I have already come:
'Tis grace hath brought me safe thus far,
    And grace will lead me home.

JOHN NEWTON

Nothing whatever pertaining to godliness and real holiness can be accomplished without grace.

AUGUSTINE

A man cannot do good before he is made good (MARTIN LUTHER); Grace groweth best in winter (SAMUEL RUTHERFORD); Grace is given of God, but knowledge is born in the market (ARTHUR H. CLOUGH).

Grace taught my wandering feet
    To tread the heavenly road;
And new supplies each hour I meet
    While pressing on to God.

Grace taught my soul to pray,
    And made my eyes o'erflow;
'Tis grace has kept me to this day,
    And will not let me go.

PHILIP DODDRIDGE

GRATITUDE

We always thank God—Giving thanks to the Father—Abounding in thanksgiving—Be thankful—With thankfulness in your hearts—Giving thanks to God—Watchful . . . with thanksgiving.

PAUL: COLOSSIANS PASSIM

In place of the bondage of commandments, the fear of divine displeasure, and anxious striving to deserve God's favour, Christianity released into man's moral experience the glad, exuberant gratitude kindled by the love that had already sought and saved; a wholly new spiritual dynamic, that motivated a goodness evoked by forgiveness and joy, and yet inherently insured against self-righteousness and pride.

ANONYMOUS

Let never day nor night unhallowed pass,
But still remember what the Lord hath done.

UNKNOWN

Gratitude is the memory of the heart (JEAN BAPTISTE MASSIEU); Some people always sigh in thanking God (ELIZABETH BARRETT BROWNING).

O Lord, that lends me life,
Lend me a heart replete with thankfulness!

WILLIAM SHAKESPEARE

I kneel not now to pray that Thou
Make white one single sin—
I only kneel to thank Thee, Lord,
For what I have not been.

HARRY KEMP

Almighty God, Father of all mercies, we Thine unworthy servants do give Thee most humble and hearty thanks for all Thy goodness and lovingkindness to us and to all men. We bless Thee for our creation, preservation, and all the blessings of this life; but above all, for Thine inestimable love in the redemption of the world by our Lord Jesus Christ; for the means of grace, and for the hope of glory. And we beseech Thee, give us that due sense of all Thy mercies that our hearts may be unfeignedly thankful, and that we shew forth Thy praise, not only with our lips, but in our lives; by giving up ourselves to Thy service, and by walking before Thee in holiness and righteousness all our days; through Jesus Christ our Lord, to whom with Thee and the Holy Ghost, be all honour and glory, world without end. Amen.

BOOK OF COMMON PRAYER

GREATNESS

Should you then seek great things for yourself? Seek them not.

JEREMIAH 45:5, NIV

No really great man ever thought himself so. . . . The test of greatness is the page of history.

WILLIAM HAZLITT

Greatness . . . may be present in lives whose range is very small.

PHILLIPS BROOKS

Great lives never go out: they go on (BENJAMIN HARRISON); Great heights are hazardous to the weak head (ROBERT BLAIR); 'Tis eminence makes envy rise (JONATHAN SWIFT); The loftiest towers rise from the ground (CHINESE PROVERB).

His the impartial vision of the great,
Who see not as they wish, but as they find.

JAMES RUSSELL LOWELL

They who grasp the world,
The kingdom and the power and the glory,
Must pay with deepest misery of spirit,
Atoning unto God for a brief brightness.

STEPHEN PHILLIPS

GUIDANCE

"I am the light of the world. No follower of mine shall wander in the dark; he shall have the light of life."

JESUS: JOHN 8:12, NEB

Keep Thou my feet, I do not ask to see
The distant scene; one step enough for me.

JOHN HENRY NEWMAN

I see my way as birds their trackless way:
I shall arrive! What time, what circuit first,
I ask not: but unless God send His hail
Or blinding fireballs, sleet or shifting snow,
In some time, His good time, I shall arrive.
He guides me and the bird. In His good time!

ROBERT BROWNING

Christ of the upward way,
   My guide divine,
Where Thou hast set Thy feet
   May I place mine:
And move and march wherever Thou hast trod,
Keeping face forward up the hill of God.

W. J. MATHAMS

Be not like a horse or a mule, without understanding,
   which must be curbed with bit and bridle,
     else it will not keep with you.
I will instruct you and teach you the way you should go;
   I will counsel you with my eye upon you.

PSALM 32:9, 8

Divine guidance, when refracted through imperfect information of the circumstances and poor understanding of our own strong prejudices, may not prove infallible; yet God is faithful, and the earnest, humble heart is not permitted to go badly astray. A hundred fascinating questions may press upon our querulous minds and our insatiable intellectual curiosity: but God does not promise to illumine the whole scenery every time we ask, but only to guide our feet, step by step into what is right. Moreover, He never guides one about the duty of another: so often His word to our interfering hearts is the word spoken by Jesus to Peter: "What is that to thee? Follow THOU me."

ANONYMOUS, JOHN 21:22, AV/KJV,
(emphasis added)

He leads us on
By paths we do not know;
Upwards He leads us, though our steps be slow;
Though oft we faint and falter on the way,
Though storms and darkness oft obscure the day,
Yet, when the clouds are gone,
We know He leads us on.

AFTER HIRAM O. WILEY

HAPPINESS

He that is of a merry heart *hath* a continual feast.

PROVERBS 15:15 AV/KJV

So long as I have stuck to Nature and the New Testament I have only got happier and happier every day.

EDWARD WILSON, OF THE ANTARCTIC

I went out yesterday for the third time this year. . . . I lay in the sun while they picked me flowerets, with a cuckoo in the distance, circling swallows overhead, broad sweeps of gentle wind slowly rustling through the trees. Need I say I was happy? . . . Nurse says there are some people downstairs who drive everywhere and admire nothing.

ALICE JAMES

The bird of paradise alights only on the hand that does not grasp.

JOHN BERRY

When one door of happiness closes, another opens; but often we look so long at the closed door that we do not see the one which has opened for us.

HELEN KELLER

Happiness is a habit: cultivate it (ELBERT HUBBARD); The attitude of unhappiness is not only painful, it is mean and ugly. . . . It but fastens and perpetuates the trouble which occasioned it, and increases the total evil of the situation (WILLIAM JAMES).

> If I have faltered more or less
> In my great task of happiness;
> If I have moved among my race
> And shown no glorious morning face;

If beams from happy human eyes
Have moved me not; if morning skies,
Books, and my food, and summer rain
Knocked on my sullen heart in vain—
Lord, Thy most pointed pleasure take
And stab my spirit broad awake;
Or, Lord, if too obdurate I,
Choose Thou, before that spirit die,
A piercing pain, a killing sin,
And to my dead heart run them in!

ROBERT LOUIS STEVENSON

HARVEST

You crown the year with your bounty,
　　and your carts overflow with abundance.
The grasslands of the desert overflow;
　　the hills are clothed with gladness.
The meadows are covered with flocks
　　and the valleys are mantled with grain;
　　they shout for joy and sing.

PSALM 65:11–13, NIV

Once more the liberal year laughs out
　　O'er richer stores than gems or gold;
Once more with harvest song and shout
　　Is Nature's boldest triumph told.

JOHN GREENLEAF WHITTIER

He that hath a good harvest may be content with some thistles.

ENGLISH PROVERB

Over the earth is a mat of green,
　　Over the green the dew;
Over the dew are the arching trees,
　　And over the trees, the blue.
Across the blue are the scudding clouds,
　　And over the clouds the sun:

> While over them all is the love of God,
> Blessing us every one.
>
> UNKNOWN

> He who observes the wind will not sow;
> and he who regards the clouds will not reap.
>
> ECCLESIASTES 11:4

> Back of the loaf is the snowy flour,
> And back of the flour is the mill;
> Back of the mill is the sun, and the shower,
> The grain, and the Father's will.
>
> UNKNOWN

"Go your way, eat the fat and drink sweet wine and send portions to him for whom nothing is prepared; for this day is holy to our Lord; and do not be grieved, for the joy of the LORD is your strength."

NEHEMIAH: NEHEMIAH 8:10

HEAVEN AND HELL

We have been born . . . to an inheritance . . . kept in heaven; "Fear him who can destroy both soul and body in hell."

PETER: 1 PETER 1:3–4;
JESUS: MATTHEW 10:28

> I never saw a moor,
> I never saw the sea;
> Yet know I how the heather looks
> And what a wave must be.
>
> I never spoke with God,
> Nor visited in heaven;
> Yet certain am I of the spot
> As if the chart were given.
>
> EMILY DICKINSON

> Of this blest man, let his just praise be given:
> Heaven was in him before he was in heaven.
>
> IZAAK WALTON, OF RICHARD STIBBES

When Christ ascended,
Triumphantly, from star to star,
He left the gates of heaven ajar.

HENRY WADSWORTH LONGFELLOW

The way to heaven out of all places is of like distance (ROBERT BURTON);
Heaven means to be one with God (CONFUCIUS).

Then, as you search with unaccustomed glance
The ranks of Paradise for my countenance,
Turn not your head along the Uranian sod
Among the bearded counsellors of God;
For if in Eden as on earth are we,
I sure shall keep a younger company:
Pass the crystalline sea, the Lampads seven—
Look for me in the nurseries of heaven.

FRANCIS THOMPSON

Some may perchance, with strange surprise
Have blundered into Paradise.
In vasty dusk of life abroad,
They fondly thought to err from God,
Nor knew the circle that they trod;
And, wandering all the night about,
Found them at morn where they set out.
Death dawned; Heaven lay in prospect wide:
Lo! they were standing by His side!

FRANCIS THOMPSON, AUTOBIOGRAPHICAL

Hell is the wrath of God—His hate of sin (P. J. BAILEY); Hell is other
people (JEAN PAUL SARTRE); The way to hell's a seeming heaven (FRANCIS
QUARLES); Hell is paved with good intentions, roofed in with lost
opportunities (PORTUGUESE PROVERB).

In short, if you don't live up to the precepts of the Gospel, but abandon
your selves to your irregular appetites, you must expect to receive your
reward in a certain place, which 'tis not good manners to mention here.

THOMAS BROWN, PREACHING IN WHITEHALL

For what, my small philosopher, is hell?
'Tis nothing but full knowledge of the truth,
When truth, resisted long, is sworn our foe
And calls eternity to do her right.

EDWARD YOUNG

Long is the way
And hard, that out of hell leads up to light.

JOHN MILTON

Then I saw that there was a way to hell, even from the gates of heaven.

JOHN BUNYAN

The mind is its own place, and in itself
Can make a heaven of hell, a hell of heaven.

JOHN MILTON

A good man, in an exclusive heaven, would be in hell.

ELBERT HUBBARD

'Tis said there were no thought of hell
    Save hell were taught; that there should be
A heaven for all's self-credible.
    Not so the thing appears to me.
'Tis heaven that lies beyond our sights,
    And hell too possible that proves;
For all can feel the God that smites,
    But ah! how few the God that loves.

FRANCIS THOMPSON

Many might go to heaven with half the labour they go to hell, if they
would but venture their industry the right way.

BEN JONSON

HISTORY

I know that everything God does will endure . . .
Whatever is has already been,

and what will be has been before;
and God will call the past to account.

ECCLESIASTES 3:14–15, NIV

Not to know what happened before one was born is always to be a child (CICERO); The historical sense involves a perception, not only of the pastness of the past but of its presence (T. S. ELIOT).

[Lessons of History] Whom the gods would destroy they first make mad with power; the mills of God grind slowly, yet they grind exceeding small; the bee fertilizes the flower it robs; when it is dark enough you can see the stars.

CHARLES BEARD, HISTORIAN

That great dust-heap called "History" (AUGUSTINE BIRRELL); An inarticulate Bible . . . a distillation of rumour . . . innumerable biographies (THOMAS CARLYLE); Little more than a register of the crimes, follies, and misfortunes of mankind (EDWARD GIBBON); God's patient explanation to man of eternal principles (CHARLES A. BEARD); The world's judgement (J. C. FRIEDRICH VON SCHILLER); The unrolled scroll of prophecy (JAMES A. GARFIELD); "My Father worketh hitherto" (JESUS: JOHN 5:17, AV/KJV).

The Deity, we know, cannot alter the past: it takes an historian to do that (WILLIAM R. INGE); Perhaps history is a thing that would stop happening if God held His breath (HERBERT BUTTERFIELD).

The church, on pilgrimage through history, is that which gives significance to history itself, looking for its consummation beyond history.

JOHN FOSTER

The deepest, the only theme of human history . . . is the conflict of scepticism with faith. All epochs that are ruled by faith, in whatever form, are glorious, elevating, fruitful. All epochs, on the other hand, in which scepticism, in whatever form, maintains a precarious triumph . . . lose their meaning for posterity . . . [as] essentially sterile.

GOETHE

It is impossible to measure the vast difference that ordinary Christian piety has made to the last two thousand years of European history: but we shall have some inkling of that difference if the world continues in its present drift towards paganism.

HERBERT BUTTERFIELD

HOLINESS

Strive for . . . the holiness without which no one will see the Lord.

HEBREWS 12:14

No amount of description really tells us anything about holiness; but an encounter with it shames and amazes, convinces and delights us, all at once.

EVELYN UNDERHILL

Purity—that immensely virile virtue (FRIEDRICH VON HÜGEL); True faith can no more be without holiness than fire without heat (JOHN OWEN); Holiness is the architectural plan upon which God buildeth up His living Temple (CHARLES H. SPURGEON); Fear God, and where you go men shall think they walk in hallowed cathedrals (RALPH WALDO EMERSON); Wherever he was there was laughter, and he taught us the gaiety of holiness (UNKNOWN, SAID OF H. R. L. SHEPPARD).

There is a feeling abroad which appears to me . . . nearer to superstition than to religion, that there should be no touching of holy things except by consecrated fingers, nor any naming of holy names except in consecrated places. As if life were not a continual sacrament since Christ brake the daily bread of it in His hands! As if the name of God did not build a church by the very naming of it! As if the word "God" were not, everywhere in His creation and at every moment in His eternity, an appropriate word! As if it *could* be uttered unfitly, if uttered devoutly!

ELIZABETH BARRETT BROWNING

HOLY SPIRIT

Any one who does not have the Spirit of Christ does not belong to him.

PAUL: ROMANS 8:9

The Spirit of truth—He will store up truth already learned; unfold truth imperfectly understood; guide into truth not yet perceived; prepare for truth still to be revealed; reinforce truth faithfully witnessed to; convince of truth unwillingly received.

JESUS: JOHN 14:17, 26, 16:14, 12, 13; 15:26, 27, 16:8

The Spirit, Christ's "other Self," is the form of the contemporary Christ in each succeeding generation.

X

Come, Holy Dove,
Descend on silent pinion,
Brood o'er my sinful soul with patient love,
Till all my being owns Thy mild dominion.
    Spirit of grace,
Reveal in me my Saviour,
That I may gaze upon His mirrored Face,
Till I reflect it in my whole behaviour.

RICHARD WILTON

With his clear insight into the central meaning of the Gospel, Paul declared that the Law had now been abolished and had been replaced by the living Spirit: but the church has never found courage to follow him.

AFTER E. F. SCOTT

One may trace in the New Testament a movement of thought concerning the Spirit: from something "shed forth" or "poured out," an element in which one might be immersed ("baptised"), a power that "comes upon" or "falls upon" Christians, to the fully *personal* view of Him, for which the Spirit calls, speaks, wills, prays, "has a mind," and loves. This movement rises to its peak in the conception of "the Spirit of Jesus," "the Spirit of Christ," relating the Spirit and the risen Jesus so closely that Paul can say, forthrightly, "the Lord is the Spirit."

ANONYMOUS

If Christ is our portrait of the Father, He is no less our portrait of the Holy Spirit. The characteristic expression of the Spirit, as seen in Christ's life, is *constructive thought* and *creative energy*.

B. H. STREETER

Not only olden ages felt
　The presence of the Lord,
Not only with the fathers dwelt
　Thy Spirit and Thy word.

Come Holy Ghost, in us arise,
　Be this Thy mighty hour;
And make Thy willing people wise
　To know Thy day of power.

THOMAS H. GILL

The blessing of the Divine Spirit will only rest on the outcome of hard, honest work. . . .

JOHN WATSON

The church has always felt that any movement (such as Montanism) which drew especial attention to the ministry of the Holy Spirit as an end in itself, was in some way out of harmony with the New Testament. The root of this feeling is the fivefold insistence of Jesus that the Spirit shall not draw attention to Himself, speak of Himself, exercise His own authority, glorify Himself, or declare "the things of the Spirit"—but only the words, authority, interests and glory of Christ himself.

ANONYMOUS: JOHN 16:13–15

Come Thou, Oh come,
Sweetest and kindliest,
Giver of tranquil rest
　Unto the weary soul;
In all anxiety
With power from heaven on high
　Console.

Come Thou, Oh come,
Help in the hour of need,
Strength of the broken reed,
　Guide of the lonely one . . .
Lead Thou us tenderly,
Till we shall find with Thee
　Our home.

LATIN, NINTH CENTURY
(translator unknown)

With Luke's works before us, the church can never again descend to a
notion of the Holy Spirit as the divine magician, the worker of tricks, the
purveyor of wonders and signs and provider of thrills. Or as an impersonal
spiritual power which Christians can manipulate at will. All this is exposed
as sub-Christian by Luke's portrait of the Spirit-born, Spirit-led, Spirit-
endowed, Spirit-filled, and Spirit-bestowing *Jesus*.

ANONYMOUS

HOPE

I know the plans I have for you, says the Lord, plans for welfare and not
for evil, to give you a future and a hope.

JEREMIAH 29:11

Hope is the power of being cheerful in circumstances which we know to
be desperate (G. K. CHESTERTON); [An] anchor of the soul (HEBREWS 6:19);
Hope is a risk that must be run (GEORGES BERNANOS); If it were not for
hopes the heart would break (THOMAS FULLER); If hopes were dupes, fears
may be liars (ARTHUR H. CLOUGH); Greet the unseen with a cheer (ROBERT
BROWNING); He fishes on who catches one (FRENCH PROVERB).

   Who brought me hither
    Will bring me hence; no other guide I seek.

JOHN MILTON

In reliance on the revealed character of God, hope looks forward with
confidence to the fulfilment of the divine purpose; it is a principle of moral
action; it inspires endurance, self-control, stability, firmness; it colours the
intellectual life, and fortifies the will.

R. L. OTTLEY

   I have not seen, I may not see
    My hopes for man take form in fact.
   But God will give the victory
    In due time; in that faith I act.
   And he who sees the future sure
   The baffling present may endure.

JOHN GREENLEAF WHITTIER

. . . That God which ever lives and loves,
One God, one law, one element,
And one far-off divine event
To which the whole creation moves.

ALFRED TENNYSON

Pessimism is a luxury no Jew can afford.

GOLDA MEIR

Reflected in the lake, I love
To see the stars of evening glow;
So tranquil in the heavens above,
So restless in the wave below.
Thus heavenly hope is all serene,
But earthly hope, how bright soe'er,
Still fluctuates o'er this changing scene,
As false and fleeting as 'tis fair.

REGINALD HEBER

'Tis always morning somewhere in the world.

RICHARD H. HORNE

HOSPITALITY

Do not neglect to show hospitality to strangers, for thereby some have
entertained angels unawares.

HEBREWS 13:2

The ornaments of this house are the friends who frequent it.

INSCRIPTION: SEIL ISLAND, ARGYLL
(RALPH WALDO EMERSON)

For whom he means to make an often guest
One dish shall serve, and welcome make the rest.

JOSEPH HALL

Hail guest! We ask not what thou art:
If Friend, we greet thee, hand and heart;

If Stranger, such no longer be;
If Foe, our love shall conquer thee.

OLD WELSH DOOR-POST WELCOME

HUMANISM

... the way of man is not in himself,
that it is not in man who walks to direct his steps.

JEREMIAH 10:23

Few pages are more tragic or ... more grotesque than those which record
the effort of civilised Europe during the last two centuries to wrest the idea
of humanity from its other-worldly foundations, and to base a humanistic
gospel on the progress of civilisation and the perfectibility of human nature.

WILLIAM G. DE BURGH

Humanism—the gospel of human control by human effort in accordance
with human ideals.

AFTER JULIAN HUXLEY

Humanistic religion is at best a culture-pattern for men sheltered from life's
poverty, pain, and bitterness, from tragedy and fear; a university product
for the university campus, which may be transplanted to the drawing-rooms
of the cultivated and protected members of an affluent society, but which
offers no help, and will scarcely survive, in the slums of the great cities, in
the wards of incurable agony, on the battlefield, or in any situation where
human hearts are brought to breaking-point.

ANONYMOUS

It is the sorry experience of mankind that ape and angel divide the empire
of Mansoul; if the angel be declared illusory, the ape reigns unopposed
(x); Human life becomes truly terrible when there ceases to be anything
above man (NICOLAS BERDYAEV); Unfortunately, humanitarianism has been the
mark of an inhuman time (G. K. CHESTERTON, ON INDUSTRIALISM).

However we explain it, one result of secular humanism has been to
depress human worth, to iron out individuality into the drab sameness of
megalopolitan culture, to make the human spirit sterile in the
incomprehensible cynicism of much modern poetry and art, to level human

experience to the mudflats of time and bound human existence by the darkness of the grave.

X

It is the God-relationship which makes a man a man.

SØREN KIERKEGAARD

The time has come for a recall to the authentic Christian humanism with which the synoptic Gospels are brimming over.

J. A. FINDLAY

HUMAN RIGHTS

"So in everything, do to others what you would have them do to you, for this sums up the Law and the Prophets."

JESUS: MATTHEW 7:12, NIV

The only valid "right" of naturalistic man in a secular world is the "right" of the fittest to struggle to survive longer than others—a merely accidental opportunity for uninhibited selfishness.

X

Rights that do not flow from duty well performed are not worth having.

MAHATMA GANDHI

Government laws are needed to give us civil rights, and God is needed to make us civil.

RALPH W. SOCKMAN

Citizenship is nothing less than the right to have rights.

EARL WARREN

Wherever there is a human being I see God-given rights inherent in that being, whatever may be the sex or complexion.

WILLIAM LLOYD GARRISON

In giving rights to others which belong to them, we give rights to ourselves and to our country.

JOHN F. KENNEDY

Every right asserted for an individual imposes—or rather, it literally *means*—a responsibility resting upon all other individuals. For that reason, each right asserted needs justification.

X

HUMILITY

"God opposes the proud,
but gives grace to the humble."

PETER: 1 PETER 5:5

Humility is the sense of our inability, even with our best intelligence and effort, to command events. There is a conceit of carrying the load of the universe, from which religion liberates us.

JOHN DEWEY

The humble man God protects and delivers; the humble He loves and comforts; to the humble He condescends; on the humble He bestows more abundant measures of His grace, and after his humiliation exalts him to glory.

THOMAS À KEMPIS

The foundation of our philosophy [i.e., Christianity] is humility (CHRYSOSTOM); If you ask me what is the first precept of the Christian religion, I will answer "First, second, and third—humility" (AUGUSTINE); Humility falls neither far nor heavily (PUBLILIUS SYRUS); Too humble is half proud (YIDDISH PROVERB); Humility is just as much the opposite of self-abasement as it is of self-exaltation (DAG HAMMARSKJÖLD); The confession of our insignificance has its remedy provided in His mercy (JOHN CALVIN, WHO INSISTED UPON AN UNMARKED GRAVE).

He that is humble ever shall
Have God to be his guide.

JOHN BUNYAN

Unless a man is always humble, always distrustful of himself, always fears his own understanding . . . his passion, his will, he will be unable to stand for very long without offence. For truth will pass him by.

MARTIN LUTHER

The fuller the ear is of rice-grain, the lower it bends; empty, it grows taller and taller.

MALAY PROVERB

No more lessen or dissemble thy merit than over-rate it; for though humility be a virtue, an affected one is not (WILLIAM PENN); Humility is to make a right estimate of one's self; it is no humility for a man to think less of himself than he ought, though it might rather puzzle him to do that (CHARLES H. SPURGEON).

According to one story, St. Francis changed clothes with a beggar. . . . In another version, he got hold of the rough brown tunic of a peasant, probably very old indeed. . . . Ten years later that makeshift costume was the uniform of five thousand men; and a hundred years later, in that for a pontifical panoply, they laid great Dante in the grave.

G. K. CHESTERTON

It needs more skill than I can tell
To play the second fiddle well.

CHARLES H. SPURGEON

Speak low to me, my Saviour, low and sweet
From out the hallelujahs, sweet and low,
Lest I should fear and fall, and miss Thee so,
Who art not missed by any that entreat.

ELIZABETH BARRETT BROWNING

The love of God created us, but the humility of God saved us.

HILDEGAARD OF BINGEN

HUMOUR

"God has made laughter for me."

SARAH: GENESIS 21:6

The laughter of man is the contentment of God (JOHN WEISS); Fun is a good thing, but only when it spoils nothing better (GEORGE SANTAYANA); No one is thoroughly well-organised that is deficient in a sense of humour (SAMUEL TAYLOR COLERIDGE).

Humour is an affirmation of dignity, a declaration of man's superiority to all that befalls him.

ROMAIN GARY

When God had finished the stars and whirl of coloured suns
He turned His mind from big things to fashion little ones,
Beautiful, tiny things (like daisies) He made, and then
He made the comical ones, in case the minds of men
　　Should stiffen and become
　　Dull, humourless and glum;
And so forgetful of their Maker be
As to take even themselves quite seriously.

F. W. HARVEY

The humorist has a good eye for the humbug; he does not always recognise the saint.

W. SOMERSET MAUGHAM

HYPOCRISY

"Beware of the leaven of the Pharisees, which is hypocrisy. Nothing is covered up that will not be revealed, or hidden that will not be known."

JESUS: LUKE 12:1-2

Hypocrisy—the subtle inner untruthfulness in which occupation with divine things is united with cunning, the lust of power, and selfishness.

R. C. EUCKEN

For neither man nor angel can discern
Hypocrisy, the only evil that walks
Invisible, except to God alone.

JOHN MILTON

Hypocrisy is the homage which vice pays to virtue (LA ROCHEFOUCAULD); The only vice that cannot be forgiven: the repentance of a hypocrite is itself hypocrisy (WILLIAM HAZLITT); Hypocrites, who point like finger-posts the way they never go (THOMAS HOOD); He hailed the power of Jesus' name, and soaked 'em twelve per cent (DOUGLAS MALLOCH); O, what a goodly outside falsehood hath! (WILLIAM SHAKESPEARE).

Veracity, integrity, form the heart of morality.

AFTER THOMAS H. HUXLEY

> He was a man
> Who stole the livery of the court of heaven
> To serve the devil in; in virtue's guise
> Devoured the widow's house and orphan's bread;
> In holy phrase transacted villainies
> That common sinners durst not meddle with.
>
> ROBERT POLLOK

> For sweetest things turn sourest by their deeds;
> Lilies that fester smell far worse than weeds.
>
> WILLIAM SHAKESPEARE

IDLENESS

Keep away from any brother who is living in idleness.

PAUL: 2 THESSALONIANS 3:6

The devil tempts all other men, but idle men tempt the devil.

TURKISH PROVERB

He lived a life of going-to-do
And died with nothing done.

J. ALBERY

If you are idle, be not solitary; if solitary, be not idle.

SAMUEL JOHNSON

Absence of occupation is not rest:
A mind quite vacant is a mind distressed.

WILLIAM COWPER

Expect poison from standing water (WILLIAM BLAKE); He is idle that might be better employed (THOMAS FULLER); Idleness is the canker of the mind (JOHN BODENHAM); Idle folk have the least leisure (CHARLES H. SPURGEON); An idle brain is the devil's shop (ENGLISH PROVERB); Laziness travels so slowly that poverty soon overtakes him (BENJAMIN FRANKLIN).

Their only labour was to kill the time;
And labour dire it is, and weary woe.

JAMES THOMSON

How dull it is to pause, to make an end,
To rust unburnished, not to shine in use—
As though to breathe were life!

ALFRED TENNYSON

IDOLATRY

Little children, keep yourselves from idols.

JOHN: 1 JOHN 5:21

Four species of idols beset the human mind: idols of the tribe, idols of the den, idols of the market, and idols of the theatre.

FRANCIS BACON

There are false *goods*, the product of men's imagination, which have no genuine reality; there are false aims towards which are directed lives that are worthless and transitory. These are idols. . . .

CHARLES GORE

If man worship not the true God, he will have his idols.

THEODORE PARKER

An idiot holds his bauble for a god.

WILLIAM SHAKESPEARE

In that day men will cast forth
their idols . . .
to the moles and to the bats.

ISAIAH: ISAIAH 2:20

IGNORANCE

My people are destroyed for lack of knowledge;
because you have rejected knowledge,
I reject you.

HOSEA 4:6

Ignorance is the mother of impudence (CHARLES H. SPURGEON); The truest characters of ignorance are vanity, pride, and arrogance (SAMUEL BUTLER I); Everybody is ignorant, only on different subjects (WILL ROGERS).

If there are two things not to be hidden, love and a cough, I say there is a third, and that is ignorance.

GEORGE ELIOT

We have become increasingly and painfully aware of our abysmal ignorance. No scientist, fifty years ago, could have realised that he was as ignorant as all first-rate scientists now know themselves to be.

ABRAHAM FLEXNER

The recipe for perpetual ignorance is to be satisfied with your opinions and content with your knowledge.

ELBERT HUBBARD

"Father, forgive them; for they know not what they do."

JESUS: LUKE 23:34

IMAGINATION

I have multiplied visions, and used similitudes.

HOSEA 12:10, AV/KJV

A man, to be greatly good, must imagine intensely and comprehensively; he must put himself in the place of another—of many others. The great instrument of moral good is the imagination.

PERCY BYSSHE SHELLEY

This is imagination: the power to see the grass grow, to feel the toothache of a child, to shudder at the fall of a bird, to thrill with fear at a blood-red sunset, to agonise with Jeremiah over truth frustrated by circumstance, to stand with David beneath the balsam trees and hear God pass by, to sing with John in exile, and with ten thousand times ten thousand and thousands of thousands "Worthy is the Lamb that was slain."

X

[Describing the curvature of the earth] The sea is a vast mountain of water, miles high . . . rising in a solid dome like the glass mountain in a fairy-tale. To have discovered that mountain of moving crystal, in which the fishes build like birds, is like discovering Atlantis.

G. K. CHESTERTON

Where there is no imagination there is cruelty, selfishness, death. Christ
. . . taught us to look on other people imaginatively, not as though they
were ciphers in a statistical abstract.

ROBERT LYND

Imagination is the air of mind (P. J. BAILEY); . . . the eye of the soul
(JOSEPH JOUBERT); . . . the mightiest lever known to the moral world
(WILLIAM WORDSWORTH); . . . more important than knowledge (ALFRED
EINSTEIN); . . . a poor substitute for experience (H. HAVELOCK ELLIS); the
human race is governed by the imagination (NAPOLEON).

> . . . Imagination, which in truth
> Is but another name for absolute power
> And clearest insight, amplitude of mind,
> And reason in her most exalted mood.

WILLIAM WORDSWORTH

We sin against our dearest, not because we do not love but because we
do not imagine.

JOHN WATSON

Truth made concrete will find its way past many a door when abstractions
knock in vain.

JAMES S. STEWART

Must then Christ perish in torment in every age to save those that have
no imagination?

GEORGE BERNARD SHAW

IMITATION

He . . . predestined [us] to be conformed to the image of his Son . . .
we . . . are . . . changed into his likeness . . . to the measure of the
stature of the fulness of Christ.

PAUL: ROMANS 8:29; 2 CORINTHIANS 3:18;
EPHESIANS 4:13

The idea of Christlikeness is so fundamental, so near to the heart of the gospel, that we come upon it in unexpected places, expressed oftentimes in surprising ways, reflected in every great doctrine of the faith, implied in every great spiritual experience. Just because it is so central we catch glimpses of it from every point on the circumference of Christian truth; because it is implied in almost everything we find it almost everywhere.

ANONYMOUS

It is incumbent to perform the works of the Master according to His similitude, and so to fulfil what scripture said as to our being made in His image and likeness . . . Christ became the perfect realisation of what God spake.

CLEMENT OF ALEXANDRIA

We were made in the likeness of God. . . . When a portrait is spoiled, the only way to renew it is for the subject to sit for the artist again. That is why Christ came . . . [that] the divine image in man might be recreated. . . . We are remade in the likeness of God's Son.

ATHANASIUS

Our determination to imitate Christ should be such that we have no time for other matters.

ERASMUS

I will give myself as a sort of Christ to my neighbour.

MARTIN LUTHER

Christ is the most perfect image of God, into which we are so renewed as to bear the image of God, in knowledge, purity, righteousness, and true holiness.

JOHN CALVIN

There can be no question of a conformity which means equality . . . Jesus Christ will reign, and men will be subject to Him, and they will always be different within, and in spite of the closest fellowship between Him and His imitators. There will be no more Christs. . . . The Unique will always be unique; the distances will remain.

KARL BARTH

Man is an imitative creature (J. C. FRIEDRICH VON SCHILLER); Example is the school of mankind (EDMUND BURKE); We need someone on whom our character may mould itself: you'll never make the crooked straight without a ruler (SENECA); The crab instructs its young, "Walk straight ahead, like me" (HINDUSTANI PROVERB); There is a difference between imitating a good man and counterfeiting him (BENJAMIN FRANKLIN).

In "imitating Christ," one thing the Christian never attempts: he never imitates the fact that Jesus had no Christ to imitate.

PAUL RAMSEY

A missionary was translating the First Epistle of John. When he came to "We shall be like Him," the native Christian scribe laid down his pen and said, "No! I cannot write these words, it is too much. Let us write, We shall kiss His feet."

G. S. BARRETT

IMMORTALITY

Our Savior Christ Jesus . . . abolished death and brought life and immortality to light through the gospel.

2 TIMOTHY 1:10

The faith of Jesus in human immortality rests upon His own experience of the character of God and the deathless nature of fellowship with Him.

UNKNOWN

Christianity has found a new basis for the hope of immortality in the fact of Christ's resurrection; a new centre for it in the personal experience of new life, prophetic of its own immortality; a new conception of it in the "Father's house" where the redeemed children of the eternal find their inheritance in security, fellowship and light.

X

If you were to destroy in mankind the belief in immortality, not only love but every living force maintaining the life of the world would at once be dried up; moreover, nothing then would be immoral, everything would be permissible, even cannibalism.

FYODOR DOSTOYEVSKY

I have good hope that there is something after death (PLATO); We feel and know that we are eternal (BARUCH SPINOZA); The universe is a stairway leading nowhere unless man is immortal (E. Y. MULLINS); He sins against this life who slights the next (EDWARD YOUNG); In the belief in immortality the rationality of the universe is at stake (B. H. STREETER).

What is at stake in the question of immortality is not man's comforting, but the validity of all his faith in righteousness, the significance of his decisions, the vindication of morality as native to the universe, the assurance of eternal justice and divine compassion, the underwriting of all man's high endeavour and spiritual travail as eternally worthwhile, and the integrity of Jesus.

ANONYMOUS

Believing as I do that man in the distant future will be a far more perfect creature . . . it is an intolerable thought that he and all other sentient beings are doomed to complete annihilation after such long-continued slow progress. To those who fully admit the immortality of the human soul, the destruction of our world will not appear so dreadful.

CHARLES DARWIN

I never have seen, and never shall see, that the cessation of the *evidence* of existence is, necessarily, evidence of the cessation of *existence*.

WILLIAM F. DE MORGAN

I believe in immortality, fundamentally, not because I vehemently crave it for myself, but because its denial seems to me to land the entire race in a hopeless situation, and to reduce philosophy to a counsel of despair.

HARRY EMERSON FOSDICK

And so beside the silent sea
I wait the muffled oar;
No harm from Him can come to me
On ocean or on shore.

I know not where His islands lift
Their fronded palms in air:
I only know I cannot drift
Beyond His love and care.

JOHN GREENLEAF WHITTIER

Awake my soul, stretch every nerve,
And press with vigour on;
A heavenly race demands thy zeal,
And an immortal crown.

PHILIP DODDRIDGE

Not as we knew them any more,
   Toilworn and sad, with burdened care,
Erect, clear-eyed, upon their brows
   Thy name they bear.

O fuller, sweeter, is that life,
   And larger, ampler, is the air:
Eye cannot see nor heart conceive
   The glory there;

Nor know to what high purpose Thou
   Dost yet employ their ripened powers,
Nor how, at Thy behest, they touch
   This life of ours.

There are no tears within their eyes;
   With love they keep perpetual tryst;
And praise, and work, and rest are one
   With Thee, O Christ.

W. CHARTER PIGGOTT

INDEPENDENCE

Each of us shall give account of himself to God.

PAUL: ROMANS 14:12

It is very easy in the world to live by the opinion of the world. It is very easy in solitude to be self-centred. But the finished man is he who in the midst of the crowd keeps with perfect sweetness the independence of solitude.

RALPH WALDO EMERSON

Not in the clamour of the crowded street,
Not in the shouts and plaudits of the throng,
But in ourselves are triumph and defeat.

HENRY WADSWORTH LONGFELLOW

Public opinion—a vulgar, impertinent, anonymous tyrant who deliberately makes life unpleasant for anyone who is not content to be the average man.

WILLIAM R. INGE

Whoso would be a man must be a non-conformist (RALPH WALDO EMERSON); The minority is always right (THOMAS H. HUXLEY); Anybody who is any good is different from anybody else (FELIX FRANKFURTER); Men are born equal, but they are also born different (ERICH FROMM); All men of one metal, but not in one mould (JOHN LYLY); A whole bushel of wheat is made up of single grains (THOMAS FULLER); Every reform was once a private opinion (RALPH WALDO EMERSON); Lean too much upon the approval of people and it becomes a bed of thorns (CHINESE PROVERB).

Among the faithless, faithful only he
Among innumerable false, unmoved,
Unshaken, unseduced, unterrified,
His loyalty he kept, his love, his zeal.

JOHN MILTON

Strongest minds
Are often those of whom the noisy world
Hears least.

WILLIAM WORDSWORTH

Thy praise or dispraise is to me alike:
One doth not stroke me, nor the other strike.

BEN JONSON

God enters by a private door into every individual.

RALPH WALDO EMERSON

We need the faith to go a path untrod,
The power to be alone, and vote with God.

EDWIN MARKHAM

Collectively we have an army, post office, police, government. . . . But we do not make love collectively, [or] marry, eat, or die; it is not collectively that we face the sorrows and the hopes, the winnings and the losings, of this world of accident and storm. No view of society can possibly be complete which does not comprise within its scope both collective organisation and individual incentive.

WINSTON SPENCER CHURCHILL

INFLUENCE

Do you not know that a little leaven leavens the whole lump?

PAUL: 1 CORINTHIANS 5:6

Every life is a profession of faith, and exercises an inevitable and silent propaganda.

HENRI AMIEL

As the Swift bore the ashes of Wycliffe into the Severn, and the Severn into the narrow seas, and they again into the ocean, so they became an emblem of his doctrine, now dispersed over the world.

THOMAS FULLER

The work an unknown good man has done is like a vein of water flowing hidden underground, secretly making the ground green.

THOMAS CARLYLE

> O may I join the choir invisible
> Of those immortal dead who live again
> In minds made better by their presence: live
> In pulses stirred to generosity,
> In deeds of daring rectitude, in scorn
> For miserable aims that end with self,
> In thoughts sublime that pierce the night like stars,
> And with their mild persistence urge man's search
> To vaster issues.

GEORGE ELIOT

To behold her is an immediate check to loose behaviour; to love her is a liberal education.

RICHARD STEELE,
OF LADY ELIZABETH HASTINGS

As for me, my bed is made: I am against bigness . . . and with the invisible molecular moral forces that work from individual to individual, stealing in through the crannies of the world like so many soft rootlets, or like the capillary oozing of water, yet rending the hardest monuments of man's pride, if you give them time.

WILLIAM JAMES

INSIGHT

The crowd said it thundered. The few, spiritually impressionable, said, "An angel spoke," The One, spiritually attuned, declared, "This voice . . . "

JOHN 12:29–30, PARAPHRASED

A moment's insight is sometimes worth a life's experience (OLIVER WENDELL HOLMES); They are ill discoverers that think there is no land when they see nothing but sea (FRANCIS BACON); A blind man will not thank you for a looking-glass (THOMAS FULLER); A blind man who sees is better than a seeing man who is blind (PERSIAN PROVERB).

He that has light within his own clear breast,
May sit i' th' centre and enjoy bright day;
But he that hides a dark soul and foul thoughts
Benighted walks under the midday sun.

JOHN MILTON

Vision is the art of seeing things invisible.

JONATHAN SWIFT

Hundreds of people can talk for one who can think, but thousands can think for one who can see. To see clearly is poetry, prophecy, religion, all in one.

JOHN RUSKIN

All around him Patmos lies
Who hath Spirit-gifted eyes.

EDITH M. THOMAS

As he that fears God fears nothing else, so he that sees God sees everything else.

JOHN DONNE

INTERDEPENDENCE

The eye cannot say to the hand, "I have no need of you," nor again the head to the feet. . . . You are the body of Christ and individually members of it.

PAUL: 1 CORINTHIANS 12:21, 27

A solitary Christian is but half a Christian (CHARLES HODGE); An insular Christian is a contradiction in terms (X); The soul of my lord shall be bound in the bundle of life with the LORD thy God (1 SAMUEL 25:29, AV/KJV); No man is an island, entire of itself; every man is a piece of the continent, a part of the main (JOHN DONNE).

> I said it in the meadow path,
>   I say it on the mountain stairs:
> The best things any mortal hath
>   Are those which every mortal shares.
>
> The air we breathe, the sky, the breeze,
>   The light without us and within,
> Life, with its unlocked treasuries,
>   God's riches, are for all to win.
>
> The grass is softer to my tread
>   For rest it yields unnumbered feet;
> Sweeter to me the wild rose red
>   Because she makes the whole world sweet.
>
> And up the radiant peopled way
>   That opens into worlds unknown
> It will be life's delight to say,
>   "Heaven is not heaven for me alone."
>
> Rich by my brethren's poverty?—
>   Such wealth were worthless! I am blest
> Only in what they share with me,
>   In what I share with all the rest.

LUCY LARCOM

JESUS CHRIST

"The word which [God] sent to Israel, preaching good news of peace by Jesus Christ (he is Lord of all) . . . how God anointed Jesus of Nazareth with the Holy Spirit and with power; how he went about doing good and healing all that were oppressed by the devil, for God was with him.

PETER: ACTS 10:36, 38

With this ambiguous earth
His dealings have been told us. These abide:
The signal to a maid, the human birth,
The lesson, and the young Man crucified. . . .

No planet knows that this
Our wayside planet, carrying land and wave,
Love and life multiplied, and pain and bliss
Bears, as chief treasure, one forsaken grave. . . .

O, be prepared, my soul!
To read the inconceivable, to scan
The million forms of God those stars unroll
When, in our turn, we show to them a Man.

ALICE MEYNELL

Tributes

He makes upon us a unique impression, the impression that in him, as in none other, God has come to us, to disclose to us his inmost heart, to condemn our sin, to call us to his service, and to create within us the life that is life indeed.

MORGAN

He is too great for our small hearts (H. G. WELLS); All history is incomprehensible without Christ (J. ERNEST RENAN); There remains the question, what righteousness really is: the method, and secret, and sweet reasonableness of Jesus (MATTHEW ARNOLD); Science has its place in life, but only Christ can save (CHARLES DARWIN, TO AN EVANGELICAL PHILANTHROPIST); Jesus, whose name is not so much written as ploughed into the history of this world (RALPH WALDO EMERSON); He breaketh not a bruised reed, nor quencheth the smoking flax: but if the wind blow, he holdeth his hands about it till it rise to a flame (SAMUEL RUTHERFORD).

> He is a path, if any be misled;
> He is a robe, if any naked be;
> If any chance to hunger, he is bread;
> If any be a bondman, he is free;
> If any be but weak, how strong is he!
>> To dead men life he is, to sick men health,
>> To blind men sight, and to the needy wealth;
> A pleasure without loss, a treasure without stealth.
>
> GILES FLETCHER, JR.

> What if, or yet, what mole, what flaw, what lapse,
> What least defect, or shadow of defect,
> What rumour tattled by an enemy
> Of inference loose? what lack of grace
> Even in torture's grasp, or sleep's, or death's?
>> Oh what amiss may *I* forgive in *Thee*,
>> Jesus, good Paragon, Thou crystal Christ?
>
> SIDNEY LANIER

However much intellectual culture advances, let the human mind expand as it will, beyond the sublimity and the moral culture of Christianity, as it gleams and glitters in the Gospels, it will never go.

GOETHE

> And so the Word had breath, and wrought
>> With human hands the creed of creeds,
>> In loveliness of perfect deeds
> More strong than all poetic thought.
>
> ALFRED TENNYSON

Jesus—a man who was completely innocent, offered himself as a sacrifice for the good of others, including his enemies, and became the ransom of the world. It was a perfect act.

MAHATMA GANDHI

The hands of Christ seem very frail,
For they were broken by a nail.
But only they reach heaven at last
Whom these frail, broken hands hold fast.

J. R. MORELAND

For ever beyond us, for ever ahead,
He leads into tomorrow, as ever He led;
No age can o'ertake Him, no time can outgrow
His pioneer spirit—He stands at the prow.

ANONYMOUS

Birth, Incarnation

This is the month, and this the happy morn,
Wherein the Son of Heaven's eternal King,
Of wedded maid and virgin mother born,
Our great redemption from above did bring;
For so the holy sages once did sing
That He our deadly forfeit should release,
And with His Father work us a perpetual peace.

JOHN MILTON

There's a song in the air,
    There's a star in the sky;
There's a mother's deep prayer
    And a Baby's low cry;
And the star rains its fire where the Beautiful sing,
For the manger at Bethlehem cradles a King.

JOSIAH G. HOLLAND

Yet if His Majesty, our sovereign lord,
Should of his own accord
Friendly himself invite,
And say, "I'll be your guest tomorrow night,"

How should we stir ourselves, call and command
All hands to work! "Let no man idle stand . . ."
Thus if the king were coming would we do;
And 'twere good reason, too;
For 'tis a duteous thing
To show all honour to an earthly king . . .
But at the coming of the King of Heaven
All's set at six and seven;
We wallow in our sin.
Christ cannot find a chamber at the inn.
We entertain Him always like a stranger,
And, as at first, still lodge Him in the manger.

ANONYMOUS, SEVENTEENTH CENTURY

I saw a stable, low, and very bare,
    A little child in a manger.
The oxen knew Him, had Him in their care,
    To men He was a stranger.
The safety of the world was lying there:
    And the world's danger.

MARY ELIZABETH COLERIDGE

Given, not lent,
And not withdrawn—once sent,
This Infant of mankind, this One,
Is still the little welcome Son.

New every year,
New born and newly dear,
He comes with tidings and a song
The ages long.

ALICE MEYNELL

Wise men seeking Jesus
    Travelled from afar,
Guided on their journey
    By a beauteous star . . .

But if we desire Him,
    He is close at hand:

For our native country
Is *our* Holy Land.

JAMES T. EAST

There fared a mother driven forth
Out of an inn to roam;
In the place where she was homeless
All men are at home.
The crazy stable close at hand
With shaking timber and shifting sand
Grew a stronger thing to abide and stand
Than the square stones of Rome.

G. K. CHESTERTON

They all were looking for a king
To slay their foes and lift them high;
Thou cam'st, a little baby-thing
That made a woman cry.

GEORGE MACDONALD

To spread the azure canopy of heaven,
And make it twinkle with those spangs of gold;
To stay the pond'rous globe of earth so even,
That it should all, and nought should it, uphold—
Lord, to Thy wisdom's nought; nought to Thy might.
But that Thou shouldst (Thy glory laid aside)
Come meanly in mortality to bide,
And die for those deserved eternal plight—
A wonder is, so far above our wit
That angels stand amazed to muse on it.

WILLIAM DRUMMOND

That glorious Form, that Light unsufferable,
And that far-beaming blaze of Majesty,
Wherewith He wont at Heaven's high council-table
To sit the midst of Trinal Unity,
He laid aside; and here with us to be
Forsook the courts of everlasting day,
And chose with us a darksome house of mortal clay.

JOHN MILTON

Augustine was later to say that in the pagan philosophers he could find parallels for everything in the New Testament except for one saying—the Word became flesh.

WILLIAM BARCLAY

Boyhood, Manhood

He came to save all . . . who through Him are born into God, infants, children, boys, young men, and old. Therefore, He passed through every stage of life: He was made an infant for infants, sanctifying infancy; a child among children, sanctifying those of this age; a young man amongst young men, an example to them and sanctifying them to the Lord; so also among the older men . . . that He might be a perfect Master for all in respect of each stage of life.

IRENAEUS

Jesus and Joseph, day after day,
Chiselled and planed and hammered away
 In the shop at Nazareth.
Mary the mother ground at the mill;
Eight little hungry mouths she must fill,
 In the home at Nazareth . . .
Games in the market—what did they play?
Weddings and funerals, that was their way,
 Boys and girls at Nazareth.
So He grew up, our Saviour dear,
Sharing the life of all of us here,
 In His home at Nazareth.

T. R. GLOVER

At work beside His father's bench,
 At play when work was done,
In quiet Galilee He lived
 The friend of everyone.
Comrade of boys and girls like us,
 Playmate so straight and true—
In all our work, in all our play,
 Make us true comrades, too.

ALICE M. PULLEN

At evening He loved to walk
Among the shadowy hills, and talk
   Of Bethlehem;
But if perchance there passed us by
The paschal lambs, He'd look at them
In silence, long and tenderly;
And when again He'd try to speak,
I've seen the tears upon His cheek.

                  JOHN BANNISTER TABB

It is not only necessary that we should know that God became man; it is
also necessary that we should know what kind of man He became.

                  ANONYMOUS

His was a commanding personality: no one dared take liberties with him
(WILLIAM R. INGE); Robust manliness and steel-tempered will-power [marked
Jesus] (OTTO BORCHERT); When His followers wished to make Jesus a king,
He shuddered, and fled as from an insult (JOHN WATSON; SEE JOHN 6:15).

          The best of men
That e'er wore earth about him was a sufferer;
A soft, meek, patient, humble, tranquil spirit,
The first true gentleman that ever breathed.

                  THOMAS DEKKER

His life was gentle, and the elements
So mixed in him that Nature might stand up
And say to all the world, "This was a man!"

        WILLIAM SHAKESPEARE, ANTONY, ON CAESAR

Ministry, Teaching

The whole of the ministry of Jesus was the working out of a life-choice
made in the solitude of the desert at the beginning. He came to win man,
but He refused to buy them, even with bread. He refused to coerce them,
even with their own weapons. He refused to overawe them, even at their
own request.

                  W. R. MALTBY

He raisèd not an army for to fight
And force religion, but did men invite

By gentle means. Twelve of the simpler sort
Served to make up His train, and kept His court.

THOMAS WASHBOURNE

The miracles of healing—what is the good of a superior sceptic throwing them away as unthinkable, at the moment when faith-healing is already a big, booming business?

G. K. CHESTERTON

Thou water turn'st to wine, fair friend of life;
Thy foe, to cross the sweet arts of thy reign,
Distils from thence the tears of wrath and strife,
And so turns wine to water back again.

RICHARD CRASHAW

[To the Centurion]

Thy God was making haste into thy roof:
    Thy humble faith and fear keeps Him aloof;
He'll be thy Guest, because He may not be:
    He'll come—into thy house? No, into thee!

RICHARD CRASHAW

Jesus is absolute master in the sphere of religion: his ideas are not words, they are laws, not thoughts but forces. He did not suggest, He asserted what He had seen; He did not propose, He commanded as one who knew there was no other way ... [He is] the objective conscience of humanity.

JOHN WATSON

Why did our blessed Saviour please to break
His sacred thoughts in parables, and speak
In dark enigmas? Whosoe'er thou be
That find'st them so, they were not spoke to thee.

FRANCIS QUARLES

Christ talked of grass, and wind, and rain,
    And fig-trees and fair weather,
And made it his delight to bring
    Heaven and the earth together ...

And yeast, and bread, and flax, and cloth,
   And eggs, and fish, and candles;
See how the whole familiar world
   He most divinely handles.

THOMAS T. LYNCH

I am the way which thou must go, the truth which thou must believe, and the life which thou must desire and hope for—the invariable and perfect way, the supreme and infallible truth, the blessed, uncreated, endless life.

THOMAS À KEMPIS, ON JOHN 14:6

Jesus stands in the way of every selfishness, leads in the path of every sacrifice. He is crucified in every act of sin, glorified in every act of holiness—the lifeblood of Christianity is Christ.

JOHN WATSON

His Passion

But shadow deepens now toward the close:
His spirit darkens with the coming doom,
While they, in whom His heart had found repose
Of sympathy in good, fold close the gloom;
For He who pours his very being forth
Divinely rich and pure for these, must hear
These even now, so nigh the end, in wrath
Dispute pre-eminence: while deadly near,
Looms Peter's base denial, and each one's broken troth.

R. B. W. NOEL

Into the woods my Master went
Clean forspent, forspent.
Into the woods my Master came,
Forspent with love and shame.
But the olives, they were not blind to Him,
The little grey leaves were kind to Him,
The thorn tree had a mind to Him,
When into the woods He came.

Out of the woods my Master went,
And He was well content.

Out of the woods my Master came
Content with death and shame.
When Death and Shame would woo Him last,
From under the trees they drew Him last,
'Twas on a tree they slew Him—last:
When out of the woods He came.

SIDNEY LANIER, NATURALIST

The cross is the outcome of his deepest mind, of his prayer life. It is more like him than anything else he ever did.

T. R. GLOVER

Oh, man's capacity
For spiritual sorrow, corporal pain
Who has explored the deepmost of that sea
With heavy links of a far-fathoming chain? . . .

One only has explored
The deepmost; but He did not die of it.
Not yet, not yet He died. Man's human Lord
Touched the extreme; it is not infinite.

But over the abyss
Of *God's* capacity for woe He stayed
One hesitating hour; what gulf was this?
Forsaken He went down, and was afraid.

ALICE MEYNELL

Seen? and yet hated Thee? They did not see;
They saw Thee not that "saw and hated" Thee:
No, no, they saw Thee not, O Life, O Love,
Who saw aught in Thee that their hate could move.

RICHARD CRASHAW ON JOHN 15:24

Desperate tides of the whole great world's anguish
Forced thro' the channels of a single heart.

F. W. H. MYERS

Rebellious fool, what hast thy folly done?
Controlled thy God? and crucified His Son?

How sweetly has the Lord of life deceived thee!
Thou shedd'st His blood, and that shed blood has saved thee.

FRANCIS QUARLES

  Mine own apostle, who the bag did bear,
  Though he had all I had, did not forbear
  To sell me also, and to put me there—
    Was ever grief like mine?
  For thirty pence he did my death devise,
  Who at three hundred did the ointment prize,
  Not half so sweet as my sweet sacrifice—
    Was ever grief like mine?

GEORGE HERBERT

  Still as of old men by themselves are priced—
  For thirty pieces Judas sold himself, not Christ.

HESTER CHOLMONDELEY

But thou, improvident Judas, since thou art
Resolved to sell a thing, whose value is
Beyond the power of arithmetic art
To reckon up—proportionate thy price
  In some more near degree; let thy demand
  Make buyers *who this Christ is* understand.
Ask all the gold that rolls on Indus' shores,
Ask all the treasures of the Eastern Sea,
Ask all the earth's yet undiscovered ore,
Ask all the gems and pearls which purest be,
  Ask Herod's 'chequer, ask the High Priest's crown,
  Ask Caesar's mighty sceptre and his throne.
Ask all the silver of the glistering stars,
Ask all the gold that flames in Phoebus' eyes,
Ask all the jewels of Aurora's tears,
Ask all the smiles and beauties of the skies.
  Ask all that can by anything be given—
  Ask bliss, ask life, ask Paradise, ask Heaven . . .

JOSEPH BEAUMONT

  To say the truth, so Judas kissed his master,
  And cried "All hail!" whereas he meant all harm.

WILLIAM SHAKESPEARE

They buy a field to bury strangers in,
Yet, with the first two such, will not begin.
True, Judas, though new to Jerusalem,
Is too much like them to be strange to them.
But since for Christ a place they will not find—
They will not find one stranger to their mind.

ANONYMOUS

Thy hands are washed, but oh, the water's spilt
That laboured to have washed thy guilt;
The flood, if any be that can suffice,
Must have its fountain in thine eyes.

RICHARD CRASHAW ON PILATE

Pilate . . . took water and washed his hands before the crowd, saying, "I am innocent of this man's blood"; [Jesus] poured water into a basin, and began to wash the disciples' feet.

MATTHEW 27:24; JOHN 13:5

Our lady stood beside the cross
      A little space apart,
And when she heard our Lord cry out
      A sword went through her heart.

HILAIRE BELLOC

"Say, bold but blessed thief,
      That in a trice
Stepped into Paradise,
And in plain day
Stol'st heaven away:
What trick could'st thou invent
To compass thy intent?
What arms?
What charms?"—
"Love, and belief."

ANONYMOUS

The man, the Christ, the soldier,
Who from his cross of pain,
Cried to the dying comrade,
"Lad, we shall meet again!"

WILLARD A. WATTLES

Blood brothers did we all become there,
And gentlemen, each one.

WILLIAM LANGLAND

Christ's cross is such a burden as sails are to a ship and wings to a bird.

SAMUEL RUTHERFORD

How life and death in Thee
Agree!
Thou hadst a virgin womb
And tomb;
A Joseph did betroth
Them both.

RICHARD CRASHAW

Resurrection, Ascension

Public was death; but power, but might,
But life again, but victory,
Were hushed within the dead of night,
The shuttered dark, the secrecy.
And all alone, alone, alone,
He rose again behind the stone.

ALICE MEYNELL

Reason and Faith at once set out
To search the Saviour's tomb;
Faith faster runs, but waits without,
As fearing to presume,

Till Reason enter in, and trace
Christ's relics round the holy place—
"Here lay His limbs, and here His sacred head,
And who was by, to make His new-forsaken bed?"

Both wonder, one believes—but while
   They muse on all at home,
No thought can tender Love beguile
   From Jesus' grave to roam.

Weeping, she stays till HE appear . . .

JOHN KEBLE

The evidence for the resurrection of Jesus is the existence of the church in that extraordinary spiritual vitality which confronts us in the New Testament. This is its own explanation of its being.

JAMES DENNEY

The New Testament writers, though they speak often of the death of Christ, never think of a dead Christ (JAMES DENNEY); The disciples did not assert merely that their Master had survived death, but that he had conquered death (E. G. SELWYN).

For the garden tomb is empty and the East is silver grey,
As the angels of the morning trumpet in another day;
See the wounded God go walking down the world's eternal way,
   For His task is never done.

STUDDERT KENNEDY

Life abides, changing but indestructible. Of this, the strong and sufficient evidence is an empty tomb within an Easter garden, a risen Lord walking with men along evening roads of sadness, and appearing in shut places with the gospel of an ever-open future; and, for contemporary evidence, the continuing fulfilment of His simple, glorious promise, "Lo, I am with you always, to the close of the age."

ANONYMOUS

Whate'er befell
   Earth is not hell:
Now, too, as when it first began,
Life is yet life, and man is man.
For all that breathe beneath the heaven's high cope
Joy with grief mixes, with despondence hope.
Hope conquers cowardice; joy, grief;
Or at the least, faith conquers unbelief.

Though dead, not dead;
Not gone, though fled;
Not lost, not vanishèd:
In the great gospel and true creed
He is yet risen indeed;
    Christ is yet risen.

ARTHUR H. CLOUGH

He is not far away:
Why do we sometimes seem to be alone;
And miss the hands outstretched to meet our own?
    He is the same today,
    As when of old He dwelt
In human form with His disciples—when
He knew the needs of all His fellowmen,
    And all their sorrow felt.
    Only our faith is dim,
So that *our* eyes are holden, and we go
All day, and until dusk, before we know
    That *we* have walked with Him.

UNKNOWN

Had Christ, the death of death, to death
Not given death by dying,
The gates of life had never been
To mortals open lying.

EPITAPH, CAMBRIDGESHIRE, ENGLAND

Bethany is barely five straight miles from Bethlehem: yet between Bethlehem's Advent and Bethany's Ascension stretches the epoch that changed the world.

X

Bright portals of the sky,
  Embossed with sparkling stars,
Doors of eternity
  With diamantine bars,
Your arras rich uphold,
  Loose all your bolts and springs,

Open wide your leaves of gold
That in your roofs may come the KING OF KINGS!

WILLIAM DRUMMOND

Historicity

The theory of a "myth-creating faith," constructing Christ out of odds and ends of contemporary hopes, superstitions and messianic expectations founders fatally on the strangeness of the resulting portrait. So far from fulfilling the longings of his generation, the Jesus of the Gospels outraged them. His birth, life, associates, and poverty, his thought, his ministry, his values, his priorities, character, claims, authority, humility, and his end, were all totally unexpected, inexplicable, and repugnant to his contemporaries, and largely so even to his disciples. Far from being the creation of existing faith, Jesus was its greatest stumblingblock, to Jew and Greek alike. No known milieu in that first century would fashion a "myth" like that. Jesus' contemporaries did not create Him, they crucified Him.

INDEBTED TO OTTO BORCHERT

Only a Christ could have conceived a Christ.

JOSEPH PARKER

Apart from a few references to Jesus or the Christian movement in non-Christian writers of the first centuries (Tacitus, Suetonius, Pliny, Celsus, Lucian, Minucius Felix), the record of Jesus is that of Christian believers, for whom its preservation was most important. The supreme significance of the story to the writers does not make it false. After a long period of sceptical research, pursuing every archaeological, literary, linguistic, and cultural clue to the historical Jesus, the sources for His life have in late years won increasing respect.

X

[The Gospel of Mark] is an authority of the first rank . . . of first-rate historical importance (VINCENT TAYLOR, AFTER MANY YEARS' INVESTIGATION); The gospel record is rooted in history . . . history and interpretation cannot in the Gospels be separated, but the control of history is everywhere present (A. M. HUNTER); The Gospels constitute certainly the reliable record of the events on which the faith [of the early church] is founded (WILLIAM BARCLAY); It is the view of many competent scholars today that the fragments of the Christian tradition which we possess . . . bear witness with singular unanimity to one single historical figure unlike any other who has ever walked among the sons of men (STEPHEN NEILL, REVIEWING A CENTURY'S RESEARCH).

There is something severely crippled about the logic that contends that there never could have been a Son of God who descended, died, and rose again for our salvation, precisely because the possibility, and the need, of such a Saviour had already occurred to minds in various parts of the world. Especially when the argument proceeds, that of course the event did not happen, because the language in which it was announced was not that of some newly-invented technical terminology, but that of familiar, existing myths! How else *could* a totally unique event ever be intelligibly described, but in terms already familiar?

ANONYMOUS

Assessments

Jesus defied classification. He was not referable to type. He was the beginning of a time.

JOHN WATSON

> Thou art the King of glory, O Christ,
> Thou art the everlasting Son of the Father;
> When Thou tookest upon Thee to deliver man
> Thou didst not abhor the virgin's womb;
> When Thou hadst overcome the sharpness of death
> Thou didst open the kingdom of heaven to all believers.
> Thou sittest at the right hand of God in the glory of the Father;
> We believe that Thou shalt come, to be our judge.

TE DEUM LAUDAMUS

If a man does not worship Christ, I do not care what he thinks of Him—he does not see what is there; and I have missed the mark completely in what I have written if I have not made it clear that all men should honour the Son even as they honour the Father. . . . For me, to worship Jesus as God is worshipped, to trust Him as God is trusted, to owe to Him what we can owe to God alone, is the essence of Christianity.

JAMES DENNEY

"Jesus is God" is not the true way to say a true thing. Jesus is man as well as God, in some way therefore both less and more than God; and consequently, a form of proposition which in our idiom suggests inevitably the precise equivalence of Jesus and God, does some kind of injustice to the truth. I have no objection at all to "Jesus is God the Son," because "the Son" introduces the very qualification of God which makes it possible to apply it to Jesus. . . . I have no hesitation in saying "Jesus was God manifest in the flesh," because "manifest in the flesh" serves the same purpose.

JAMES DENNEY

Jesus—the near end of God; the human face of God.

X

At the turning of the earth beneath the waxing moon, the immeasurable surge of the ocean flows from the China Sea southwards through the Pacific, around the Cape of Africa into the South Atlantic, moving on westwards and north towards the Caribbean to fall at last in single waves upon the shores of Mexico Bay. To calculate that immense thrust, to measure the inconceivable tidal surge, defeats thought, baffles imagination. Yet each final breaker truly represents, and originates in, that world-encircling energy. Even so, in Christ the measureless ocean of the Godhead washes our human shore—not, certainly, all there is of God, but all we can comprehend, or appreciate, or need.

INDEBTED TO HARRY EMERSON FOSDICK

So far from being on the same road as we are, ahead, but not too far, and for the time being only, Christ is the object of Christian worship. . . . He transcends the category of religious genius. . . Christ is Mediator, and Redeemer, not only the Sovereign but the Saviour of men.

N. H. G. ROBINSON

I say, the acknowledgement of God in Christ
Accepted by thy reason, solves for thee
All questions in the earth and out of it,
And has so far advanced thee to be wise.

ROBERT BROWNING

In the Word made flesh, the divine thought is expressed, the divine message is conveyed, divine power is communicated (as at creation), and the meaning of all things is at last made luminous.

X

With all the advantage of centuries of hindsight sifting varying opinions about Jesus, our conviction concerning Him must remain an act of faith. But that is no mere "decision so to think," no wilful "will to believe": it comprises a value-judgement, that Christ and all He stood for is morally right, good, and beautiful; a truth-judgement, that the claims of Jesus and those made for Him by his closest followers are valid and worthy of trust; and an empirical judgement, that his grace and power have *in fact* been confirmed in our personal experience and in our observation of his grace in other lives.

ANONYMOUS

He comes to us, as of old by the lakeside he came to those men who knew him not. He speaks to us the same words, "Follow thou me!" and sets us to the tasks which he has to fulfil for our time. He commands. And to those who obey him, he will reveal himself in the toils, the conflicts, the sufferings, which they shall pass through in his fellowship, and, as an ineffable mystery, they shall learn in their own experience who he is.

ALBERT SCHWEITZER, CLOSING *QUEST OF
THE HISTORICAL JESUS*

> The love of Christ, in the Gospels and today—
>> confronts suffering and issues in healing;
>> confronts bewilderment and brings enlightenment;
>> confronts penitence and assures forgiveness;
>> confronts despair and kindles hope;
>> confronts weakness and works redemption;
>> confronts loneliness and offers fellowship;
>> confronts sin and makes expiation;
>> confronts lovelessness and burns with anger;
>> confronts rejection and assents to death;
>> confronts death and overcomes it.
> Jesus is love's portrait, done to the life—and death.

ANONYMOUS

It is said that God is love and needs no propitiation; what John teaches is that God is love and therefore provides the propitiation (G. S. BARRETT ON 1 JOHN); There is no sublimation of the historical into "ethical" or "spiritual" principles, or into "eternal facts," which absolves us from all obligation to a Saviour who came in blood (JAMES DENNEY); It is perilously easy, on the subject of the cross, to sound impeccably orthodox and mean nothing (X).

Once a blurred and indistinct view of Christ's atonement is accepted in the church, it is more than likely that the next generation will arrive at the ultimate obscurity of one of whom it could be said, "R— believed that Christ did something or other which, somehow or other, had some connection or other with salvation."

X

> But if the wanderer his mistake discern,
> Judge his own ways, and sigh for a return,
> Bewildered once, must he bewail his loss
> For ever and for ever? NO—the cross! . . .
> There and there only is the power to save;
> There no delusive hope invites despair,
> No mockery meets you, no deception there:
> The spells and charms that blinded you before
> All vanish there, and fascinate no more.
>   I am no preacher; let this hint suffice:
> The cross once seen is death to every vice;
> Else He that hung there suffered all his pain,
> Bled, groaned, and agonised, and died, in vain.

WILLIAM COWPER

Testimony

Without Christ I should be an atheist.

ALBRECHT RITSCHL

> Thou art our Holy Lord,
> The all-subduing Word,
>   Healer of strife;
> Thou didst Thyself abase
> That from our sin's disgrace

Thou mightest save our race,
And give us life.

CLEMENT OF ALEXANDRIA

In fancy I stood by the shore, one day,
Of the beautiful murm'ring sea:
I saw the great crowds as they thronged the way
Of the Stranger of Galilee.
I saw how the man who was blind from birth
In a moment was made to see;
The lame was made whole by the matchless skill
Of the Stranger of Galilee.
    And I felt I could love Him for ever,
    So gracious and tender was He:
    I claimed Him that day as my Saviour,
    This Stranger of Galilee.

C. H. MORRIS

In the sunset's flare the heavens declare
    I know not what;
Mine eyes I lift where the hill mists drift
    And they help me not.
For gold I sought in the mines of thought,
    But the grains were few;
Then the life that smiled in a little Child
Its full word spoke in a heart that broke,
    And I knew.

UNKNOWN

Star whose light shines o'er me,
Rock on which I stand,
Guide who goes before me
    To my fatherland;
Daily bread reviving,
Spring that cheers my heart,
Goal to which I'm striving—
    All, O Lord, Thou art!
Faith—a shining beacon,
Hope—lest I lose heart,

Love that cannot weaken—
All, O Lord, Thou art!

CORNELIUS KRUMMACHER,
TRANS. FRANK HOUGHTON

Yea, through life, death, through sorrow and through sinning,
Christ shall suffice me, for He hath sufficed;
Christ is the end, for Christ was the beginning:
Christ the beginning, for the end is Christ.

F. W. H. MYERS

If Thou, O God, the Christ didst leave,
In Him, not Thee, I do believe;
To Jesus, dying all alone,
To His dark cross, not Thy bright throne,
My hopeless hands will cleave.

But if it was Thy love that died,
Thy voice that in the darkness cried,
The print of nails I long to see
In *Thy* hands, God, who fashioned me;
Show me *Thy* piercèd side.

EDWARD SHILLITO

"Raise but the stone, and thou shalt find me there;
Or cleave the wood, and there am I. I say
Wherever there is one alone, yea there,
Am I in him." These Thy new words, today
I heard, still darkly hid, and looked—and there,
Where I so long had thought Thou hadst no part,
I found Thee hiding with me in my heart.

NORMAN AULT, QUOTING
OXYRHYNCHUS PAPYRUS

I see His blood upon the rose,
And in the stars the glory of His eyes,
His body gleams amid eternal snows,
His tears fall from the skies.

I see His face in every flower;
The thunder, and the singing of the birds

Are but His voice—and carven by His power,
Rocks are His written words.

All pathways by His feet are worn,
His strong heart stirs the ever-beating sea:
His crown of thorns is twined with every thorn,
His cross is every tree.

           J. M. PLUNKETT

The night was dark, the shadows fell
Far as the eye could see:
I gave my hand to the human Christ
And He walked in the dark with me.

Out of the darkness we came at length,
Our feet on the dawn-warmed sod,
And I knew by the light in His wondrous eyes
That I walked with the Son of God.

           LAUCHLAN MACLEAN WATT

A Christless cross no refuge were for me:
A crossless Christ—no Saviour would he be:
But, O Christ crucified, I rest in Thee.

           UNKNOWN

Christ means to me the best kind of a friend, as well as Leader, who is
giving me in this world ten times—nay, the proverbial hundredfold as good
times as I could enjoy in any other way.

           WILFRED GRENFELL, OF LABRADOR

Thou art my Way: I wander if Thou fly;
Thou art my Light: if hid, how blind am I!
Thou art my Life: if Thou withdraw I die . . .
Thou art the pilgrim's path, the blind man's eye,
The dead man's life; on Thee my hopes rely;
If Thou remove, I err, I grope, I die.

           FRANCIS QUARLES

Heaven above is softer blue,
Earth around is sweeter green:
Something breathes in every hue

Christless eyes have never seen.
Birds with gladder songs o'erflow,
Flowers with deeper beauties shine,
Since I know, as now I know,
I am His, and He is mine.

G. WADE ROBINSON

Response to Christ

Let folly praise that fancy loves, I praise and love that Child
Whose heart no thought, whose tongue no word,
    whose hand no deed defiled.
I praise Him most; I love Him best; all praise and love is His;
While Him I love, in Him I live, and cannot live amiss ...
To love Him, life: to leave Him, death: to live in Him, delight;
He mine by gift, I His by debt, thus each to other due;
First friend He was, best friend He is; all times will
    prove Him true.

ROBERT SOUTHWELL

We find Thee—yea, we find Thee every day,
In mangers and on crosses by the way;
Yea, even our own soul's darkest agony
May be a Cave of Bethlehem for Thee.

FATHER ANDREW

Light of the world, for ever, ever shining,
    There is no change in Thee;
True light of life, all joy and health enshrining,
    Thou canst not fade or flee.
Light of the world, undimming and unsetting,
    O shine each mist away!
Banish the fear, the falsehood, and the fretting,
    Be our unchanging Day.

HORATIUS BONAR

If Jesus Christ were to come today, people wouldn't even crucify him.
They would ask him to dinner, hear what he had to say, and make fun
of it (THOMAS CARLYLE); To call Jesus " Lord" is orthodoxy, and to call
Him "Lord, Lord" is piety; but to call Jesus "Lord, Lord" and do not
the things that He says, is blasphemy (LESLIE WEATHERHEAD).

The Gospels bring home to us Christ's living presence, and in that presence all superstition and unreality are superfluous, and fade away as we kneel in wonder.

ERASMUS

Thou O my Jesus, Thou didst me upon the cross embrace,
For me didst bear the nails and spear, and manifold disgrace;
And griefs and torments numberless, and sweat of agony;
E'en death itself—and all for one who was Thine enemy.
Then why, O blessed Jesus Christ, should I not love Thee well?
Not for the sake of winning heaven, or of escaping hell;
Not with the hope of gaining aught, nor seeking a reward;
But as Thyself hast lovèd me, O ever-loving Lord.
E'en so I love Thee.

FRANCIS XAVIER

And didst Thou love the race that loved not Thee?
    And didst Thou take to heaven a human brow?
Dost plead with man's voice by the marvellous sea?
    Art Thou his kinsman now?

O God, O kinsman loved, but not enough!
    O Man with eyes majestic after death,
Whose feet have toiled along our pathways rough,
    Whose lips drawn human breath!

By that one likeness which is ours and Thine,
    By that one nature which doth hold us kin,
By that high heaven where, sinless, Thou dost shine
    To draw us sinners in;

By Thy last silence in the judgement hall,
    By long foreknowledge of the deadly tree,
By darkness, by the wormwood and the gall,
    I pray Thee, visit me.

Come, lest this heart should, cold and cast away,
    Die ere the Guest adored she entertain—
Lest eyes that never saw Thine earthly day
    Should miss Thy heavenly reign.

JEAN INGELOW

None other Lamb, none other Name,
   None other hope in heaven or earth or sea,
None other hiding-place from guilt and shame,
   None beside Thee!

My faith burns low, my hope burns low;
   Only my heart's desire cries out in me,
By the deep thunder of its want and woe,
   Cries out to Thee.

Lord Thou art life, though I be dead;
   Love's fire Thou art, however cold I be:
Nor heaven have I, nor place to lay my head,
   Nor home, but Thee.

CHRISTINA ROSSETTI

If we never sought, we seek Thee now;
   Thine eyes burn through the dark, our only stars;
We must have sight of thorn-pricks on Thy brow,
   We must have Thee, O Jesus of the scars . . .

The other gods were strong, but Thou wast weak;
   They rode, but Thou didst stumble to a throne;
But to our wounds God's wounds alone can speak—
   And not a god has wounds, but Thou alone.

EDWARD SHILLITO, DURING WAR

JEWS

He is not a real Jew who is one outwardly. . . . He is a Jew who is one inwardly. . . . His praise is not from men but from God.

PAUL: ROMANS 2:28–29, PUNNING ON
JUDAH = PRAISE

Hath not a Jew eyes? hath not a Jew hands, organs . . . fed with the same food, hurt with the same weapons. If you prick us do we not bleed? If you tickle us do we not laugh? If you poison us do we not die? And if you wrong us, shall we not revenge?

WILLIAM SHAKESPEARE

The Jews are among the aristocracy of every land. If a literature is called rich in the possession of a few classic tragedies, what shall we say to a national tragedy lasting for fifteen hundred years, in which the poets and actors were also the heroes?

GEORGE ELIOT

Yes, I am a Jew; and when the ancestors of the right honourable gentleman were brutal savages in an unknown island, mine were priests in the temple of Solomon.

BENJAMIN DISRAELI,
(speaking in Parliament)

> A people still, whose common ties are gone,
> Who, mixed with every race, are lost in none.

GEORGE CRABBE

To the Christian, the Jew is the incomprehensibly obdurate man who declines to see what has happened; and to the Jew, the Christian is the incomprehensibly daring man who affirms in an unredeemed world that its redemption has been accomplished.

MARTIN BUBER

JOY

Rejoice in the Lord always. I will say it again: Rejoice!

PAUL: PHILIPPIANS 4:4, NIV

This is the most significant fact about Jesus' joy, that the sources of it were not at the mercy of men or circumstances.

HARRY EMERSON FOSDICK

I defy any man to do something for somebody, comfort them, help them, and not come back happier and full of joy. This is cause and effect.

HENRY DRUMMOND

> Not by appointment do we meet Delight
> And Joy; they heed not our expectancy;

But round some corner in the streets of life
They, on a sudden, clasp us with a smile.

GERALD MASSEY

Sing out, my soul, thy songs of joy;
Such as a happy bird will sing,
Beneath a rainbow's lovely arch
In early spring.

W. H. DAVIES

He who bends to himself a joy
Does the wingèd life destroy;
But he who kisses the joy as it flies
Lives in eternity's sunrise.

WILLIAM BLAKE

A sorrow shared is half a trouble, but joy that's shared is joy made double.

ENGLISH PROVERB

JUDGEMENT

"With the judgement you pronounce you will be judged."

JESUS: MATTHEW 7:2

Divine

Every hour is the last hour (WILLIAM BARCLAY); Every event is a judgement of God (J. C. FRIEDRICH VON SCHILLER); A God all mercy is a God unjust (EDWARD YOUNG).

Our sense of living at the end of a world epoch, and of witnessing the reaction of a moral universe against the wickedness and folly of mankind, is no illusion, but one more testimony to the unescapable truth that this world comes to an end (sooner or later, and for each of us at death) and leaves us exposed to the final realities. . . . Our life can hardly be said to make sense unless each of us is to be given at some moment, soon or late, an understanding of himself as he really is. . . . This is the last judgement.

C. H. DODD, IN 1945

God hides from man the reckoning day, that he
May fear it ever for uncertainty:
That being ignorant of that one he may
Expect the coming of it every day.

ROBERT HERRICK

A robust morality refuses to believe that it does not matter whether a man
has lived like the apostle Paul or like the emperor Nero; there must be
one place for St. John, who was Jesus' friend and another for Judas
Iscariot, who was His betrayer.

JOHN WATSON

God will not look you over for medals, degrees, or diplomas, but for scars
(ELBERT HUBBARD); We shall not be asked what we have read, but what
we have done (THOMAS À KEMPIS).

The wrath of God is revealed from heaven against all ungodliness and
wickedness of men. . . . They are without excuse. . . . Therefore God gave
them up. . . . God gave them up. . . . God gave them up.

PAUL: ROMANS 1:18, 20, 24, 26, 28

Such was the last of Jesus' parables. . . . By their love, and by their love
alone, would this Judge judge mankind—the gentlest, the sternest, the most
inexorable judgement ever to be passed on man.

MIDDLETON MURRY

Human

For all right judgement of any man, it is . . . essential to see his good
qualities before pronouncing on his bad (THOMAS CARLYLE); He who decides
a case with the other side unheard, though he decide justly, is himself
unjust (SENECA); Do not hear one and judge two (GREEK PROVERB); Don't
judge any man until you have walked two moons in his moccasins
(AMERICAN INDIAN PROVERB); He hath good judgement who relieth not wholly
on his own (THOMAS FULLER).

He only judges right who weighs, compares,
And, in the sternest sentence which his voice
Pronounces, ne'er abandons charity.

WILLIAM WORDSWORTH

They have a right to censure, that have a heart to help (WILLIAM PENN);
Who reproves the lame must go upright (SAMUEL DANIEL).

> Still mark if vice or nature prompts the deed,
> Still mark the strong temptation, and the need.
>
> JOHN LANGHORNE

Woe to him . . . who has no court of appeal against the world's
judgement (THOMAS CARLYLE); Weigh, do not merely count, men's
judgements (SENECA); When you are evil spoken of, go on living so nobly
that the slander cannot be believed (UNKNOWN).

"Do not give dogs what is sacred; do not throw your pearls to pigs . . .
they may trample them under their feet, and then turn and tear you to
pieces."

> JESUS: MATTHEW 7:6, NIV

Neither give Aesop's cock a gem, who would be better pleased and
happier if he had a barley corn.

> FRANCIS BACON

> The sinner's own fault? So it was . . .
> Clearly his own fault. Yet I think
>   My fault in part, who did not pray,
>   But lagged, and would not lead the way.
> I, haply, proved his missing link.
>   God help us both . . .
>
> CHRISTINA ROSSETTI

How awful to reflect that what people say of us is true.

> L. PEARSALL SMITH

JUSTICE

> Let justice roll down like waters,
>   and righteousness like an everflowing stream.
>
> AMOS 5:24

Truth is justice's handmaid, freedom its child, peace its companion, safety walks in its steps, victory follows in its train; it is the brightest emanation of the Gospel; it is the attribute of God.

SYDNEY SMITH

Justice is like the kingdom of God: not without us as a fact, it is within us as a great yearning.

GEORGE ELIOT

Justice is truth in action (BENJAMIN DISRAELI) . . . the right of the weakest (JOSEPH JOUBERT) . . . the interest of the stronger (PLATO); Where justice reigns, 'tis freedom to obey (JAMES MONTGOMERY); He hurts the good who spares the bad (PUBLILIUS SYRUS); Justice must tame whom mercy cannot win (GEORGE SAVILE).

To no one will we deny justice, to no one will we delay it (MAGNA CARTA, A.D. 1215); National injustice is the surest road to national downfall (WILLIAM E. GLADSTONE).

> And earthly power doth then show likest God's
> When mercy seasons justice . . .
>
> Sparing justice feeds iniquity . . .

WILLIAM SHAKESPEARE

KINDNESS

Be kind to one another; The . . . kindness of God our Savior.

EPHESIANS 4:32, TITUS 3:4

Be the living expression of God's kindness, in your face, your eyes, your smile, your greeting. Give not only your care but your heart.

MOTHER TERESA OF CALCUTTA

'Twas a thief said the last kind word to Christ;
Christ took the kindness and forgave the theft.

ROBERT BROWNING

To do him any wrong was to beget
A kindness from him, for his heart was rich.

ALFRED TENNYSON

Fierce for the right he bore his part
In strife with many a valiant foe;
But laughter winged his polished dart,
And kindness tempered every blow.

WILLIAM WINTER OF I. H. BROMLEY

That best portion of a good man's life,
His little, nameless, unremembered acts
Of kindness and of love.

WILLIAM WORDSWORTH

KINGDOM OF GOD

Jesus came into Galilee, preaching the gospel of God, and saying, "The time is fulfilled, and the kingdom of God is at hand. . . ."

MARK 1:14–15

The very programme of Christianity, as it is often understood, is to establish the kingdom of God on earth by the concentrated effort of all good men. To Jesus this conception would have been meaningless, and repellent. The kingdom as he knew it was God's: men could no more establish it than they could make the sun rise.

E. F. SCOTT

> O Jesus, King most wonderful,
> Thou conqueror renowned;
> Thou sweetness most ineffable
> In whom all joys are found—
> When once Thou visitest the heart,
> Then truth begins to shine;
> Then earthly vanities depart,
> Then kindles love divine.

BERNARD OF CLAIRVAUX

Jesus slowly built up the new kingdom. . . . A formalist must be born again; the slave of riches must sell all he had; a man in the toils of a darling sin must pluck out his right eye to enter the kingdom of God. . . . The eight men of the beatitudes divide the kingdom of God. . . . The kingdom can only rule over willing hearts; it advances by individual conversion, and stands in individual consecration.

JOHN WATSON

God has set up two forms of rule, the spiritual, which makes Christians through the Holy Spirit subject to Christ; and the secular, which restrains the wicked. . . . The secular rule can also be called the kingdom of God. He intends it to stand, and us to be obedient in it. But it is only *the kingdom of His left hand*. The kingdom of His right hand, which He rules himself, not placing in it father, king, executioner, jailer, but dwelling in it himself, is that in which the gospel is preached to the poor.

MARTIN LUTHER

> Thy kingdom come! On bended knee
>   The passing ages pray;
> And faithful souls have yearned to see
>   On earth that kingdom's day.

But the slow watches of the night
Not less to God belong;
And for the everlasting right
The silent stars are strong.

FREDERICK L. HOSMER

The kingdom of heaven is to me the great existing reality which is to renew the earth.

F. D. MAURICE

My business, because I am a theologian . . . is to show that economics and politics . . . must have a ground beneath themselves; that society is not to be made anew by arrangements of ours, but is to be regenerated by finding the law and ground of its order and harmony—the only secret of its existence—in God.

F. D. MAURICE

Many solicitously enquire who is greatest in the kingdom of heaven, who utterly neglect the only important enquiry, whether they themselves shall be thought worthy to be numbered among the least. To be the least, where all are great, is to be great.

THOMAS À KEMPIS

Where in life's common ways
With cheerful feet we go;
Where in His steps we tread
Who trod the way of woe;
Where He is in the heart,
City of God, thou art.

FRANCIS T. PALGRAVE

KNOWLEDGE

"Woe to you lawyers! for you have taken away the key of knowledge; you did not enter yourselves, and you hindered those who were entering."

JESUS: LUKE 11:52

It often comes into my mind to go round all the Universities of Europe
. . . crying out every where like a madman, and saying to all the learned
men whose learning is so much greater than their love, "Ah, what a
multitude of souls is shut out of heaven through your fault."

FRANCIS XAVIER

God does not want your cleverness—or your ignorance (JOHN CLIFFORD);
"The most saintly of the learned and most learned of the saints" (POPULAR
TRIBUTE TO THOMAS AQUINAS); They know enough who know how to learn
(HENRY ADAMS); Grace is given of God, but knowledge is bought in the
market (ARTHUR H. CLOUGH); What man knows is everywhere at war with
what he wants (JOSEPH WOOD KRUTCH); We don't know one millionth of
one per cent about anything (THOMAS EDISON); We have too many experts,
not enough leaders (UNKNOWN).

It is no less true in this human kingdom of knowledge than in God's
kingdom of heaven, that no man shall enter into it except he become first
as a little child.

FRANCIS BACON

Sit down before the fact as a little child; be prepared to give up every
preconceived notion, follow humbly and to whatever abysses Nature leads,
or you shall learn nothing.

THOMAS H. HUXLEY

To know that we know what we know, and that we do not know what
we do not know—that is true knowledge.

CONFUCIUS

Knowledge and wisdom, far from being one,
Have oft-times no connection. Knowledge dwells
In heads replete with thoughts of other men;
Wisdom in minds attentive to their own.
Knowledge is proud that he has learned so much;
Wisdom is humble that he knows no more.

WILLIAM COWPER

Knowledge, when wisdom is too weak to guide her,
Is like a headstrong horse, that throws the rider.

FRANCIS QUARLES

Let us never think or maintain that a man can search too far . . . in the book of God's word or in the book of God's works . . . but . . . let men beware that they do not unwisely mingle or confound these learnings together.

FRANCIS BACON, "the sentence which established science's independence of religion"

To be proud of knowledge is to be blind with light (BENJAMIN FRANKLIN); If the great things of religion are *rightly understood*, they will affect the heart (JONATHAN EDWARDS); What science has done hitherto is to improve the means for achieving unimproved or actually deteriorated ends (ALDOUS HUXLEY).

> Let knowledge grow from more to more,
>   But more of reverence in us dwell;
>   That mind and soul, according well,
> May make one music as before.
>
> ALFRED TENNYSON

No man can know God unless God has taught him; that is to say, that without God, God cannot be known.

> IRENAEUS

> We believe that in all ages
> Every human heart IS human;
> That in even savage bosoms
> There are longings, strivings, yearnings
> For the good they comprehend not;
> That the feeble hands and helpless
> Groping out into the darkness
> Touch God's right hand in that darkness,
> And are lifted up and strengthened.
>
> HENRY WADSWORTH LONGFELLOW

A humble knowledge of thyself is a surer way to God than a deep search after learning.

> THOMAS À KEMPIS

Did not your father . . .
    do justice and righteousness?
He judged the cause of the poor and needy . . .
Is not this to know me?
               says the LORD.

            JEREMIAH 22:15–16

LAW

God . . . sending his own Son . . . in order that the just requirement of the law might be fulfilled in us.

PAUL: ROMANS 8:3–4

Jesus' enemies were unable to bring any direct charge against Him, but in their main contention they were right; the "fulfilment" which He gave to the law involved in the long run its dissolution.

E. F. SCOTT

There is but one law for all, namely that law which governs all law, the law of our Creator, the law of humanity, justice, equity—the law of nature, and of nations.

EDMUND BURKE

Where is there any book of the law so clear to each man as that written in his heart? (LEO TOLSTOI); The man who does no wrong needs no law (MENANDER); No laws, however stringent, can make the idle industrious, the thriftless provident, or the drunken sober (SAMUEL SMILES).

Two things fill the mind with ever new and increasing admiration and awe, the oftener and the more steadily we reflect on them: the starry heavens above, and the moral law within. I have not to search for them. . . . I see them before me, and connect them directly with the consciousness of my existence.

IMMANUEL KANT

Adam was but human: this explains it all. He did not want the apple for the apple's sake; he wanted it only because it was forbidden.

MARK TWAIN

The fruit of the Spirit is love, joy, peace, patience, kindness, goodness, faithfulness, gentleness, self-control; against such there is no law.

PAUL: GALATIANS 5:22–23, NIV

LIFE

What is your life?

JAMES 4:14

I am convinced that the world is not a mere bog in which men and women trample themselves in the mire and die. Something magnificent is taking place here amid the cruelties and tragedies; and the supreme challenge to intelligence is that of making the noblest and best in our curious heritage prevail.

CHARLES A. BEARD (HISTORIAN)

Life is a boundless privilege . . . an ecstasy . . . an experiment (RALPH WALDO EMERSON) . . . a preparation for the future (ELBERT HUBBARD) . . . a mission—religion, science, philosophy all agree in this, that every existence is an aim (GUISEPPE MAZZINI) . . . a voyage, homeward bound (HERMAN MELVILLE).

Life can only be understood backwards, but it must be lived forwards (SØREN KIERKEGAARD); We now demand to be personally conducted through life, all risks to be taken by someone else (WILLIAM R. INGE); We break up life into little bits and fritter it away (SENECA); The residue of life is short: live as on a mountain (MARCUS AURELIUS); Life: a whim of several million cells to be you for a while (GRAHAM STORR); A man may live long yet live very little (MICHEL DE MONTAIGNE).

> It is not growing like a tree
> In bulk doth make man better be;
> Or standing long, an oak, three hundred year . . .
> In small proportions we just beauties see:
> And in short measures life may perfect be.
>
> BEN JONSON

We live in deeds, not years; in thoughts, not breaths;
In feelings, not in figures on a dial.

We should count time by heart-throbs. He most lives
Who thinks most, feels the noblest, acts the best.

P. J. BAILEY

I live for those who love me, for those who know me true;
For the heaven that smiles above me, and awaits my spirit too;
For the cause that lacks assistance, for the wrong that
    needs resistance,
For the future in the distance, and the good that I can do.

G. L. BANKS

Two children in two neighbour villages,
Playing mad pranks along the healthy leas;
Two strangers meeting at a festival;
Two lovers whispering by an orchard wall;
Two lives bound fast in one with golden ease;
Two graves grass-green beside a grey church-tower,
Washed with still rains, and daisy-blossomed;
Two children in one hamlet born and bred—
So runs the round of life from hour to hour.

ALFRED TENNYSON

So long as faith in freedom reigns
And loyal hope survives,
And gracious charity remains
To leaven lowly lives;
While there is one untrodden tract
For intellect or will,
And men are free to think and act,
Life is worth living still.

ALFRED AUSTIN

LOVE

Beloved, if God so loved us, we also ought to love one another.

JOHN: 1 JOHN 4:11

God's Love

God is love. That is the one supreme piece of good news which every New Testament writer is, in his different manner, concerned to publish to the world.

JOHN BAILLIE

God is love;
If God is love, then life is good;
If God is love, then love is right;
If God is love, then tomorrow is a promise.

1 JOHN 4:8, 18, 7, 17

The love of God is never idle (ANGELA OF FOLIGNO); Love was our Lord's meaning (JULIAN OF NORWICH); The love of God is an indrawing and outpouring tide (JOHANNES RUYSBROECK); Love is God's essence, power His attribute; therefore is His love greater than His power (RICHARD GARNETT); God's love is more concerned with the development of a man's character than with the promotion of his comfort (J. IRELAND HASLER).

Ah, fondest, blindest, weakest,
I am He whom thou seekest!
Thou dravest love from thee, who dravest Me.

FRANCIS THOMPSON

He did not begin to love us because of what we were, and he will go on loving us in spite of what we are.

UNKNOWN

Love for God:

True love of God often consists in a firm, dry resolution to give up everything for Him.

FRANCOIS FÉNELON

God is the only goal worthy of man's efforts; the fitting end of human existence is a loving union with God.

AUGUSTINE

Some people are for seeing God with their eyes, as they can see a cow (which thou lovest for the milk, and for the cheese, and for thine own profit). Thus do all those who love God for the sake of outward riches or of inward comfort; they do not love aright, but seek only themselves and their own advantage.

MEISTER ECKHART

Love thy God, and love Him only:
And thy breast will ne'er be lonely.
In that one great Spirit meet
All things mighty, grave, and sweet . . .
Mortal!—love that Holy One,
Or dwell for aye alone.

AUBREY DE VERE

For Jesus, nothing is allowed to take precedence over the first and greatest commandment. The second is like unto it, but with Him it is never allowed to obscure, or to exhaust, the first. And to *love* God means unwavering trust, implicit obedience, reverence for God's name, His day, His house; worship, constant communion, and abounding joy in God himself.

ANONYMOUS, MATTHEW 22:35–39

Love for Others

The Greeks had a word for it: "Eros" (physical love) is all take; "Philia" (friendship) is give and take; "Agape" (Christian love) is all give.

G. B. CAIRD

The content of *agape* was supplied, from the outset, by reference to the concrete action of Jesus Christ upon the field of history. . . . It is strictly true, in the history of thought and language, that we know what *agape* means from the fact that Christ laid down His life for us.

C. H. DODD

Love, and do what you will. Whether you keep silence . . . exclaim . . . correct . . . forbear . . . do it in love: from that root nothing but good can spring . . . Love, and you cannot but do well; use discipline . . . harshness . . . but in love.

AUGUSTINE

If I love my neighbour as myself, I regale myself with his prosperity, even as I share the bitter cup of his adversity; I am honoured in his praise, promoted in his advancement, gladdened in his joy, even as I am humbled in his shame or distressed in his sin.

ROBERT LAW

The powerful means for achieving true happiness is to spread out from oneself, in every direction, a whole spider's web of love, and to catch in it everything that comes along—whether it is an old woman or a child, a girl or a policeman.

LEO TOLSTOI

To love a thing means wanting it to live (CONFUCIUS); Our love of our neighbour is a sort of cradle of our love to God (AUGUSTINE); See in everyone you meet the image of Christ (ERASMUS); It is generous to ignore someone else's mistakes: quite the opposite to imitate them (ERASMUS); True charity is universal; without picking and choosing it loves all men in God, and treats its neighbour without respect of persons (MARTIN LUTHER); We must love one another or die (W. H. AUDEN); Let a man be what he may, he is still to be loved because God is loved (JOHN CALVIN); Love is an act of endless forgiveness, a tender look which becomes a habit (PETER USTINOV).

> For love is but the heart's immortal thirst
> To be completely known and all forgiven.

HENRY VAN DYKE

The loving of men which can exist apart from loving God is not at all love as Jesus meant it—love of divine quality, undemanding, deep, and enduring.

X

Love grasps not at her rights, refuses to take offence, has no memory for injuries. . . . All tolerance is she, all trustfulness, all hope, all strong endurance.

PAUL: 1 CORINTHIANS 13:5, 7, WAY'S TRANSLATION

Charity may cause a man to be fierce, and wickedness may cause him to speak smoothly. A boy may be struck by his father, and have fair words from a slave-dealer—it is charity that strikes and wickedness that ingratiates.

AUGUSTINE

The man who lives according to God ... owes "a perfect hatred" to evil men; not that he should hate the man on account of his fault, nor love the fault because of the man, but he should hate the fault and love the man.

AUGUSTINE

He drew a circle that shut me out—
Heretic, rebel, a thing to flout.
But love and I had the wit to win:
We drew a circle that took him in.

EDWIN MARKHAM

We may without undue tension of speech, speak of goodness as love in conduct; of truth as love in thought; of beauty as love in self-expression in whatever medium.

RICHARD ROBERTS

Call him not heretic whose works attest
His faith in goodness by no creed confessed.
Whatever in love's name is truly done
To free the bound and lift the fallen one,
Is done to Christ. Whoso in deed and word
Is not *against* Him, labours *for* the Lord.

JOHN GREENLEAF WHITTIER

He that shuts out love in turn shall be
Shut out from love, and on her threshold lie
Howling in the outer darkness.

ALFRED TENNYSON

Love is the condition in which the happiness of another person is essential to your own.

R. A. HEINLEIN

A leaf may hide the largest star
From love's uplifted eye;
    A mote of prejudice out-bar
A world of charity.

JOHN BANNISTER TABB

Love is all we have, the only way
That each can help the other.

EURIPIDES, FIFTH CENTURY B.C.

True love's the gift which God has given
To man alone beneath the heaven.

WALTER SCOTT

Love is indeed a transcendent excellence, an essential and sovereign good;
it maketh the heavy burden light, and the rugged path smooth. . . . Love
delights in the communication of good, and with swiftness equal to thought
diffuses its blessings with impartiality and ardour; it is courageous and
patient, faithful and prudent, longsuffering and generous, and never seeketh
itself. Love is circumspect, humble, and equitable; not soft and effeminate,
fickle and vain, but sober, chaste, constant, and persevering, peaceful and
calm, thankful to God, resigned to God's will—for in this fallen life love
is not exempt from pain.

THOMAS À KEMPIS

God regardeth more the degree of love with which we act than what, or
how much, we have performed. He doth much, and well, who constantly
preferreth the good of all to the gratification of his own will.

THOMAS À KEMPIS

Every act of reconciliation is in direct line with the current of things; every
sincere word of forgiveness we ever speak is a word of God; every
generous deed is a service of God's kingdom; every bridge of
understanding, friendship, sympathy, that we throw across some gulf of
race, resentment, prejudice, or pride, is an act of God. That sounds
extravagant only to those who have not grasped the Christian message, that
God is love; that every one that loves is born of God; that he that dwells
in love dwells in God—because God himself is love.

ANONYMOUS

MAGNANIMITY

The Bereans were of more noble character . . . for they received the message with great eagerness and examined the Scriptures every day to see if what Paul said was true.

ACTS 17:11, NIV

God gave Solomon wisdom and very great insight, and a breadth of understanding as measureless as the sand on the seashore.

1 KINGS 4:29, NIV

Faith, Hope, Love—each is intrinsically an enlarging of the soul, an outgoing of the human spirit upwards, forwards, outwards, to a liberated life. By faith the soul rebels against the limitation of its powers; by hope, against the limitation of its horizon; by love, against the limitation of self-absorption. By the faith He implants, the hope He imparts, the love He inspires, Christ opens the prison of belittling, world-bound selfishness to send the soul forth upon endless errands, discoveries, and adventurings. He came that we might have larger life.

X

No sadder proof can be given by a man of his own littleness than disbelief in great men (THOMAS CARLYLE); He wants worth that dares not praise a foe (JOHN DRYDEN); Of all virtues, magnanimity is the rarest (WILLIAM HAZLITT); The pettiness of a mind can be measured by the pettiness of its adoration, or its blasphemy (ANDRÉ GIDE); To the mean eye all things are trivial (THOMAS CARLYLE); Small minds are much distressed by little things (LA ROCHEFOUCAULD); He who knows only his own side of the case, knows little of that (JOHN STUART MILL); Beware of the man of one book (BENJAMIN DISRAELI); A blackbird singing where the boundaries meet sounds the same from either side (UNKNOWN).

The most fatal illusion is the narrow point of view. Since life is growth and motion, a fixed point of view kills anybody who has one.

BROOKS ATKINSON

It is with narrow-souled people as with narrow-necked bottles: the less they have in them, the more noise they make in pouring it out.

ALEXANDER POPE

During war, soldiers sought permission to bury a dead comrade in a churchyard, but the priest sadly refused consent for one unbaptised to occupy "consecrated ground." They laid their comrade just outside the boundary. Returning later, before leaving the area, they could not find the place, until the priest arrived, and with tears explained that he, deeply worried by his refusal, had moved the churchyard fence with his own hands, to enclose the lonely grave in "consecrated ground."

X

Broadmindedness is the result of flattening highmindedness out.

GEORGE E. B. SAINTSBURY

MAN

What is man that you are mindful of him,
the son of man that you care for him?

PSALM 8:4, NIV

Jesus came out, wearing the crown of thorns and the purple cloak. "Behold the Man!" said Pilate.

JOHN 19:5, NEB

Jesus believed in man: therein he differed from the pessimists of his day. The Pharisees regarded the mass of people as moral refuse; with Jesus the common people were the raw material for the kingdom of God, rich in possibilities of sainthood.

JOHN WATSON

[Jesus] was the first to bring the value of every human soul to the light, and what He did no one can any more undo.

ADOLPH HARNACK

How poor, how rich, how abject, how august,
How complicate, how wonderful, is man! . . .
Distinguished link in being's endless chain,
Midway from nothing to Deity! . . .
Though sullied and dishonoured, still divine . . .
An heir of glory, a frail child of dust . . .
O what a miracle to man is man . . .
An angel's arm can't snatch me from the grave:
Legions of angels can't confine me there.

EDWARD YOUNG

Man is a reed, the weakest thing in Nature, but a thinking reed (BLAISE PASCAL); The mind is the man (FRANCIS BACON).

Man—The measure of all things (PROTAGORAS) . . . Heaven's masterpiece (FRANCIS QUARLES) . . . An ingenious assembly of portable plumbing (CHRISTOPHER MORLEY) . . . A little soul carrying around a corpse (EPICTETUS) . . . A fallen god who remembers the heavens (X) . . . A problem that must puzzle the devil (ROBERT BURNS) . . . The glory, jest, and riddle of the world (ALEXANDER POPE) . . . A god in ruins (RALPH WALDO EMERSON) . . . A machine into which we put what we call food to produce what we call thought (ROBERT INGERSOLL) . . . A phenomenon (TEILHARD DE CHARDIN) . . . The playground for innumerable brawling micrococci (NGAIO MARSH) . . . The organic container equipped with organs and capacities, into which society pours ideas, experiences, myths, moralities and propaganda, to be manipulated by educationists, psychiatrists, and social engineers into socially acceptable responses or eliminated (X) . . . That animal called man (JONATHAN SWIFT) . . . A noble animal (THOMAS BROWNE) . . . A political animal (ARISTOTLE) . . . A religious animal (EDMUND BURKE) . . . A gaming animal (CHARLES LAMB) . . . A social animal (BARUCH SPINOZA) . . . A tool-making animal (BENJAMIN FRANKLIN) . . . An animal that bargains (ADAM SMITH) . . . The only animal that blushes—or needs to (Mark Twain) . . . An animal that reasons, laughs, weeps, cooks, and cannot assimilate death (X) . . . A story-telling animal (UMBERTO ECO) . . . A make-believe animal (WILLIAM HAZLITT) . . . The aristocrat among animals (HEINRICH HEINE) . . . The only animal for whom his own existence is a problem (ERICH FROMM) . . . When perfected, the best of animals; when separated from law and justice, the worst of all (ARISTOTLE).

Man, biologically considered . . . is the most formidable of all the beasts of prey, the only one that preys systematically on its own species.

WILLIAM JAMES

Why should anything go right, even [scientific] observation and deduction, [if] they are both movements in the brain of a bewildered ape?

AFTER G. K. CHESTERTON

The sane man knows that he has a touch of the beast, a touch of the devil, a touch of the saint, a touch of the citizen. The really sane man knows that he has a touch of the madman.

G. K. CHESTERTON

What a piece of work is man! How noble in reason! How infinite in faculty! In form, in moving, how express and admirable! In action, how like an angel! In apprehension, how like a god! The beauty of the world, the paragon of animals! And yet, to me, what is this quintessence of dust?

WILLIAM SHAKESPEARE

Know then thyself, presume not God to scan,
The proper study of mankind is man.
Placed in this isthmus of a middle state
A being darkly wise and rudely great:
With too much knowledge for the sceptic side,
With too much weakness for the stoic's pride,
He hangs between; in doubt to act or rest;
In doubt to deem himself a god, or beast;
In doubt his mind or body to prefer;
Born but to die, and reas'ning but to err . . .
Chaos of thought and passion, all confused;
Still by himself abused, or disabused;
Created half to rise, and half to fall,
Great lord of all things, yet a prey to all.

ALEXANDER POPE

The proper study of mankind is Christ.

ANONYMOUS

The greatest enemy to man is man (ROBERT BURTON); Man's inhumanity to man makes countless thousands mourn (ROBERT BURNS); The trouble with man is man (JAMES THURBER).

Man's unhappiness, as I construe, comes of his greatness; it is because there is an infinite in him, which with all his cunning he cannot quite bury under the finite.

THOMAS CARLYLE

> Not only cunning casts in clay:
> Let Science prove we are, and then
> What matters Science unto men,
> At least to me? I would not stay.
>
> Let him, the wiser man who springs
> Hereafter, up from childhood shape
> His action like the greater ape:
> But I was born to other things.

ALFRED TENNYSON

> Love, hope, fear, faith—these make humanity;
> These are its sign, its note, and character.

ROBERT BROWNING

That principle [conscience] by which we . . . approve or disapprove our own heart . . . gives us a further view of the nature of man. Neither can any human creature be said to act conformably to his constitution of nature unless he allows to that supreme principle the absolute authority which is due to it.

JOSEPH BUTLER

[Evangelical social reformers] appeal always and everywhere from the miserable reality to the human conscience. They make one see the man in the criminal, the brother in the Negro . . . They introduced a new personage into the social and political world . . . *the fellow man*, [who] never more will leave the stage.

M. Y. OSTROGORSKI

Beneath the dingy uniformity of international fashions in dress, man remains
what he has always been, a splendid fighting animal, a self-sacrificing hero,
and a blood-thirsty savage.

WILLIAM R. INGE

In the average human brain there are as many separate living cells as there
are stars in the Milky Way—some ten thousand million. That coincidental
correspondence is somehow symbolic of the amazing power of the human
mind to apprehend the fathomless splendours of the universe.

X

In thy lone and long night watches, sky above and sea below,
Thou didst learn a higher wisdom than the babbling
    schoolmen know;
God's stars and silence taught thee, as His angels only can,
That the one sole sacred thing beneath the cope of heaven is Man.

JOHN GREENLEAF WHITTIER

To offer man only what is human is to betray him . . . for by the
principal part of him, which is the mind, man is called to something better
than a purely human life.

JACQUES MARITAIN

[The reputed sceptic] Voltaire must have the credit that he hated injustice,
hated cruelty, hated senseless repression, hated hocus-pocus. But if men
cannot live on bread alone, still less can they do so on disinfectants.

ALFRED NORTH WHITEHEAD

Sigmund Freud spoke of three offences against man's conception of himself.
Copernicus gave the cosmic offence, Darwin the biological offence, and
Freud himself the psychological offence to man's traditional high regard for
the powers of man. It might be added that, in the reduction of man, Karl
Marx provided the cultural offence.

PAUL RAMSEY

Humanity's long climb, from supposed primeval slime to "civilisation" by
means of "illusory ideals," has led only to urbanised man crowded into
city anthills, his moral struggles but "a trouble of ants in the gleam of a
million suns," "a murmur of gnats in the gloom," a rat race without

goals, ideals, standards, depth, or fulfilment, but only a void which he tries desperately to fill with drugs, stimulants, artificial excitements, and subhuman animality. Thus man strives to stifle the nagging suspicion that he and the world he inhabits are alike meaningless, irrational, inimical to his welfare, and doomed to nuclear self-destruction.

X

Man's only relief in this century from the many-sided process of self-denigration was the "long step for mankind" taken on the surface of the moon—a long and costly step which in fact led nowhere.

ANONYMOUS

God give us men: a time like this demands
Strong minds, great hearts, true faith, and ready hands!
Men whom the lust of office does not kill;
Men whom the spoils of office cannot buy;
Men who possess opinions, and a will;
Men who love honour, men who cannot lie.

JOSIAH G. HOLLAND

There are but two kinds of men: the righteous who believe they are sinners, and the sinners who believe themselves righteous.

BLAISE PASCAL

'Twas much, that man was made like God before;
But, that God should be made like man, much more.

JOHN DONNE

MARRIAGE

Marriage is honourable; let us all keep it so.

HEBREWS 13:4, NEB

The first bond of society is marriage (SENECA); On what pretence can man have interdicted marriage, which is a law of nature? It is as though we were forbidden to eat, to drink, to sleep (MARTIN LUTHER).

Except Thou build it, Father,
The house is built in vain;

> Except Thou, Saviour, bless it,
>   The joy will turn to pain:
> But nought can break the union
>   Of hearts in Thee made one;
> And love Thy Spirit hallows
>   Is endless love begun.

JOHN ELLERTON

It is not marriage that fails; it is people that fail. All that marriage does is to show people up.

HARRY EMERSON FOSDICK

> O love divine and tender,
>   That through our homes dost move,
> Veiled in the softened splendour
>   Of holy household love:
> A throne without Thy blessing
>   Were labour without rest;
> And cottages possessing
>   Thy blessedness are blest.

JOHN S. B. MONSELL

A man's friend likes him but leaves him as he is; his wife loves him and is always trying to turn him into somebody else.

G. K. CHESTERTON

MARTYRDOM

Men who have risked their lives for the sake of our Lord Jesus Christ.

ACTS 15:26

As they were stoning Stephen, he prayed, "Lord Jesus, receive my spirit" . . . "Lord, do not hold this sin against them." And when he had said this, he fell asleep.

ACTS 7:59–60 OF STEPHEN, PROTOMARTYR

Though I am alive while I write to you, yet I am eager to die for the sake of Christ . . . Stand firm, as does an anvil which is beaten. It is the part of a noble athlete to be wounded, yet to conquer . . . Let none of you be found as a deserter. May I have joy of you forever.

IGNATIUS, MARTYRED C. 110

[Called upon to curse Christ]: Eighty and six years have I served Him, and He hath done me no wrong; how then can I blaspheme my King who saved me? [And at the stake, in the sports arena at Smyrna]: Make me a true athlete of Jesus Christ, to suffer and to conquer; an anvil, Lord, let me be an anvil, smitten but standing firm.

POLYCARP, MARTYRED C. 155

No right-thinking person falls away from piety to impiety.

JUSTIN MARTYR, MARTYRED 167

A purpose so well-founded, and a will which hath once devoted itself to God, can never be altered . . . You have your orders, obey them; the case admits of no consideration.

CYPRIAN, MARTYRED 258

[Mocking his torturers]: Turn me over now, I am well roasted on one side.

LAWRENCE, MARTYRED 258

I will not give the king the things that are God's. You threaten me in vain. Were all the swords in England drawn against me, you could not scare me from my obedience to God. I am no traitor, but a priest of God.

THOMAS À BECKET, MARTYRED 1170

My answer is, that forasmuch as mine own conscience cannot be satisfied, I do absolutely refuse the Oath [declaring royal supremacy]. At the execution ground he read: This is life eternal, that they may know Thee, the only true God, and Jesus Christ whom Thou hast sent, [adding] Here is learning enough for me to my life's end . . . In Thee, O Lord, have I put my trust.

JOHN FISHER, MARTYRED 1535

Play the man, Master Ridley; we shall this day light such a candle by God's grace in England as I trust shall never be put out.

HUGH LATIMER, MARTYRED 1555

We are in good health, thanks be to God; and yet the manner of using us doth change as sour ale in summer . . . With all our evil reports, grudges, and restraints, we are merry . . . As you know, we are no fewer than three, and I dare say every one well contented with his portion. Thus fare you well. We shall, by God's grace, one day meet together, and be merry. [At the stake]: So long as the breath is in my body, I will never deny my Lord Christ and His known truth. God's will be done in me.

NICHOLAS RIDLEY, MARTYRED 1555

Now I come to the great thing that troubleth my conscience more than any thing I ever said or did in my life . . . things written by my hand contrary to the truth which I thought in my heart, and written for fear of death . . . And forasmuch as my hand offended in writing contrary to my heart, my hand therefore shall be the first punished; for if I come to the fire, it shall be the first burned.

THOMAS CRANMER, MARTYRED 1556, FIRST HOLDING HIS HAND WITHIN THE FLAMES

I felt that I was being dragged away to be murdered; but I sang "Safe in the arms of Jesus," and laughed at the very agony of my situation . . . I am quite broken down and brought low, but comforted by Psalm 27— "Though a host should encamp against me, my heart shall not fear" . . . I was upheld by the 30th Psalm, which came with great power.

JAMES HANNINGTON, BISHOP, CENTRAL AFRICA, MURDERED 1885

Shall we Christians forget that our faith comes from God? I refuse to waver in my faith, still more to jeopardise the beliefs of other Christians and weaken the faith of other believers. It is my duty to speak my mind. I pray God that He may take pity on my weakness and grant me supernatural courage to remain steadfast unto death. At some future date I may lose control of myself; let me insure myself in advance against failure, by taking advantage of this moment, when I am completely lucid, to repudiate solemnly anything I or they may say under these circumstances.

JOHN TUNG, AT A DEMONSTRATION IN CHUNGKING, WEEKS BEFORE MARTYRDOM, C. 1946

MERCY

Blessed are the merciful, for they shall obtain mercy.

JESUS: MATTHEW 5:7

We do pray for mercy;
And that same prayer doth teach us all to render
The deeds of mercy.

WILLIAM SHAKESPEARE

Mercy the wise Athenians held to be
Not an affection, but a deity.

ROBERT HERRICK

Now there suddenly broke in on him like a sunrise a sense of God's
mercy—deeper than the fore-ordination of things, like a great mercifulness
. . . Out of the cruel North most of the birds had flown south from
ancient instinct, and would return to keep the wheel of life moving.
Merciful! But some remained, snatching safety by cunning ways from the
winter of death. Merciful! Under the fetters of ice and snow there were the
little animals lying snug in holes, and fish under the frozen streams, and
bears asleep in their lie-ups, and moose stamping out their yards, and
caribou rooting for their grey moss. Merciful! And human beings, men,
women and children, fending off winter and sustaining life by an instinct
old as that of the migrating birds. Lew nursing like a child one whom he
had known less than a week . . . Johnny tormented by anxiety for his
brother, but uncomplainingly sticking to the main road of his duty . . .
Surely, surely, behind the reign of law and the coercion of power, there
was a deep purpose of mercy.

JOHN BUCHAN

Cowards are cruel, but the brave love mercy, and delight to save.

JOHN GAY

Teach me to feel another's woe.
To hide the fault I see;
That mercy I to others show,
That mercy show to me.

ALEXANDER POPE

My friend, judge not me . . .
Betwixt the stirrup and the ground
Mercy I asked, mercy I found.

EPITAPH BY WILLIAM CAMDEN

Why, all the souls that were, were forfeit once;
And He that might the vantage best have took
Found out the remedy. How would you be
If He, which is the top of judgement, should
But judge you as you are? O! think on that,
And mercy then will breathe within your lips
Like man new made.

WILLIAM SHAKESPEARE

MIDDLE AGE

All the people were praising God for what had happened. For the man
who was miraculously healed was over forty years old.

ACTS 4:21–22, NIV

The middle-aged, who have lived through their strongest emotions, but are
yet in the time when memory is still half passionate, should be a sort of
natural priesthood, whom life has disciplined and consecrated to be the
refuge and the rescue of early stumblers and victims of despair.

GEORGE ELIOT

I saw then in my dream that they . . . came into a certain country,
whose air naturally tended to make one drowsy . . . Here *Hopeful* began
to be very dull and heavy of sleep; wherefore he said, " . . . I can
scarcely hold up mine eyes; let us lie down here, and take one nap."
"By no means," said *Christian*, "lest, sleeping, we never awake more . . .
Do you not remember that one of the shepherds bid us beware of the
Enchanted Ground? Let us not sleep . . . but . . . watch, and be sober."

When saints do sleepy grow, let them come hither . . .
Saints' fellowship, if it be managed well,
Keeps them awake, and that in spite of hell.

JOHN BUNYAN

Virtuous and wise he was, but not severe;
He still remembered that he once was young.

JOHN ARMSTRONG

O Lord, revive thy work in the midst of the years.

HABAKKUK 3:2, AV/KJV

MIRACLES

He did not do many mighty works there, because of their unbelief.

MATTHEW 13:58

When our fathers were being led captive to Persia, the pious priests . . .
took some of the fire of the altar and secretly hid it . . . After many years
. . . Nehemiah . . . sent the descendants of the priests . . . they reported to
us that they had not found fire but thick liquid . . . Nehemiah ordered the
priests to sprinkle the liquid on the wood . . . When . . . the sun . . .
shone out, a great fire blazed up, so that all marveled . . . The king
investigated the matter, and enclosed the place and made it sacred.

2 MACCABEES 1:19–22, 34

A mouse is miracle enough to stagger sextillions of infidels (WALT WHITMAN);
Every believer is God's miracle (P. J. BAILEY); I should not be a Christian
but for the miracles (AUGUSTINE); The age of miracles now is (THOMAS
CARLYLE); Things mysterious are not necessarily miracles (GOETHE); Religion
seems to have grown an infant with age, and requires miracles to nurse it,
as it had in its infancy (JONATHAN SWIFT); It is impossible for a miracle to
be impossible (J. DICKSON CARR); The science of tomorrow is the
supernatural of today (AGATHA CHRISTIE).

Science has had its revenge on scepticism. A man in Voltaire's time did
not know what miracle he would next have to throw up. A man in our
time does not know what miracle he will next have to swallow (G. K.
CHESTERTON); If you could reason by pure logic for the occurrence of
miracles, they would not be miracles, would they? (ELLIS PETERS).

For martyrdoms, I reckon them amongst miracles, because they seem to
exceed the strength of human nature; and I may do the like of superlative
and admirable holiness of life.

FRANCIS BACON

We must not sit down and look for miracles; up, and be doing, and the Lord will be with thee.

JOHN ELIOT (SEE JUDGES 6:13–16)

MISSIONS

Truly I perceive that God shows no partiality, but in every nation any one who fears him and does what is right is acceptable to him.

ACTS 10:34–35

When the kingdom comes in its greatness it will fulfil every religion and destroy none.

JOHN WATSON

> Thine is the mystic life great India craves,
> Thine is the Parsee's sin-destroying beam,
> Thine is the Buddhist's rest from tossing waves,
> Thine is empire of vast China's dream . . .
>
> Thine is the Roman's strength without his pride,
> Thine is the Greek's glad world without its graves,
> Thine is Judea's law, with love beside,
> The truth that censures and the grace that saves . . .
>
> Some seek a Father in the heavens above;
> Some ask a human image to adore;
> Some crave a Spirit vast as life and love:
> Within Thy mansions we have all, and more—
>   Gather us in.

GEORGE MATHESON

Extension or extinction is the Master's ultimatum.

UNKNOWN

While piety imagined God as the Father of a few and the Judge of the rest, humanity was belittled, slavery defended, missions counted an impertinence. When He is recognised as the universal Father, and the outcasts of humanity as His prodigal children, every effort of love will be stimulated, and the kingdom of God will advance by leaps and bounds.

JOHN WATSON

The nerve of missionary endeavour is the conviction that in the Christian revelation there is something distinctive and vital, which the world cannot do without.

J. H. OLDHAM

The Christianising of men, of all men, in all their relations, is not so much a matter of interest to the church, as a matter of life or death for the world.

J. E. MCFADYEN

In every age, the spread of Christianity has been the work, not of the generality of Christians, but of the more devoted few.

JOHN FOSTER, CHURCH HISTORIAN

Go to the people. Live with them. Learn from them. Love them. Start with what they know, build with what they have.

LAO TSE

MORALITY

The LORD is righteous, he loves righteous deeds;
the upright shall behold his face.

PSALM 11:7

Morality did not begin by one man saying to another, "I will not hit you if you do not hit me"; there is no trace of such a transaction. There *is* a trace of both men having said, "We must not hit each other in the holy place." They gained their morality by guarding their religion.

G. K. CHESTERTON

Morality without religion is only a kind of dead reckoning, an endeavour to find our place on a cloudy sea (HENRY WADSWORTH LONGFELLOW);
Religion without morality is mere ceremony substituting for conscience, ritual for righteousness, sacrament for saintliness (X).

The true meaning of religion is . . . morality touched by emotion (MATTHEW ARNOLD) . . . morality in eternal perspective and furnished with incentives (X).

If your morals make you dreary, depend upon it they are wrong.

ROBERT LOUIS STEVENSON

Moral principles are the deposit of the race's long experience that well-being and well-doing are inseparable. Humanity has discovered, slowly, painfully, at great cost, that welfare and behavior are inextricably linked; has perceived that this is the innate structure of human experience; and has deduced that since God so arranged things, the moral "laws" are ultimately divine. Any individual, any generation may deny this analysis, defy the inherited moral insights: but only to rediscover the moral constitution of things again, by the slow, painful, costly way that man has already trodden.

ANONYMOUS

MUSIC

David also commanded . . . to appoint . . . the singers who should play loudly on musical instruments, on harps and lyres and cymbals, to raise sounds of joy.

1 CHRONICLES 15:16

Music strikes in me a deep fit of devotion, and a profound contemplation of the First Composer.

THOMAS BROWNE

But God has a few of us whom he whispers in the ear;
The rest may reason and welcome: 'tis we musicians know.

ROBERT BROWNING

Music is well said to be the speech of angels (THOMAS CARLYLE); Among all the arts, music alone can be purely religious (MADAME ANNE-LOUISE-GERMAINE DE STAËL).

The man that hath no music in himself,
Nor is not moved with concord of sweet sounds,
Is fit for treasons, stratagems, and spoils;
The motions of his spirit are dull as night,
And his affections dark as Erebus.
Let no such man be trusted.

WILLIAM SHAKESPEARE

All composers speak to me, and I listen. Bach speaks to God, and I overhear.

UNKNOWN

Whether the angels play only Bach in praising God, I am not quite sure; I am sure however that *en famille* they play Mozart.

KARL BARTH, FROM HIS OBITUARY

God is its author, and not man; He laid
The key-note of all harmonies; He planned
All perfect combinations, and He made
Us so that we could hear and understand.

J. G. BRAINARD

The harp at Nature's advent strung
Has never ceased to play;
The song the stars of morning sung
Has never died away.

JOHN GREENLEAF WHITTIER

Where dwells the beauty? In the horsehair and the catgut? In the breath of the woodwind or the percussion of the drum? In the vibration of the air, or the mind of the composer, the appreciation of the audience? Or in all together kindling distant memories of heaven?

X

There is sweet music here that softer falls
Than petals from blown roses on the grass . . .
Music that gentlier on the spirit lies
Than tired eyelids upon tired eyes;
Music that brings sweet sleep down from the blissful skies.

ALFRED TENNYSON

We are the music-makers,
    We are the dreamers of dreams,
Wandering by lone sea breakers,
And sitting by desolate streams;
World-losers and world-forsakers,
On whom the pale moon gleams:
Yet we are the movers and shakers
Of the world for ever, it seems.

ARTHUR S. O'SHAUGHNESSY

NATURE

God saw all that he had made, and it was very good.

GENESIS 1:31, NIV

O world as God has made it! All is beauty.

ROBERT BROWNING

To St. Francis, Nature is a sister, and even a younger sister: a little, dancing sister, to be laughed at as well as loved.

G. K. CHESTERTON

Nature as a whole is a progressive realisation of purpose, strictly comparable to the realisation of purpose in any single plant or animal.

JOHN DEWEY

> To him who in the love of Nature holds
> Communion with her visible forms, she speaks
> A various language; for his gayer hours
> She has a voice of gladness, and a smile
> And eloquence of beauty, and she glides
> Into his darker musings, with a mild
> And healing sympathy, that steals away
> Their sharpness, ere he is aware.

WILLIAM CULLEN BRYANT

The most beautiful, the most profound emotion is the sensation of the mystical . . . He to whom this emotion is a stranger, who can no longer wonder, and stand rapt in awe, is as good as dead.

ALBERT EINSTEIN

The study of Nature is intercourse with the Highest Mind (JEAN LOUIS AGASSIZ); Laws of nature are God's thoughts thinking themselves out in the orbits and the tides (C. H. PARKHURST); Nature is "religious" only as it manifests God (X); Nature is the living, visible garment of God (GOETHE); . . . the glass reflecting God (EDWARD YOUNG).

After the great volumes of God and the scriptures, study, in the second place, that great volume of the works and the creatures of God.

FRANCIS BACON

And this our life, exempt from public haunt,
Finds tongues in trees, books in the running brooks,
Sermons in stones, and good in everything.

WILLIAM SHAKESPEARE

The perfections of Nature show that she is the image of God; her defects show that she is only his image.

BLAISE PASCAL

All are but parts of one stupendous Whole,
Whose body Nature is, and God the soul;
That changed through all, and yet in all the same,
Great in the earth as in the ethereal frame,
Warms in the sun, refreshes in the breeze,
Glows in the stars, and blossoms in the trees; . . .
As full, as perfect, in a hair as heart;
As full, as perfect, in vile man that mourns
As the rapt Seraph that adores and burns.
To Him no high, no low, no great, no small;
He fills, he bounds, connects, and equals all!

ALEXANDER POPE

Those honour Nature well who teach that she can speak on everything, even on Theology.

BLAISE PASCAL

I have learned
To look on Nature, not as in the hour

Of thoughtless youth, but hearing oftentimes
The still, sad music of humanity.

WILLIAM WORDSWORTH

Nature, with folded hands, seemed there
Kneeling at her evening prayer.

HENRY WADSWORTH LONGFELLOW

This world, after all our science and sciences, is still a miracle, wonderful,
inscrutable, magical, and more, to whosoever will think of it.

THOMAS CARLYLE

For the comforting warmth of the sun that my body embraces,
For the cool of the waters that run through the shadowy places;
For the balm of the breezes that brush my face with their fingers
For the vesper-hymn of the thrush when the twilight lingers;
For the long breath, the deep breath, the breath of a heart
     without care,
I will give thanks, and adore Thee, God of the open air!

HENRY VAN DYKE

Talk not of temples, there is one
     Built without hands, to mankind given;
Its lamps are the meridian sun
     And all the stars of heaven;
Its walls are the cerulean sky,
     Its floor the earth so green and fair,
The dome its vast immensity:
     All Nature worships there.

DAVID VEDDER

Forth in the pleasing Spring
Thy beauty walks, Thy tenderness and love . . .
Then comes Thy glory in the summer-months,
With light and heat refulgent. Then Thy sun
Shoots full perfection through the swelling year: . . .
Thy bounty shines in Autumn unconfined,
And spreads a common feast for all that lives.
In Winter, awful Thou! with clouds and storms
Around Thee thrown, tempest o'er tempest rolled,

Majestic darkness! . . .
    Mysterious round! what skill, what force divine,
Deep felt in these appear.

JAMES THOMSON

I don't believe you can really find the *heart* of God in Nature unless you have first found Him somewhere else.

RITA SNOWDEN

Nature, to be commanded, must be obeyed (FRANCIS BACON); Nature is hitting back; not with the old weapons—floods, plagues, holocausts. We can neutralise them. She's fighting back with strange instruments called neuroses. She's deliberately inflicting mankind with the jitters (ROBERT E. SHERWOOD); Respected, Nature is a splendid servant; abused, she becomes a relentless enemy (X).

The spiritual landscape in which the godly live: God's love the sky, overarching all; God's faithfulness the scudding clouds; God's righteousness the massive mountain backdrop; His judgements the unfathomable sea; embracing all, the shade of His unceasing care; enriching all, the bounty of His gifts, the river of divine delight, the springing fountain of life; irradiating all, the clear daylight of divine illumination.

PSALM 36:5–9, PARAPHRASE

NEIGHBOUR

Love thy neighbour as thyself.

LEVITICUS 19:18, MATTHEW 19:19, AV/KJV

Love thy neighbour (THALES); Love your neighbour, yet pull not down your hedge (GEORGE HERBERT); Good fences make good neighbours (ROBERT FROST); Every man's neighbour is his looking-glass (ENGLISH PROVERB); Withdraw thy foot from thy neighbour's house; lest he be weary of thee, and *so* hate thee (PROVERBS 25:17, AV/KJV).

There is an idea abroad among moral people that they should make their neighbours good. One person I have to make good—myself. My duty to my neighbour is much more nearly expressed by saying that I have to make him happy, if I may.

ROBERT LOUIS STEVENSON

To God be humble, to thy friend be kind,
And with thy neighbour, gladly lend and borrow;
His chance tonight, it may be thine tomorrow.

WILLIAM DUNBAR

"Lord, who is my neighbour?"
   "The Samaritan."
"Sound the pipe and tabor! Welcome such a man!"
"Lord, who is my neighbour?"
   "He the thieves beset."
"Though he cause me labour, I will love him yet."
"Lord, who is my neighbour?"
   "The Levite and the Priest."
"Even those I may bear, though I'll love them least."
"Lord, who is my neighbour?"
   "Dear one, I am he."
"Lord, ah no! I pray, bare not thy face to me."

UNKNOWN, LUKE 10:29

NEW YEAR

"This month shall be . . . the first month of the year for you . . . a memorial day . . . a feast to the LORD . . . for on this very day I brought your hosts out of the land of Egypt.

EXODUS 12:2, 14, 17

At the door . . . where I will meet with you, to speak there to you.

EXODUS 29:42

Drop the last year into the silent limbo of the past. Let it go, for it was imperfect, and thank God that it can go.

BROOKS ATKINSON

Ring out, wild bells, to the wild sky,
   The flying cloud, the frost light;
   The year is dying in the night,
Ring out, wild bells, and let him die.

Ring out the old, ring in the new,
 Ring happy bells across the snow:
 The year is going, let him go;
Ring out the false, ring in the true . . .

Ring out old shapes of foul disease;
 Ring out the narrowing lust of gold;
 Ring out the thousand wars of old,
Ring in the thousand years of peace.

Ring in the valiant men and free,
 The larger heart, the kindlier hand;
 Ring out the darkness of the land;
Ring in the Christ that is to be.

ALFRED TENNYSON

In the beginning God . . . In the beginning was the Word.

GENESIS 1:1; JOHN 1:1

Father, let me dedicate
All this year to Thee,
In whatever worldly state
Thou wouldst have me be;
Not from sorrow, pain, or care,
Freedom dare I claim;
This alone shall be my prayer:
"Glorify Thy name."

LAWRENCE TUTTIETT

OATH

Do not swear at all, either by heaven, for it is the throne of God, or by the earth, for it is his footstool.

JESUS: MATTHEW 5:34–35

Jesus stands by the stall, watching some small sale . . . The buyer swears "on his head" that he will not give more than so much; then "by the altar," he won't get the thing. "By the earth" it isn't worth it; "by the heaven" the seller gave that for it. So the battle rages, and at last the bargain is struck . . . Neither believes the other . . . And by Heaven, and by Him who sits on the Throne, men swear falsely for an anna or two . . . In later days Jesus told his followers to swear not at all—to stick to Yes and No.

T. R. GLOVER

Oaths are the fossils of piety (GEORGE SANTAYANA); You may depend upon it, the more oath-taking the more lying, generally, among people (SAMUEL TAYLOR COLERIDGE).

I'll take thy word for faith, not ask thine oath;
Who shuns not to break one will sure crack both.

WILLIAM SHAKESPEARE

Oaths terminate, as Paul observes, all strife;
Some men have surely then a peaceful life!

WILLIAM COWPER

When a man takes an oath . . . he's holding his own self in his own hands. Like water. And if he opens his fingers *then*—he needn't hope to find himself again.

ROBERT BOLT

OBEDIENCE

To obey is better than sacrifice.

SAMUEL: 1 SAMUEL 15:22

In vain do we break the alabaster box if we do not obey.

ROBERT LAW

I cast one look at the fields,
    Then set my face to the town;
He said, "My child, do you yield?
    Will you leave the flowers for the crown?"

Then into his hand went mine,
    And into my heart came he;
And I walk in a light divine
    The path I had feared to see.

GEORGE MACDONALD

The attitude which "Thy will be done" expresses is not one of resignation, but that of soaring aspiration, of joyful dedication to a high adventure.

UNKNOWN

We must do the thing we must
    Before the thing we may;
We are not fit for any trust
    Till we can and do obey.

GEORGE MACDONALD

I argue not
Against Heaven's hand or will, nor bate a jot
Of heart or hope; but still bear up and steer
Right onward.

JOHN MILTON

The man who does something under orders is not unhappy; he is unhappy who does something against his will (SENECA); Obedience alone gives the right to command (RALPH WALDO EMERSON); Dispose of me according to the wisdom of Thy pleasure; Thy will be done, though in my own undoing (THOMAS BROWNE).

I'll go where you want me to go, dear Lord,
    O'er mountain or plain or sea;
I'll say what you want me to say, dear Lord,
    I'll be what you want me to be.

MARY BROWN

Cheered by the presence of God, I will do, at the moment and without anxiety, according to the strength which he shall give me, the work that his providence assigns to me. The rest I will leave: it is not my affair.

FRANÇOIS FÉNELON

Choose for us, God, nor let our weak preferring
    Cheat our poor souls of good Thou hast designed;
Choose for us, God, Thy wisdom is unerring,
    And we are fools, and blind.

W. H. BURLEIGH

Choose Thou for me my friends,
    My sickness or my health;
Choose Thou my cares for me,
    My poverty or wealth.
Not mine, not mine the choice
    In things or great or small;
By Thou my guide, my strength,
    My wisdom, and my all.

HORATIUS BONAR

With parted lips and outstretched hands
And listening ears, Thy servant stands:
Call Thou early, call Thou late,
To Thy great service dedicate.

CHARLES H. SORLEY

Why do you call me "Lord, Lord," and not do what I tell you?

JESUS: LUKE 6:46

OPPORTUNITY

Be very careful, then, how you live . . . making the most of every opportunity, because the days are evil.

PAUL: EPHESIANS 5:15–16, NIV

Each morning is a fresh beginning, and God watches, full of His everlasting hope that we'll take Christian advantage of it.

VICTOR CANNING

A wise man will make more opportunities than he finds (FRANCIS BACON); No great man ever complains of want of opportunity (RALPH WALDO EMERSON); Opportunities are seldom labelled (J. A. SHEDD); He who will not when he may may not when he will (ENGLISH PROVERB).

Man's extremity is God's opportunity.

JOHN FLAVEL

Four things come not back: the spoken word, the spent arrow, time past, the neglected opportunity.

IBN AL-KHATTAB OMAR

There is a tide in the affairs of men
Which, taken at the flood, leads on to fortune;
Omitted, all the voyage of their life
Is bound in shallows and in miseries.

WILLIAM SHAKESPEARE

PAIN

Although [Jesus] was a Son, he learned obedience through what he suffered.

HEBREWS 5:8

To keep me from being too elated ... a thorn was given me in the flesh, a messenger of Satan, to harass me.

PAUL: 2 CORINTHIANS 12:7

How bitter that cup
No heart can conceive,
Which He drank quite up
That sinners might live:
His way was much rougher
And darker than mine;
Did Jesus thus suffer,
And can I repine?

JOHN NEWTON

Although today He prunes my twigs with pain,
    Yet doth His blood nourish and warm my root:
Tomorrow I shall put forth buds again,
    And clothe myself with fruit.

CHRISTINA ROSSETTI, ON JOHN 15:2

I thank Thee, Lord, that all our joy
    Is touched with pain;
That shadows fall on brightest hours,
    That thorns remain:
So that earth's bliss may be our guide,
    And not our chain.

ADELAIDE A. PROCTER

It changed the soul of one to sour
And passionate regret;
To one it gave unselfish power
To love, and to forget.

SELDEN L. WHITCOMB

PARENTHOOD

In the same way, you husbands must conduct your married life with
understanding: pay honour to the woman's body, not only because it is
weaker, but also because you share together in the divine grace of
engendering new life. Given this mutual respect and consideration, your
prayers will not be hindered.

PETER: 1 PETER 3:7, NEB, further paraphrased

God could not be everywhere, so He made mothers (JEWISH PROVERB);
Judicious mothers will always keep in mind that they are the first book
read, and the last put aside, in every child's library (C. LENOX REMOND).

What the mother sings to the cradle goes all the way down to the coffin
. . . We never know the love of our parents until we have become
parents . . . The mother's heart is the child's schoolroom.

HENRY WARD BEECHER

Schoolmasters and parents exist to be grown out of.

JOHN WOLFENDEN

I kneel before the Father, from whom all fatherhood in heaven and on
earth derives its name.

PAUL: EPHESIANS 3:14–15, NIV margin

PAST

"You who pursue deliverance . . .
look to the rock from which you were hewn,
and to the quarry from which you were digged."

ISAIAH: ISAIAH 51:1

What is past is past: there is a future left to all men who have the virtue to repent, the energy to atone.

EDWARD G. E. BULWER-LYTTON

The past is prologue (WILLIAM SHAKESPEARE) . . . a bucket of ashes (CARL SANDBURG) . . . the faultful past (ALFRED TENNYSON).

Even God cannot change the past (AGATHON FIFTH CENTURY B.C.); This only is denied, even to God: the power to undo the past (ARISTOTLE); Not heaven itself upon the past has power (JOHN DRYDEN); I will restore to you the years which the swarming locust has eaten (JOEL 2:25).

> Nor deem the irrevocable past
>   As wholly wasted, wholly vain,
> If, rising on its wrecks at last,
>   To something nobler we attain.

HENRY WADSWORTH LONGFELLOW

Those who cannot remember the past are condemned to repeat it.

GEORGE SANTAYANA

Do not ask why the old days were better than these; for that is a foolish question.

ECCLESIASTES 7:10, NEB

PATIENCE

May you be strengthened with all power . . . for all endurance and patience.

PAUL: COLOSSIANS 1:11

Patience . . . alike to the pagan and the Christian world, to the Oriental and the Occidental mind, is the greatest virtue of man.

GEORGE E. WOODBERRY

Dare to look up to God and say, "Use me henceforward as Thou wilt; I am of one mind with Thee; I am Thine; I ask exemption from nothing that pleases Thee; lead me where Thou wilt; clothe me in any dress Thou choosest."

EPICTETUS

You must be patient with your own impatience.

FRANÇOIS FÉNELON

Patience is love waiting for its opportunity (UNKNOWN); "It's dogged as does it" (ANTHONY TROLLOPE); Patience is the art of hoping (VAUVENARGUES); Patience and diligence, like faith, remove mountains (WILLIAM PENN); Patience . . . the principal part of faith (GEORGE MACDONALD); I can plod, I know the meaning of patience (WILLIAM CAREY, WAITING SEVEN YEARS FOR A CONVERT); Our patience will achieve more than our force (EDMUND BURKE); Sorrow and silence are strong, and patient endurance is Godlike (HENRY WADSWORTH LONGFELLOW); At least bear patiently, if thou canst not joyfully (THOMAS À KEMPIS); I worked with patience, which means almost power (ELIZABETH BARRETT BROWNING); Armed with stubborn patience as with triple steel (JOHN MILTON); Patience is sorrow's salve (CHARLES CHURCHILL); The patient overcome (WILLIAM LANGLAND); Whosoever is out of patience is out of possession of his soul (FRANCIS BACON); A wise man does not try to hurry history (ADLAI STEVENSON).

Come what, come may
Time and the hour run through the roughest day.

WILLIAM SHAKESPEARE, ELIZABETH FRY

Faith will outlast the bitter hour,
Hope will outshine the darkest fear,
Love will outmatch the strongest power
That threatens all the soul holds dear:
For faith will conquer, hope abide,
And love will reign the Throne beside,
When sin, and fear, and death, have died.

ANONYMOUS

The road from Ur to Canaan, from aspiration to achievement, from promise to fulfilment, is paved with persistence, trodden with patience—or we never arrive.

X, GENESIS 11:31, 12:5, AV/KJV

That's best
Which God sends. 'Twas His will: it is mine.

OWEN MEREDITH

Doth God exact day-labour, light denied,
I fondly ask; but patience, to prevent
That murmur, soon replies, God doth not need
Either man's work or His own gifts; who best
Bear His mild yoke, they serve Him best . . .
They also serve, who only stand and wait.

JOHN MILTON, ON HIS BLINDNESS

How poor are they that have not patience!
What wound did ever heal but by degrees?

WILLIAM SHAKESPEARE

I murmured because I had no shoes, until I met a man who had no feet.

PERSIAN PROVERB

An' I thowt 'twur the will o' the Lord, but Miss Annie, she said it wur draains.

ALFRED TENNYSON

Impatience is not the best counsellor, nor haste the best advocate (ELLIS PETERS); There are times when patience proves at fault (ROBERT BROWNING).

PATRIOTISM

If I forget you, O Jerusalem,
  let my right hand wither!
Let my tongue cleave to the roof of my mouth,
  if I do not remember you,
if I do not set Jerusalem
  above my highest joy!

PSALM 137:5-6

God gave all men all earth to love;
  But since our hearts are small,
Ordained for each one spot should prove
  Belovèd over all.

RUDYARD KIPLING

Men did not love Rome because she was great: she was great because they had loved her.

G. K. CHESTERTON

To make us love our country, our country ought to be lovely (EDMUND BURKE); Indeed, I tremble for my country when I reflect that God is just (THOMAS JEFFERSON); Patriotism—a lively sense of collective responsibility (RICHARD ALDINGTON).

Patriotism has become a mere national self-assertion, a sentimentality of flag-cheering with no constructive duties.

H. G. WELLS

The best of patriots is he who tills the soil.

CADOC OF WALES, SIXTH CENTURY

PAUL

Our beloved brother Paul.

2 PETER 3:15

A man little of stature, thin-haired upon the head, crooked in the legs, of good state of body, with eyebrows joining and a nose somewhat crooked; full of grace, for sometimes he appeared like a man, and sometimes had the face of an angel.

PAUL AND THECLA, MID-SECOND CENTURY

Because of what he grasped and taught, the church passed the frontiers of Palestine and left Judaism behind. Because of what he did, the church survived the collapse of Rome and lived on through the dark ages. Because of what he experienced and movingly told and courageously argued out, the revelation that had come in Christ was translated, expounded, and established as a world faith.

X

The epistles of Paul show us the elder brother of the parable, broken down by the father's love, now leaving home and its secure delights to go out into far countries—Cyprus, Pisidia, Macedonia, Greece, Rome—to seek out those brothers who still lingered among the husks and the swine.

AFTER C. H. DODD

Among the greatest of Christians, staunchest of friends, most intrepid of adventurers, most dauntless of sufferers, profoundest of teachers, apostle extraordinary, pastor of all churches in all generations, most winsome of saints, Paul of Tarsus, strict Jew and freeman of Rome, evangelist of the world, soldier and slave and lover of Jesus Christ his Lord.

X

While many figures of the past are unintelligible and incomprehensible he is as human as if he had walked in upon us out of the street (UNKNOWN); One of the most influential teachers of mankind (JAMES STALKER); An exceptional man, the maker of an epoch (T. R. GLOVER); By far the greatest figure of his time (G. B. CAIRD); At no time has the Christian church contained a more original or creative mind (JAMES S. STEWART); Paul thunders, and lightens, and speaks sheer flame (ERASMUS).

Here, if anywhere, the style is the man . . . We have to realise that Paul is one of the great writers of Greece, and of the world . . . He has a great range of living allusion and metaphor. The flaming individuality of his mind is through all his style, in the tangents . . . the hyperbole . . . his superlatives . . . a series of explosions . . . the amazing vocabulary, the striking metaphors, the compressed wordpictures, the popular phrase, the Septuagint echoes, terms of his own coining.

T. R. GLOVER, CLASSICAL SCHOLAR

In Paul the language of the heart is born again. Since the hymn of Cleanthes, nothing so intimate, nothing so splendid, had been written as Paul's hymn to love. Those two hymns of love to God and love to men [Romans 8:31—39 and 1 Corinthians 13] have given again to the Greek language what had been lost for centuries, the intimacy and the enthusiasm of the mystic.

EDUARD NORDEN; CLEANTHES,
300—220 B.C.

Christ, I am Christ's! and let the name suffice you.
Ay, for me, too, He greatly hath sufficed.
Lo, with no winning words would I entice you:
Paul has no honour, and no friend, but Christ!

F. W. H. MYERS

PEACE

"Blessed are the peacemakers"; The peace of God, which passes all understanding, will keep your hearts and your minds in Christ Jesus . . . And the God of peace will be with you.

JESUS: MATTHEW 5:9;
PAUL: PHILIPPIANS 4:7, 9

Outward

The peace of which Jesus speaks is not a negative thing. It is an achievement of creative minds, the triumph of the human spirit over discord, confusion, and strife.

UNKNOWN

Since wars begin in the minds of men, it is in the minds of men that the defences of peace must be constructed.

UNESCO CONSTITUTION

Earth shall be fair, and all her people one:
Not till that hour shall God's whole will be done.

CLIFFORD BAX

Where there is peace, God is (GEORGE HERBERT); Peace is liberty in tranquillity (CICERO); Peace hath her victories, no less renowned than war (JOHN MILTON); No one can have peace longer than his neighbour pleases (DUTCH PROVERB); If we will have peace without a worm in it, lay we the foundations of justice and righteousness (OLIVER CROMWELL); Arms alone are not enough to keep the peace: it must be kept by men (JOHN F. KENNEDY); Peace cannot be kept by force; it can only be achieved by understanding (ALBERT EINSTEIN).

Inward

Peace that the world has not to give
    Is theirs who do the Saviour's will;
Help Thou us more to Him to live,
    And with His peace our spirits fill.

JOHN E. BODE

That peace which the world cannot give.

BOOK OF COMMON PRAYER

Thou hast touched me and I have been translated into Thy peace.

AUGUSTINE

But sometimes through the soul of man,
Slow moving o'er his pain,
The moonlight of a perfect peace
Floods heart and brain.

WILLIAM SHARP

Peace begins just where ambition ends (EDWARD YOUNG); We should have
much peace if we would not busy ourselves with the sayings and doings
of others (THOMAS À KEMPIS).

The Navajo word is *hozro*—a sort of blend of being in harmony with
one's environment, at peace with one's circumstances, content with the
day, devoid of anger, and free from anxieties.

TONY HILLERMAN

Drop Thy still dews of quietness
    Till all our strivings cease;
Take from our souls the strain and stress,
And let our ordered lives confess
    The beauty of Thy peace.

Breathe through the heats of our desire
    Thy coolness and Thy balm;
Let sense be dumb, let flesh retire,
Speak through the earthquake, wind, and fire,
    O still, small voice of calm.

JOHN GREENLEAF WHITTIER

By the faith that flowers show when they bloom unbidden;
By the calm of the river's flow to a goal that is hidden;
By the trust of the tree that clings to its deep foundation;
By the courage of wild birds' wings on the long migration,
(Wonderful secret of peace that abides in Nature's breast!)
Teach me how to confide, and live my life, and rest.

HENRY VAN DYKE

Peace? Perfect peace? in this dark world of sin?
    The blood of Jesus whispers peace within.
Peace? perfect peace? by thronging duties pressed?
    To do the will of Jesus, this is rest.
Peace? perfect peace? the future all unknown?
    Jesus we know, and He is on the throne.
Peace? perfect peace? death shadowing us and ours?
    Jesus has vanquished death and all its powers.

EDWARD H. BICKERSTETH

Father, hear the prayer we offer:
    Not for ease that prayer shall be,
But for strength, that we may ever
    Live our lives courageously.

Not for ever by still waters
    Would we idly quiet stay;
But would smite the living fountains
    From the rocks along our way.

L. MARIA WILLIS

Certainly it is heaven upon earth to have a man's mind move in charity,
rest in providence, and turn upon the poles of truth.

FRANCIS BACON

PERSECUTION

"Blessed are you when men revile you and persecute you and utter all
kinds of evil against you falsely on my account. Rejoice."

JESUS: MATTHEW 5:11–12

The more you mow us down, the more quickly we grow; the blood of Christians is fresh seed.

TERTULLIAN

The anvil is not afraid of the hammer.

CHARLES H. SPURGEON

It is a heretic that makes the fire,
Not she which burns in 't.

WILLIAM SHAKESPEARE

Your lordships demand a simple answer. Here it is, plain and unvarnished. Unless I am convicted of error by the testimony of scripture or . . . by manifest reasoning I stand convicted by the scriptures to which I have appealed, and my conscience is taken captive by God's word, I cannot and will not recant anything, for to act against our conscience is neither safe for us, nor open to us. God help me. Amen.

MARTIN LUTHER

To persecute
Makes a faith hated, and is furthermore
No perfect witness of a perfect faith
In him which persecutes.

ALFRED TENNYSON

A single zealot may become a persecutor, and better men be his victims.

THOMAS JEFFERSON

'Tis man's perdition to be safe
When for the truth he ought to die.

RALPH WALDO EMERSON

During these years, in sheer terror we may sometimes have felt as though we were falling into the bottomless abyss . . . But there is a Power that sustains us; we are borne up by God the Father's everlasting arms . . . It is the tenth week now that I wait for the opening of my prison door; and looking back and around I am amazed at the good cheer that I have felt for weeks . . . an answer to so many prayers.

GERMAN PASTORS IN PRISON, 1933–1937

Everything is in a golden glory ... I have returned completely to the open arms of our Lord and Saviour [by a condemned colonel]; I have now a new understanding of the figure of Jesus ... the measureless love he felt for all men [by a boy]; Where will God's will lead us now? He himself stands always at the end of the road. "God's children journey inviolable, garbed in light"—even to Dachau [by a pastor]; I shall waken you in the morning with laughter [by a student writing home]; We are sheltered in the hands of God [by another student].

LETTERS FROM GERMAN PRISONS, 1937–
1944, EDITED BY PASTOR GOLLWITZER

PERSEVERANCE

A righteous man falls seven times, and rises again;
but the wicked are overthrown by calamity.
PROVERBS 24:16

The perseverance of the saints is nothing else than the patience of God.
X

Our courteous Lord does not want his servants to despair, even when they sin: for our falling does not hinder his loving.
JULIAN OF NORWICH

It is far, far more God who must hold us, than we who must hold him.
FRIEDRICH VON HÜGEL

To persevere, trusting in what hopes he has, is courage in a man; the coward despairs (EURIPIDES); By perseverance the snail reached the Ark (CHARLES H. SPURGEON); Blossom by blossom the Spring begins (MARY MCMULLEN); Even the woodpecker owes his success to the fact that he uses his head and keeps pecking away (COLEMAN COX).

Perseverance is more prevailing than violence; many things which cannot be overcome together yield when taken little by little.
PLUTARCH

God is with those who persevere.
THE KORAN

PERSUASION

Let your speech always be gracious, seasoned with salt [wit], so that you may know how you ought to answer every one.

PAUL: COLOSSIANS 4:6

Too much zeal offends, where indirectness works (EURIPIDES); Soft words are hard arguments (THOMAS FULLER).

Who overcomes
By force, hath overcome but half his foe.

JOHN MILTON

People are generally better persuaded by the reasons which they have themselves discovered than by those which have come into the mind of others.

BLAISE PASCAL

Yet hold it more humane, more heavenly, first
By winning words to conquer willing hearts,
And make persuasion do the work of fear.

JOHN MILTON

PETER

Peter was grieved because [Jesus] said to him the third time, "Do you love me?" And he said to him, "Lord, you know everything; you know that I love you."

JOHN 21:17

Thou hast the art on't, Peter, and canst tell
To cast thy nets on all occasions well;
When Christ calls, and thy nets would have thee stay,
To cast them well's to cast them quite away.

RICHARD CRASHAW

Peter, fleeing from persecution in Rome, met Christ on the road and asked him, "Lord, where are you going?" Christ answered, "I am coming to be crucified again"; thereupon Peter turned back to meet his martyrdom.

DONALD ATTWATER, CITING THE
APOCRYPHAL ACTS OF PETER

The Saviour looked on Peter. Ay, no word,
No gesture of reproach; the Heavens serene,
Though heavy with armed justice, did not lean
Their thunders that way: the forsaken Lord
Looked only, on the traitor . . .
And Peter, from the height of blasphemy—
"I never knew this man"—did quail and fall
As knowing straight THAT GOD; and turnèd free
And went out speechless from the face of all,
And filled the silence, weeping bitterly.

I think that look of Christ might seem to say:
"Thou Peter! art thou then a common stone
Which I at last must break my heart upon, . . .
And do thy kisses, like the rest, betray?
The cock crows coldly; go, and manifest
A late contrition, but no bootless fear!
For when thy final need is dreariest
Thou shalt not be denied, as I am here;
My voice to God and angels shall attest,
Because I know this man, let him be clear."

ELIZABETH BARRETT BROWNING

PHILOSOPHY

See to it that no one takes you captive through hollow and deceptive philosophy, which depends on human tradition and the basic principles of this world rather than on Christ.

PAUL: COLOSSIANS 2:8, NIV

Philosophy begins in wonder, and at the end . . . the wonder remains.

ALFRED NORTH WHITEHEAD

The object of studying philosophy is to know one's own mind, not other people's (WILLIAM R. INGE); A philosophy is characterised more by the formulation of its problems than by its solution of them (SUSAN K. LANGER); It is a great advantage for a system of philosophy to be substantially true (GEORGE SANTAYANA); Philosophy is the highest music (PLATO).

Bishop Berkeley destroyed this world in one volume octavo, and nothing remained after his time but mind; which experienced a similar fate from the hand of Mr. Hume in 1739.

SYDNEY SMITH

There once was a man who said "God
Must think it exceedingly odd
    If He finds that this tree
    Continues to be
When there's no one about in the Quad."

RONALD A. KNOX,
ON GEORGE BERKELEY'S PHILOSOPHY

Dear Sir, Your astonishment's odd:
I am always about in the Quad.
    And that's why the tree
    Continues to be,
Since observed by, yours faithfully, God.

ANONYMOUS

Philosophy will clip an angel's wings,
Conquer all mysteries by rule and line,
Empty the haunted air and gnomèd mine—
Unweave a rainbow . . .

JOHN KEATS

PILGRIMAGE

These all died in faith, not having received the promises, but having seen them afar off . . . and confessed that they were strangers and pilgrims on the earth.

HEBREWS 11:13, AV/KJV

Ancient man was ever a pilgrim: modern man is a mere pedestrian.

ANONYMOUS

> Who would true valour see
> Let him come hither;
> Once here will constant be,
> Come wind, come weather.
> There's no discouragement
> Shall make him once relent
> · His first avowed intent
> To be a pilgrim.

JOHN BUNYAN

> Give me my scallop-shell of quiet,
> My staff of faith to walk upon,
> My scrip of joy, immortal diet,
> My bottle of salvation,
> My gown of glory, hope's true gage,*
> And thus I'll make my pilgrimage.

WALTER RALEIGH, *(pledge, guarantee)

POLITICS

Be subject for the Lord's sake to every human institution, whether it be to the emperor . . . or to governors . . . Fear God. Honour the emperor.

PETER: 1 PETER 2:13–14, 17

Those who would treat politics and morality apart will never understand the one or the other (JOHN MORLEY); We cannot safely leave politics to politicians (HENRY GEORGE); Politics and theology are the only two really great subjects (HARRIET GROTE); Public office is a public trust (W. CADWALADER HUDSON).

Minorities . . . are almost always in the right.

SYDNEY SMITH

Puritanism, believing itself quick with the seed of religious liberty, laid without knowing it the egg of democracy (JAMES RUSSELL LOWELL); Democracy meant not "I'm as good as you are" but "You're as good as

I am" (THEODORE PARKER); Democracy . . . has the obvious disadvantage of merely counting votes instead of weighing them (WILLIAM R. INGE); Democracy—the notion that a man's liberty consists in giving his vote at election hustings and saying, "Behold, now I too have my 20,000th part of a Talker in our National Palaver" (THOMAS CARLYLE).

[H. W. Nevinson] believed in democracy because he believed in the common man. But he never understood by democracy the tyranny of the mass mind.

J. L. HAMMOND

Tradition means giving votes to our ancestors—the democracy of the dead (G. K. CHESTERTON); Democracy means government by discussion, but it is only effective if you can stop people talking (CLEMENT ATTLEE).

"Thus says the LORD of hosts, the God of Israel, to all the exiles . . . Build houses and live in them; plant gardens and eat their produce. Take wives and have sons and daughters . . . do not decrease. But seek the welfare of the city where I have sent you into exile, and pray to the LORD on its behalf, for in its welfare you will find your welfare."

JEREMIAH: JEREMIAH 29:4–7

POWER

[To Pilate] "You would have no power over me unless it had been given you from above."

JESUS: JOHN 19:11

The property of power is to protect (BLAISE PASCAL); Power tends to corrupt, and absolute power corrupts absolutely (LORD ACTON); The exercise of power and the sense of power are quite separate experiences: "When I am weak, than am I strong"—2 Corinthians 12:10 (ANONYMOUS); The silent, irresistible forces of the frost can fracture iron and split the hardest stone (X).

The innocent moon, that nothing does but shine,
Moves all the labouring surges of the world.

FRANCIS THOMPSON

Thrice blest is he to whom is given
    The instinct that can tell
That God is on the field when He
    Is most invisible.

FREDERICK W. FABER

O it is excellent
To have a giant's strength; but it is tyrannous
To use it like a giant.

WILLIAM SHAKESPEARE

PRAISE

Praise the LORD!
Praise God in his sanctuary;
praise him in his mighty firmament!
Praise him for his mighty deeds;
praise him according to his exceeding greatness . . .
Let everything that breathes praise the LORD!
Praise the LORD!

PSALM 150:1−2, 6

We praise Thee, O God:
We acknowledge Thee to be the Lord.
All the earth doth worship Thee:
The Father everlasting . . .
Heaven and earth are full of the majesty of Thy glory . . .
The glorious company of the apostles praise Thee:
The goodly fellowship of the prophets praise Thee:
The noble army of martyrs praise Thee:
Thy holy church throughout all the world doth acknowledge
    Thee . . .

TE DEUM LAUDAMUS, FOURTH CENTURY

Praise, my soul, the King of heaven,
    To His feet thy tribute bring;
Ransomed, healed, restored, forgiven,
    Who like thee His praise should sing?

Praise Him!
Praise the everlasting King.

HENRY F. LYTE

Thou who art beyond the farthest
    Mortal eye can scan,
Can it be that Thou regardest
    Songs of sinful man?
Can we know that Thou art near us
And wilt hear us?
    Yea, we can.

FRANCIS POTT

Let all the world in every corner sing:
    "My God and King!"
The heavens are not too high;
His praise may thither fly:
The earth is not too low;
His praises there may grow.
Let all the world in every corner sing:
    "My God and King!"

GEORGE HERBERT

God! what a glorious morning:
The sky is a delicate blue;
And the muted grey of the soft brushed clouds
Shadows a world that's new.

The air, new washed by the dew fall,
Hangs out on the green to dry;
And the dappled leaves of the sap-surged trees
Quiver as I pass by.

The work of the day is beginning
In the city of smoke and grey;
But I cherish the image of new-made Eden—
God! what a glorious day!

GLENDA WHITE

PRAYER

"If you knew . . . you would have asked . . . and he would have given."

JESUS: JOHN 4:10

I have been driven many times to my knees by the overwhelming conviction that I had nowhere else to go.

ABRAHAM LINCOLN

The power to pray comes with praying. You know "Of ourselves we know not what to ask, but the Spirit helpeth our infirmities." But He helpeth us when we are trying to pray, not when we are not trying.

E. B. PUSEY: ROMANS 8:26

The praying Christ is the supreme argument for prayer (JAMES S. STEWART); Prayer is the homing of the soul, a sixth and deepest sense that guides us Godward . . . friendship with God (GEORGE ARTHUR BUTTRICK); True prayer is asking God for what He wants (WILLIAM BARCLAY); The best prayer is to rest in the goodness of God (JULIAN OF NORWICH); [Prayer] is not our own effort to get into touch with a God far away, but part of the deep silent work of God Himself within us, to which we need to open up, generously, receptively (AFTER OLIVE WYON); Prayer is the heart and centre of all religion (FRIEDRICH HEILER); Of all mental exercises, earnest prayer is the most severe (SAMUEL TAYLOR COLERIDGE); The wish to pray is a prayer in itself (GEORGES BERNANOS); Certain thoughts are prayers; there are moments when, whatever be the attitude of the body, the soul is on its knees (VICTOR HUGO); With God is an immeasurable reservoir of grace and power and love: each instant-prayer just turns the tap (J. O. HAGGER); Prayer is a mighty instrument, not for getting man's will done in heaven but for getting God's will done on earth (ROBERT LAW).

Prayer is the soul's sincere desire,
   Uttered or unexpressed,
The motion of a hidden fire
   That trembles in the breast.
Prayer is the burden of a sigh,
   The falling of a tear,
The upward glancing of an eye
   When none but God is near.

JAMES MONTGOMERY

Prayer is the peace of our spirit, the stillness of our thoughts, the evenness of recollection, the seat of meditation, the rest of our cares, the calm of our tempest . . . the issue of a quiet mind . . . the daughter of charity and the sister of meekness.

JEREMY TAYLOR

Prayer, the church's banquet, Angels' age,
God's breath in man returning to his birth,
The soul in paraphrase, heart in pilgrimage,
The Christian plummet sounding heaven and earth;

Softness, and peace, and joy, and love, and bliss,
Exalted manna, gladness of the best,
Heaven in ordinary, man well dressed,
The milky way, the bird of Paradise . . .

Church bells beyond the stars heard, the soul's blood,
The land of spices, something understood.

GEORGE HERBERT

The object of prayer is not to persuade God to do something different from what He intended, but to free His hand to do that which can only be done for free men with their co-operation.

CHARLES GORE

To pray is to desire what God would have us desire (FRANÇOIS FÉNELON); God is not a cosmic bell-boy for whom we can press a button to get things (HARRY EMERSON FOSDICK); Prayer as a means to effect a private end is theft and meanness (RALPH WALDO EMERSON).

Why therefore should we do ourselves this wrong,
Or others, that we are not always strong—
That we are sometimes overborne with care,
That we should ever weak or heartless be,
Anxious, or troubled, when with us is prayer,
And joy and strength and courage are with Thee?

RICHARD C. TRENCH

God's Word, and the prayers of Christians, sustain the world (MARTIN LUTHER); Pray as if all depended on God's doing: act as if all depended on your own (IGNATIUS OF ANTIOCH); It is impossible to isolate the practice of prayer from the rest of life (OLIVE WYON); "Coming in on a wing and a prayer" (RADIO SIGNAL BY WARTIME BRITISH PILOT); Only obedience rationalises prayer (WILLIAM CAREY); You cannot pray a lie (MARK TWAIN); Do not pray for tasks equal to your powers—pray for power equal to your tasks (PHILLIPS BROOKS); Do you wish to find out the really sublime?—Repeat the Lord's prayer (NAPOLEON); Ah, yes, there are times when all pray (WINSTON SPENCER CHURCHILL).

> Prayer to a heart of lowly love
> Opens the gate of heaven above.
> Ah, prayer is God's high dwelling-place,
> Wherein His children see His face.
> From earth to heaven we build a stair:
> The name by which we call it—prayer.
> Love's rain, the Spirit's holy ray,
> And tears of joy, are theirs who pray.
>
> NARAYAN VAMAN TILAK, (TRANS., NICOL MACNICOLL)

That "unwritten" saying of Jesus: "Ask for the big things and the little things shall be added unto you"—what a criticism of our small ideas!

T. R. GLOVER

> Two went to pray—or rather say
> One went to brag, the other to pray.
> One stands up close and treads on high
> Where the other dares not send his eye;
> One nearer to God's altar trod,
> The other, to the altar's God.
>
> RICHARD CRASHAW

To pray together, in whatever tongue or ritual, is the most tender brotherhood of hope and sympathy that men can contract in this life.

MADAME ANNE-LOUISE-GERMAINE DE STAËL

> Be not afraid to pray—to pray is right.
> Pray, if thou canst, with hope; but ever pray

Though hope be weak, or sick with long delay;
Pray in the darkness, if there be no light . . .
Whate'er is good to wish, ask that of Heaven,
Though it be what thou canst not hope to see:
Pray to be perfect, though material leaven
Forbid the spirit so on earth to be;
But if for any wish thou darest not pray,
Then pray to God to cast that wish away.

HARTLEY COLERIDGE

My soul, cheer up; what if the night be long?
Heaven finds an ear when sinners find a tongue;
Thy tears are morning showers . . .

FRANCIS QUARLES

What various hindrances we meet
In coming to the mercy seat!
Yet who, that knows the worth of prayer,
But wishes to be often there!

Have you no words? Ah! think again.
Words flow apace when you complain,
And fill your fellow-creature's ear
With the sad tale of all your care.

Were half the breath thus vainly spent
To Heaven in supplication sent,
Your cheerful song would oftener be
"Hear what the Lord has done for me."

WILLIAM COWPER

Pray for my soul. More things are wrought by prayer
That this world dreams of. Wherefore, let thy voice
Rise like a fountain for me night and day.
For what are men better than sheep or goats
That nourish a blind life within the brain,
If, knowing God, they lift not hands of prayer
Both for themselves and those that call them friend?
For so the whole round earth is every way
Bound by gold chains about the feet of God.

ALFRED TENNYSON

Answers to Prayer

God is always listening (WILLIAM BARCLAY); Give us grace to listen well (JOHN KEBLE).

Unless there is some impediment on our part, we shall infallibly obtain what we ask, or something else more expedient for us, or it may be both together.

LORENZO SCUPOLI

Even on the "material" level, God answers prayer in varied ways. He may change the situation about which we pray, as when He delivered Peter from prison. He may show us how to change the situation, as when Moses, complaining of defeat at Ai, was told to get off his knees and purify the people. He may leave the situation unchanged but change us within it, as when He enabled Paul and Silas to sing through the darkness and pain of Philippi's prison. Or He may leave the situation and ourselves unchanged, but make plain his deeper purposes to our understanding, as when Paul was led "most gladly" to accept his "thorn in the flesh."

ANONYMOUS

Who rises from prayer a better man, his prayer is answered.

GEORGE MEREDITH

It may never be mine,
    The loaf or the kiss or the kingdom
        Because of beseeching;
But I know that my hand
    Is an arm's length nearer the sky
        For reaching.

FRANCIS QUARLES

Character must be won, not prayed for.

B. H. STREETER

A man prayed concerning his neighbour, "O Lord, take away this wicked person!" And God said, "Which?"

AFTER AUGUSTINE

God answers sharp and sudden on some prayers,
And thrusts the thing we have prayed for in our face—
A gauntlet with a gift in't.

ELIZABETH BARRETT BROWNING

When the gods wish to punish us, they answer our prayers.

OSCAR WILDE

Did not God
Sometimes withhold in mercy what we ask,
We should be ruined at our own request.

HANNAH MORE

Prayers

Without adoration, public prayer is not reverently offered to God; without
thanksgiving, it is not worthy to be offered; without confession, it is not
truly ours; without petition, it is hardly prayer at all; without intercession,
not Christian prayer; without closing submission to God's will, it borders
upon superstitious self-assertion.

ANONYMOUS

Almighty God, unto whom all hearts be open, all desires known, and from
whom no secrets are hid, cleanse the thoughts of our hearts by the
inspiration of thy Holy Spirit, that we may perfectly love thee, and
worthily magnify thy holy name, through Christ our Lord. Amen.

BOOK OF COMMON PRAYER

O Lord, our heavenly Father, almighty and everlasting God, who hast
safely brought us to the beginning of this day, defend us in the same with
thy mighty power; and grant that this day we fall into no sin, neither run
into any kind of danger; but that all our doings, being ordered by thy
governance, may be righteous in thy sight, through Jesus Christ our Lord.
Amen.

BOOK OF COMMON PRAYER

The God of peace who brought again from the dead our Lord Jesus, the
great shepherd of the sheep, by the blood of the eternal covenant, equip
you with everything good that you may do his will, working in you that
which is pleasing in his sight, through Jesus Christ . . . Amen.

HEBREWS 13:20–21

If I am right, thy grace impart
Still in the right to stay;
If I am wrong, O teach my heart
To find the better way!

ALEXANDER POPE

O God, who art the author of peace and lover of concord, in knowledge of whom standeth our eternal life, whose service is perfect freedom: defend us thy humble servants in all assaults of our enemies; that we, surely trusting in thy defence, may not fear the power of any adversaries; through the might of Jesus Christ our Lord. Amen.

BOOK OF COMMON PRAYER

O God our Father, who hast reconciled us to thyself by Jesus Christ, help us to trust in thee at all times, and never to doubt thy promises and love. May our minds ever be open to thy truth, our hearts strengthened to love thee more, our wills made obedient to thine, and our hands prepared to serve thee in the world. In our duties, grant us thy help; in our dangers, thy protection; in our difficulties, thy guidance; and in our sorrow, thy peace. May thy grace be sufficient for us, and thy strength made perfect in our weakness; and bring us at last to thine eternal kingdom, through Jesus Christ our Lord. Amen.

UNKNOWN

Teach us, good Lord, to serve thee as thou deservest; to give, and not to count the cost; to fight, and not to heed the wounds; to toil, and not to seek for rest; to labour, and not to ask for any reward, save that of knowing that we do thy will; through Jesus Christ our Lord. Amen.

IGNATIUS LOYOLA

A good prayer, though often used, is still fresh and fair in the ears and eyes of Heaven.

THOMAS FULLER

And help us, this and every day,
To live more nearly as we pray.

JOHN KEBLE

PREACHING

"If you utter what is precious, and not what is worthless,
you shall be as my mouth.

JEREMIAH 15:19

Preaching is the manifestation of the incarnate word from the written word
by the spoken word (BERNARD MANNING); In the beginning was the sermon
(MARTIN DIBELIUS, ON CHRISTIAN ORIGINS); Great sermons lead the people to
praise the preacher; good preaching leads the people to praise the Saviour
(CHARLES G. FINNEY).

We who utter the Word are like organ pipes giving the tune, but here
and there in a cottage sits a simple inward soul who, by his secret
prayers, fills us with the breath of the Spirit, with its power and blessing,
both for ourselves and others.

GERHARD TERSTEEGEN

Through the apostolic preaching men were still encountering God in Christ.
The missionary proclamation of the mighty acts of redemption was in fact
a continuation of the divine redeeming activity; it was something more than
a religious lecture that was going on: it was God in action to judge and
save men by confrontation with the living Christ. So all down the
centuries.

JAMES S. STEWART

God's word is like wheat that nourishes, like fire that kindles, like a
hammer that breaks even rock in pieces.

SO JEREMIAH: JEREMIAH 23:28–29

I preached as never sure to preach again,
And as a dying man to dying men.

RICHARD BAXTER

We have no right to constrain others by any other means than by the
preaching of the word . . . I will preach and talk and write against these
things, but no one will I attempt to force. We have to preach the word;
but the consequences should be left to God alone in His pleasure.

MARTIN LUTHER

If God give us success, then to the feet of Jesus let our sheaves be carried; if it be His will that we should fail, to the same dear Lord let us flee, who knows what it is to see His life fall into the ground.

JOHN WATSON

A frigid people can chill the most fiery soul, while a hundred warm-hearted folk can make a plain man eloquent.

JOHN WATSON

Would I describe a preacher . . .
I would express him simple, grave, sincere;
In doctrine uncorrupt; in language plain,
And plain in manner; decent, solemn, chaste,
And natural in gesture . . .
      . . . affectionate in look,
And tender in address, as well becomes
A messenger of grace to guilty men.

WILLIAM COWPER

Christian saw the picture of a very grave person. It had eyes lifted up to heaven, the best of books was in his hand, the law of truth was written upon his lips, the world was behind his back, he stood as if he pleaded with men, and a crown of gold did hang over his head.

JOHN BUNYAN

Provoked by a curious phrase from some obscure passage of Holy Writ, the young preacher weaves artistically his intricate web of tenuous ideas, upon which no positive purpose or firm conclusion dare hang. Perceiving the thinness of the resulting fabric, he proceeds to accumulate adjectives, search out similes, multiply metaphors, and adduce appropriate anecdotes, until the gossamer thread of thought snaps under the weight of the glistening dew of ornament, and collapses in the dust.

ANONYMOUS, PARAPHRASING JOHN HENRY
NEWMAN ON INDIAN LOVELETTERS

How the heart listened while he pleading spoke!
While on the enlightened mind, with winning art,
His gentle reason so persuasive stole
That the charmed hearer thought it was his own.

JAMES THOMSON

Once in seven years I burn all my sermons; for it is a shame if I cannot write better sermons now than I did seven years ago.

JOHN WESLEY

Take heed lest your example contradict your doctrine, lest you unsay with your lives what you say with your tongues. Such a little thing on your part may cut the throat of many a sermon.

RICHARD BAXTER

Young man, I think I can tell you what is wrong. For the last half-hour you have been trying to get something out of your head instead of trying to get something into mine.

JOSEPH PARKER

Eloquence is the power to translate a truth into language perfectly intelligible to the person to whom you speak (RALPH WALDO EMERSON); The finest eloquence is that which gets things done (DAVID LLOYD GEORGE); True eloquence consists in saying all that is necessary and nothing else (LA ROCHEFOUCAULD); Eloquence persuades by sweetness, not by authority (BLAISE PASCAL).

He can compress the most words into the smallest ideas of any man I ever met (ABRAHAM LINCOLN); It is terrible to speak well and be wrong (SOPHOCLES); On the whole, it may be better for the sake of his people for the average [preacher] not to go to the Holy Land, unless he has great self-control (JOHN WATSON); There is endless merit in a man's knowing when to have done (THOMAS CARLYLE); Blessed is the man who, having nothing to say abstains from giving us wordy evidence of the fact (GEORGE ELIOT); Take care, not that the listener may understand if he will, but that he must understand, whether he will or not (QUINTILIAN).

If you your ears would keep from jeers,
   These things keep meekly hid:
Myself and me, or my and mine,
   Or how I do, or did.

W. E. NORRIS, ATTRIBUTED

He who talks upon plain gospel themes in a farmer's kitchen, and is able to interest the carter's boy and the dairymaid, has more of the minister in him than the prim little man who keeps prating about being cultured, and means by that—being taught to use words which nobody can understand.

CHARLES H. SPURGEON

Every time you present a truth, picture it; if you would persuade, portray; don't argue, imagine; don't define, depict; the quickest way past the ears is through the eyes, and the short way to the heart is through imagination; no man ever possesses a truth until he "sees" it for himself.

ANONYMOUS

I praise the heart and pity the head of him,
And refer myself to Thee instead of him.

ROBERT BROWNING

Men must be taught as if you taught them not,
And things unknown proposed as things forgot.

ALEXANDER POPE

God calleth preaching folly. Do not grudge
To pick out treasures from an earthen pot.
The worst speak *something* good: if all want sense,
God takes a text and preacheth patience.

GEORGE HERBERT

PREJUDICE

God shows no partiality.

PAUL: ROMANS 2:11

A prejudice is—a vagrant opinion without visible means of support (AMBROSE BIERCE) . . . the child of ignorance (WILLIAM HAZLITT).

Dogs bark at people they do not know! (HERACLITUS); Knowledge humanizes mankind; reason inclines to mildness; prejudices eradicate every tender disposition (CHARLES LOUIS DE S. MONTESQUIEU).

Father, Mother, and Me
Sister, and Auntie say

All the people like us are WE,
And everyone else is THEY.

RUDYARD KIPLING

There is no king who has not had a slave among his ancestors, and no slave who has not had a king among his.

HELEN KELLER

Everyone is a prisoner of his own experiences; no one can eliminate prejudices—just recognise them (EDWARD R. MURROW); Fortunately for serious minds, a bias recognised is a bias sterilised (A. E. HAYDON).

PRIDE

I bid every one among you not to think of himself more highly than he ought to think.

PAUL: ROMANS 12:3

There are two sorts of pride: one in which we approve ourselves, the other in which we cannot accept ourselves.

HENRI AMIEL

To have a thing is little, if you're not allowed to show it,
And to know a thing is nothing unless others know you know it.

CHARLES NEAVES

When a proud man hears another praised he thinks himself injured (ENGLISH PROVERB); The proud are always most provoked by pride (WILLIAM COWPER); Pride and grace dwell never in one place (THOMAS FULLER); "God *opposes* the proud" (PETER: 1 PETER 5:5, EMPHASIS ADDED).

Pride,
However disguised in its own majesty,
Is littleness.

WILLIAM WORDSWORTH

Of all the causes which conspire to blind
Man's erring judgement, and misguide the mind,

What the weak head with strongest bias rules
Is Pride, the never-failing vice of fools.

ALEXANDER POPE

PRIESTHOOD

You are . . . a royal priesthood . . . built into a spiritual house to be a
holy priesthood, to offer spiritual sacrifices acceptable to God.

PETER: 1 PETER 2:9, 5

Luther put the layman on his theological feet [proclaiming] a single human
estate and the priesthood of all believers.

WILLIAM R. INGE

All Christians whatsoever belong to the "religious" class; there is no
difference between them except as they do different work . . . Baptism
makes us all priests . . . Those who exercise secular authority have all
been baptised like the rest of us; therefore they are priests and bishops.

MARTIN LUTHER

God's representative requires—
Of an ambassador the just address,
A Father's tenderness, a shepherd's care,
A leader's courage, which the cross can bear,
A Ruler's awe, a watchman's wakeful eye,
A pilot's skill, the helm in storms to ply,
A fisher's patience, and a labourer's toil,
A guide's dexterity to disembroil,
A prophet's inspiration from above,
A teacher's knowledge, and a Saviour's love.

THOMAS KEN

The clergyman is expected to be a kind of human Sunday.

SAMUEL BUTLER II

PROGRESS

Not that I have already . . . been made perfect, but I press on.

PAUL: PHILIPPIANS 3:12, NIV

Growth is the only evidence of life (JOHN HENRY NEWMAN); Stretch your foot to the length of your blanket (PERSIAN PROVERB); The shell must break before the bird can fly (ALFRED TENNYSON); Never leave growing till the life to come (ROBERT BROWNING).

Thank God! a man can grow!
He is not bound
With earthward gaze to creep along the ground:
Though his beginnings be but poor and low,
Thank God a man can grow!

UNKNOWN

O my brave soul!
O farther, farther sail!
O daring joy, but safe—are they not all the seas of God?
O farther, farther, farther sail.

WALT WHITMAN

Not enjoyment, and not sorrow,
Is our destined end or way;
But to act that each tomorrow
Find us farther than today.

HENRY WADSWORTH LONGFELLOW

Build thee more stately mansions, O my soul,
  As the swift seasons roll!
Leave thy low-vaulted past!
Let each new temple, nobler than the last,
Shut thee from heaven with a dome more vast,
  Till thou at length art free,
Leaving thine outgrown shell by life's unresting sea.

OLIVER WENDELL HOLMES

Advance is possible only when it is conjoined with abiding—abiding in fellowship with God and in fidelity to the facts of the faith.

J. IRELAND HASLER, SUMMARISING 1 JOHN

If every year we did but extirpate one vice, we should soon become perfect; but we experience the sad reverse. We find that we were more contrite, pure, humble, obedient in the beginning of our conversion than after many years profession of a religious life: and . . . it is now thought to be a ground of comfort, and even of boast, if a man at the close of this mortal state is able to retain some degree of his first ardour.

THOMAS À KEMPIS

Onward the chariot of the Untarrying moves;
    Nor day divulges Him, nor night conceals;
Thou hearest the echo of unreturning hooves,
    And thunder of irrevocable wheels.

WILLIAM WATSON

Our chief want in life is someone who shall make us do what we can.

RALPH WALDO EMERSON

Progress, man's distinctive mark alone,
    Not God's, and not the beasts': God is, they are;
Man partly is, and wholly hopes to be.

ROBERT BROWNING.

The fatal metaphor of progress, which means leaving things behind us, has utterly obscured the real idea of growth, which means leaving things inside us.

G. K. CHESTERTON

But it is written in the heart of man:
Thou shalt no larger be than thy desire.

LASCELLES ABERCROMBIE

So the grand oaks grow
That once were acorns; so the grand deeds, too,
That once were only dreams.

MARIANNE FARNINGHAM

New occasions teach new duties,
Time makes ancient good uncouth;

> They must upward still and onward,
> Who would keep abreast of truth.

JAMES RUSSELL LOWELL

> New times demand new measures and new men;
> The world advances, and in time outgrows
> The laws that in our fathers' day were best;
> And, doubtless, after us some purer scheme
> Will be shaped out by wiser men than we.

JAMES RUSSELL LOWELL

There is no greater disloyalty to the great pioneers of human progress than to refuse to budge an inch from where they stood.

WILLIAM R. INGE

Is it progress if a cannibal uses knife and fork?

STANISLAW LEC

To live with fear and not be afraid is the final test of maturity.

EDWARD WEEKS

PROVIDENCE

In everything God works for good with those who love him, who are called according to his purpose.

PAUL: ROMANS 8:28

Nothing happens by chance, but by the far-sighted wisdom of God (JULIAN OF NORWICH); Providence provides for the provident (W. G. BENHAM); There's a divinity that shapes our ends, rough-hew them how we will (WILLIAM SHAKESPEARE); God's gifts put man's best dreams to shame (ELIZABETH BARRETT BROWNING); Whom God will help no man can hinder (ENGLISH PROVERB); The man whom heaven helps has friends enough (EURIPIDES); The Almighty has his own purposes (ABRAHAM LINCOLN); A greater power than we can contradict hath thwarted our intents (WILLIAM SHAKESPEARE).

A person who strives to be godly will always have enough to get along.

ERASMUS

Hast thou not seen
How thine entreaties have been
Granted in what He ordaineth?

JOACHIM NEANDER

When all Thy mercies, O my God,
  My rising soul surveys,
Transported with the view I'm lost
  In wonder, love, and praise . . .

Unnumbered comforts on my soul
  Thy tender care bestowed
Before my infant heart conceived
  From whence those comforts flowed.

When in the slippery paths of youth
  With heedless steps I ran,
Thine arm unseen conveyed me safe
  And brought me up to man.

Ten thousand thousand precious gifts
  My daily thanks employ:
Nor is the least a cheerful heart
  That tastes those gifts with joy.

JOHN ADDISON

Know well, my soul, God's hand controls
  Whate'er thou fearest;
Round Him in calmest music rolls
  Whate'er thou hearest.
What to thee is shadow to Him is day,
  And the end He knoweth;
And not on a blind and aimless way
  Thy spirit goeth.

UNKNOWN

It never will rain roses; when we want to have more roses we must plant more trees (GEORGE ELIOT); Every drunken skipper trusts to Providence; but one of the ways of Providence with drunken skippers is to run them on the rocks (GEORGE BERNARD SHAW); There are many scapegoats for our sins, but the most popular is providence (MARK TWAIN); I do not believe in a fate that falls on men however they act; but I do believe in a fate that falls on them unless they act (G. K. CHESTERTON).

"Providence?" said the old woman, "Don't yew talk to me about Providence! I've had enough o' Providence. First he took my 'usband, and then he took my 'taters; but there's One above as'll teach him to mend his manners, if he don't look out."

DOROTHY SAYERS

Any natural or "accidental" event—a falling tile, a child's death—may have a quite simple explanation on the level of material, meteorological, medical analysis; and yet enter into an onlooker's or a father's experience laden with a moral and religious significance determined by his total background and attitude, as a "providence" if the event affects his own life, or other lives, for *good*, and seems related to life's highest purposes; or as a "judgement" if its effects are evil, and appear related in any way to his sinful intention or his bad conscience at the time. To a mind accustomed to the religious interpretation of daily experience, "providence" and "judgement," like "guidance" and "warning," signify the religious value attached to ordinary events by the basic premise that nothing happens entirely outside the directive or permissive will of God.

ANONYMOUS

The only possible guarantee of the progress of man as a free agent would be an overruling Providence which can, by infinite mercy, wisdom and judgement, take note of the choices of man and adjust itself to them, to achieve its own purposes.

H. G. WOOD

He who, from zone to zone,
Guides through the boundless sky thy certain flight,
In the long way that I must tread alone
Will lead my steps aright.

WILLIAM CULLEN BRYANT

All as God wills, who wisely heeds
To give or to withhold,
And knoweth more of all my needs
Than all my prayers have told!

Enough, that blessings undeserved
    Have marked my erring track;
That wheresoe'er my feet have swerved
    His chastening turned me back;

That more and more a providence
    Of love is understood,
Making the springs of time and sense
    Sweet with eternal good. . . .

And so the shadows fall apart,
    And so the west winds play:
And all the windows of my heart
    I open to the day.

JOHN GREENLEAF WHITTIER

PRUDENCE

The simple believes everything, but the prudent looks where he is going.

PROVERBS 14:15

No one tests the depth of a river with both feet (ASHANTI PROVERB); No wise man stands behind an ass (TERENCE).

Early and provident fear is the mother of safety (EDMUND BURKE); Precaution is better than cure (EDWARD COKE); Where the road bends abruptly, take short steps (ERNEST BRAMAH); Take things always by their smoothest handle (THOMAS JEFFERSON).

Set thy sails warily,
Tempests will come;
Steer thy course steadily,
    Christian steer home!

CAROLINE SOUTHEY

He that is *over*-cautious will accomplish little.

J. C. FRIEDRICH VON SCHILLER

"The master commended the dishonest steward for his prudence; for the sons of this world are wiser in their own generation than the sons of light."

JESUS: LUKE 16:8

QUIETNESS

"In returning and rest you shall be saved;
in quietness and in trust shall be your strength."

ISAIAH 30:15

That blessed mood,
In which the burden of the mystery,
In which the heavy and the weary weight
Of all this unintelligible world,
Is lightened.

WILLIAM WORDSWORTH

[To be aware of God] requires a mind that is not subject to passion, but a serene and quiet posture, where there is no tumult of imagination. There is no genuine and proper effect of religion where the mind of man is not composed, sedate, and calm.

BENJAMIN WHICHCOTE

Let us forget ourselves; let us rest quietly in God and find our peace in him . . . I know a back door that leads me into a kingdom that cannot be shaken, and there I can rest my spirit.

GERHARD TERSTEEGEN

Still waters are the deepest; the shallowest brooks brawl the most.

CHARLES H. SPURGEON

RACISM

He created every race of men of one stock, to inhabit the whole earth's surface.

PAUL: ACTS 17:26, NEB

The broken heart, whether of Jew or gentile, was a broken heart to Jesus; the wounds of the Samaritan were human wounds to Him.

W. FEARON HALLIDAY

> Not for myself I make this prayer,
>   But for this race of mine,
> That stretches forth from shadowed places
>   Dark hands for bread and wine.

COUNTÉE CULLEN

If I were to go to heaven, and God said, "Aggrey, I am going to send you back; would you like to go as a white man?" I would reply, "No, I have work to do as a black man that no white man can do. Please send me back as black as you can make me."

JAMES E. AGGREY OF AFRICA AND AMERICA

Some people took to hate, we took to song; some people took to anger, we took to laughter. In the darkest part of the night, when everybody else might have despaired, we looked up, and we sang, long before our white brothers thought of an airplane, "Swing low, sweet chariot, coming for to carry me home."

JAMES E. AGGREY OF AFRICA AND AMERICA

But our Captain counts the image of God nevertheless His image, cut in ebony as if done in ivory.

THOMAS FULLER, SEVENTEENTH CENTURY

For mercy has a human heart,
　　Pity a human face;
And love, the human form divine,
　　And peace the human dress.

Then every man, of every clime,
　　That prays in his distress,
Prays to the human form divine
　　Love, mercy, pity, peace.

And all must love the human form
　　In heathen, Turk, or Jew;
Where mercy, love and pity dwell,
　　There God is dwelling too.

WILLIAM BLAKE

REASON

Always be prepared to give an answer to everyone who asks you to give
the reason for the hope that you have.

PETER: 1 PETER 3:15, NIV

He who will not reason is a bigot, he who cannot is a fool, and he who
dares not is a slave.

WILLIAM DRUMMOND

Sure he that made us with such large discourse,
Looking before and after, gave us not
That capability and godlike reason
To fust in us unused.

WILLIAM SHAKESPEARE

The last function of reason is to recognise that there are an infinity of
things which surpass it.

BLAISE PASCAL

A mind all logic is like a knife all blade, which makes the hand bleed
that used it.

TAGORE

Whoever knows Jesus Christ knows the reason of everything.

BLAISE PASCAL

REFORM

The time of reformation.

HEBREWS 9:10

Every generation needs regeneration (CHARLES H. SPURGEON); Reform must come from within . . . you cannot legislate for virtue (JAMES GIBBONS); The beginning of compunction is the beginning of a new life (GEORGE HERBERT); Every revolution was first a thought in one man's mind (RALPH WALDO EMERSON); Moderate reformers always hate those that go beyond them (JAMES A. FROUDE); Extreme reformers despise all moderates (X); To innovate is not to reform (EDMUND BURKE); To make a crooked stick straight we bend it the contrary way (MICHEL DE MONTAIGNE).

Every reform, however necessary, will by weak minds be carried to an excess, which will itself need reforming (SAMUEL TAYLOR COLERIDGE); Every reform movement has a lunatic fringe (THEODORE ROOSEVELT).

I am in earnest—I will not equivocate—I will not excuse—I will not retreat a single inch—and I *will* be heard.

WILLIAM LLOYD GARRISON

> For him who fain would teach the world
> The world holds fate in fee;
> For Socrates the hemlock cup,
> For Christ, Gethsemane.

DON MARQUIS

Erasmus forwarded the Reformation positively, by reviving classical, Biblical, and patristic studies; negatively, by exposing pitilessly with a mordant wit the ignorance and bigotry of the monks, as well as the obscurantism of the schoolmen.

J. ATKINSON

Erasmus laid the egg, Luther hatched it (SIXTEENTH-CENTURY SAYING); There would assuredly have occurred a Catholic Reformation had Protestantism never developed (A. G. DICKENS); The numerous religious reforms in the south of Europe were not entirely the work of the Counter-reformation, [but derived in part from] "the religion of pure inwardness." (WILLIAM R. INGE).

Realising that only by seeing the Christian ethic in its noblest forms will the world be convinced of its truth, [post-Reformation Catholic leaders] met the situation, not by exhortations to Christian duty, but by teaching people to pray. The galaxy of saints who adorn the period shows how right they were.

G. W. O. ADDLESHAW

Luther showed at this time a marked concern for the immorality of the nobility, the vulgarity of the peasants . . . That God could be so unreal, and faith so ineffective in the lives of evangelical men gave Luther much distress of mind . . . Spite of clear preaching, the people showed little change in their lives and morals . . . It galled him that Wittenberg, the cradle of the Reformation should bear such meagre fruits of spirituality and morality . . . How little changed the human heart, for all the torrents of the gospel that had flowed through Wittenberg!

J. ATKINSON

God is decreeing some new and great period in His church, even to the reforming of the Reformation itself.

JOHN MILTON, IN 1644

RELIGION

The kind of religion which is without stain or fault in the sight of God our Father is this: to go to the help of orphans and widows in their distress and keep oneself untarnished by the world.

JAMES: JAMES 1:27, NEB

It is well said that a man's religion is the chief fact with regard to him, the thing a man does practically lay to heart, and know for certain, concerning his vital relations to this mysterious universe, and his duty and destiny there (THOMAS CARLYLE); Science without religion is lame: religion without science is blind (ALBERT EINSTEIN); Religion—that voice of the deepest human experience (MATTHEW ARNOLD); Over the gray world, ruined by deluge and death, religion has sought ever—and found—the arching rainbow of hope (A. E. HAYDON).

Some have argued that religion is the fulfilment of duty, reducing it to morality; some, that religion is acceptance of revealed truth, resolving religion into knowledge; some, that religion is a state of feeling, dissolving it into emotion. Neither can exclude the other two; all three cannot exhaust religion.

AFTER JOHN WATSON

The fact of the religious vision, and its history of persistent expansion, is our one ground for optimism.

ALFRED NORTH WHITEHEAD

Christianity began in something that happened, in a deed that was done, in a life that was lived. In the beginning was the deed: "Go thou and do likewise." So presented, Christianity is . . . quite the most convincing religion ever offered to the intellect or the heart.

L. P. JACKS

The essence of all religion consists, not in the solution of riddles, but in the conviction that all of value will be preserved.

HARALD HÖFFDING

The soul of man to God is as a flower to the sun; it opens at its approach, and shuts when it withdraws. Religion puts the soul in a right posture toward God, for we are thereby renewed in the spirit of our minds.

BENJAMIN WHICHCOTE

Man attains in religion, as truly as elsewhere . . . in proportion as he seeks not too directly, not feverishly and strainingly, but in a largely subconscious, waiting, genial, expansive, endlessly patient, sunny manner.

FRIEDRICH VON HÜGEL

The various modes of worship which prevailed in the Roman world were all considered by the people as equally true, by the philosophers as equally false, and by the magistrates as equally useful.

EDWARD GIBBON

Among my patients in the second half of life, that is, over thirty-five, there has not been one whose problem in the last resort was not that of finding a religious outlook.

CARL G. JUNG

[The world's monster problems] can only be successfully met in the light of, and with the aid of, a new organisation of thought and belief, a new dominant pattern of ideas . . . Man must reunify his life within the framework of a satisfactory idea-system . . . [must] build a system of thought and belief which will provide . . . a supporting framework for his present existence . . . an ultimate or ideal goal . . . a guide and directive for practical action and planning.

JULIAN HUXLEY

Anyone can create a new religion; all he needs is self-confidence and a supply of foolscap.

JOHN WATSON

At first sight, ours has been a bad century for religion, with war, fanaticism, sectarian bitterness, underlining its worst characteristics. Yet it has seen outstanding examples of the true religious spirit, too. In Albert Schweitzer, "living out his golden sermon on the edge of the primeval forest"; in Mother Teresa, incarnating the compassion of Christ for India's unwanted; in Toyohiko Kagawa, pitting his frail physique against the massed evils of Kobe. In Father Huddleston, too, confronting racial oppression embodied in State policy; Charles Péan defeating almost alone the corruption of a prison slum and snatching Devil's Island from the devil; "Mother Maria" (Elizabeth Pilenko) of Russia, sharing the fate (perhaps actually take the place) of a Jewess in the line for the Ravensbrück gas chambers; the Abbé Pierre, with scorching indignation demanding housing for the homeless of Paris. Yet again in Pope John XXIII, bringing new life and truth to revitalise ancient tradition—all dedicated to the Christian ideal "that there may be a few less people suffering in the world, and that God will be a little less misunderstood."

ANONYMOUS

Whether from a demand for explanation of things he cannot understand, or from reflection upon the orderliness of the universe, or from consideration of the nature of his own moral obligation and experience, or from the objective portrayal of his inmost ideals, or fears, or from the experienced incompleteness of human personality, or from age-old inherited traditions of ritual, ceremonial, and cultic legend—or from any other "cause" which we care to isolate or invent, it is entirely beyond question that historically man has been "a religious animal." It has been the invariable fruit of his individual and corporate experience that he should seek earnestly, or conjure up, a God to worship, trust, and obey.

X

REPENTANCE

"I tell you, there will be more joy in heaven over one sinner who repents than over ninety-nine righteous persons who need no repentance."

JESUS: LUKE 15:7

By repentance we are made clean, by compassion we are made ready, and by yearning for God we are made worthy.

JULIAN OF NORWICH

I seek no more to alter things, or mend,
Before the coming of so great a Friend:
Come not to find, but *make* this troubled heart
A dwelling worthy of Thee as Thou art.
I bid Thee welcome, boldly, in the name
Of Thy great glory—and my want and shame.

HANDLEY G. C. MOULE

Confession of our faults is the next thing to innocence (PUBLILIUS SYRUS); How else but through a broken heart may Lord Christ enter in? (OSCAR WILDE); Amendment is repentance (THOMAS FULLER); To do it no more is the truest repentance (MARTIN LUTHER); It's no use crying over spilt milk, it only makes it salty for the cat (UNKNOWN).

The prodigal: Sick of home—homeless—homesick—home.

ANONYMOUS

What's in prayer but this twofold force,
To be forestallèd, ere we come to fall,
Or pardoned, being down? Then I'll look up . . .
My fault is past; but O, what form of prayer
Can serve my turn? "Forgive me my foul murder"?
That cannot be, since I am still possessed
Of those effects for which I did the murder; . . .
May one be pardoned and retain the offence? . . .
      What then? what rests?
Try what repentance can—what can it not?
Yet what can it, when one can not repent?
O wretched state!

WILLIAM SHAKESPEARE

Remorse is as the heart in which it grows:
If that be gentle, it drops balmy dews
Of true repentance; but if proud and gloomy
It is the poison tree that, pierced to the inmost
Weeps only tears of poison.

SAMUEL TAYLOR COLERIDGE

"Would a man 'scape the rod?"
      Rabbi ben Karshook saith,
"See that he turn to God
      The day before his death."

"Ay, could a man inquire
      When it shall come!" I say.
The Rabbi's eye shoots fire—
      "Then let him turn today!"

ROBERT BROWNING

Drop, drop slow tears
And bathe those beauteous feet
Which brought from heaven
The news and Prince of peace.
Cease not, wet eyes,
His mercies to entreat;
To cry for vengeance
Sin doth never cease.
In your deep floods

Drown all my faults and fears,
Nor let His eye
See sin, but through my tears.

PHINEHAS FLETCHER

RESPONSIBILITY

"What do you people mean by quoting this proverb . . .

"'The fathers eat sour grapes,
and the children's teeth are set on edge"?

. . . For every living soul belongs to me. . . . The soul who sins is the one who will die.

EZEKIEL 18:2, 4, NIV

"From everyone who has been given much, much will be demanded" (JESUS: LUKE 12:48, NIV); Who are you, to judge someone else's servant? To his own master he stands or falls (PAUL: ROMANS 14:4, NIV).

We make guilty of our disasters the sun, the moon, and the stars, as if we were villains by necessity, fools by heavenly compulsion, knaves, thieves, by spherical predominance, drunkards, liars and adulterers by an enforced obedience of planetary influence . . .

The fault, dear Brutus, is not in our stars,
But in ourselves, that we are underlings.

WILLIAM SHAKESPEARE

Charity rightly seeks extenuating excuses for wrongdoers who "never had a chance," whose background, circumstances, environment, and weak nature were all against them from the start: but charity over-reaches herself and becomes sentimental, unkind, even contemptuous, when she denies to any soul its personal dignity, free choice, and human responsibility.

ANONYMOUS

"Am I my brother's keeper?"

CAIN: GENESIS 4:9

REST

Come to me, all who labor and are heavy laden, and *I will give* you rest. Take my yoke upon you, and learn from me . . . and *you will find* rest for your souls.

> JESUS: MATTHEW 11:28–29
> (emphasis added)

Thou hast created us for Thyself, and our heart knows no rest until it repose in Thee.

> AUGUSTINE

We are not at rest, because we will seek it in things so little there is no rest in them; God the all mighty, all wise, all good—He is true rest.

> JULIAN OF NORWICH

> There is a point of rest
> At the great centre of the cyclone's force,
>   A silence at its secret source—
> A little child might slumber undistressed,
>   Without the ruffle of one fairy curl
> In that strange central calm amid the mighty whirl.
>
> So in the centre of these thoughts of God,
> Cyclones of power, consuming glory-fire,
> There, there we find a point of perfect rest
>   And glorious safety. There we see
>   His thoughts to usward, thoughts of peace
> That stoop to tenderest love; that still increase
> With increase of our need; that never change,
> That never fail, or falter, or forget . . .
>   "For I am poor and needy, yet
> The Lord Himself, Jehovah, thinketh on me."

> FRANCES RIDLEY HAVERGAL

Go where thou wilt, rest is not to be found but in humble submission to the divine will.

> THOMAS À KEMPIS

REVIVAL

They were all filled with the Holy Spirit and spoke the word of God with boldness . . . And with great power the apostles gave their testimony to the resurrection of the Lord Jesus, and great grace was upon them all.

ACTS 4:31, 33

While it was yet twilight a figure appeared . . . dark against the fading darkness. For it was the end of a long stern night, a night of vigil, not unvisited by stars. Francis stood with his hands lifted, . . . about him was a burst of birds singing, and behind him was the break of day.

G. K. CHESTERTON ON FRANCIS OF ASSISI

Awake, O Lord, as in the time of old!
　　Come down, O Spirit, in Thy power and might!
For lack of Thee our hearts are strangely cold,
　　Our minds but blindly grope toward the light.

Make us to be what we profess to be:
　　Let prayer be prayer, and praise be heartfelt praise;
From unreality O set us free
　　And let our words be echoed by our ways.

HENRY TWELLS

Revive Thy work, O Lord,
　　Disturb this sleep of death;
Quicken the smouldering embers now
　　By Thine almighty breath.

Revive Thy work, O Lord,
　　Create soul-thirst for Thee;
And hungry for the bread of life
　　O may our spirits be.

ALBERT MIDLANE

Look at the great historic advances of the Spirit! The Reformation was not a formal repeat of Pentecost. The Wesley revival was not an outward duplicate of the Reformation. And the revival associated with Sankey and Moody had, in method, no great historic precedent. The Spirit can always be as original as the circumstances demand. Thus it is a serious mistake to try to standardise the methods of the Spirit.

T. G. DUNNING

REWARD

Henceforth there is laid up for me the crown of righteousness, which the Lord, the righteous judge, will award to me on that Day; and not only to me but also to all who have loved his appearing.

PAUL: 2 TIMOTHY 4:8

Jesus retained the idea of moral reward, but denied any human claim upon God, any assertion of individual merit. God is no man's debtor, and in any case, the first shall be last, the last first. The prospect of reward is thus not the main Christian motive for godliness: attempts to bribe or frighten the irreligious fail because one has to be religious to believe in them. Nevertheless, men do look for some worthwhile outcome, for themselves, for others, and for God, from their struggles, self-discipline, and sacrifice.

X

The reward of one duty is the power to fulfil another (GEORGE ELIOT); The reward of a thing rightly done is to have done it (SENECA); Not in reward, but in the strength to strive, the blessing lies (J. T. TROWBRIDGE).

> No gate of pearl, no branch of palm I merit,
>   Nor street of shining gold—
>
> Suffice it if—my good and ill unreckoned,
>   And both forgiven through thy abounding grace—
> I find myself by hands familiar beckoned
>   Unto my fitting place.
>
> Some humble door among Thy many mansions,
>   Some sheltering shade, where sin and striving cease,
> And flows for ever through heaven's green expansions
>   The river of Thy peace.

JOHN GREENLEAF WHITTIER

When all is said, we cannot, in a world that is ruled by purpose and links an effect with every cause, escape from the concept of reward. Action by which nothing is gained is futile.

E. F. SCOTT

O happy servant he,
    In such a posture found!
He shall his Lord with rapture see,
    And be with honour crowned.

Christ shall the banquet spread
    With His own royal hand,
And raise that favoured servant's head
    Amidst the angelic band.

                    PHILIP DODDRIDGE

RIGHT

Let no one deceive you. He who does right is righteous, as [Christ] is
righteous.

                    JOHN: 1 JOHN 3:7

No one can have a true idea of right until he does it; any genuine
reverence for it until he has done it often and with cost; any peace
ineffable in it till he does it always and with alacrity.

                    JAMES MARTINEAU

Be sure you are right, then go ahead (DAVID CROCKETT); He will hew to
the line of right, let the chips fall where they will (R. CONKLING ON ULYSSES
S. GRANT); Because right is right, to follow right were wisdom, in the scorn
of consequence (ALFRED TENNYSON); Do what thou oughtest, come what
come can (GEORGE HERBERT); They are slaves who dare not be in the right
with two or three (JAMES RUSSELL LOWELL).

    I trust in God—the right shall be the right
    And other than the wrong, while He endures.

                    ROBERT BROWNING

    Wrong ever builds on quicksands, but the Right
    To the firm centre lays its moveless base.

                    JAMES RUSSELL LOWELL

SAINT

To the church of God which is at Corinth . . . called to be saints . . .

PAUL: 1 CORINTHIANS 1:2

The transition from the good man to the saint is a sort of revolution; by which one for whom all things illustrate and illuminate God becomes one for whom God illustrates and illuminates all things.

G. K. CHESTERTON

I have known in my life five saints . . . All found the supernatural world so natural that it did not occur to them to talk about it much.

EVELYN UNDERHILL

Saints are not made for haloes, or for inward thrills: they are made to become focus points of light and power . . . a good mother, a good neighbour, a good constructive force in society, a fragrance and a blessing.

RUFUS M. JONES

Not all the saints are canonised (F. C. GILL); The great saints in their eagle strength . . . (THÉRÈSE OF LISIEUX); We want saints who, by abandoning rank and wealth, and by living humble, loving lives, will hold up to derision our false gods (DONALD HANKEY); Saint: a dead sinner revised and edited (AMBROSE BIERCE); It is easier to make a saint out of a libertine than out of a prig (GEORGE SANTAYANA); He hath a daily beauty in his life that makes me ugly (WILLIAM SHAKESPEARE).

He was penniless, he was parentless, he was to all appearances without a trade or a plan or a hope in the world; and as he went under the frosty trees, he burst suddenly into song.

G. K CHESTERTON ON FRANCIS OF ASSISI

God's saints are shining lights . . .
They are indeed our pillar-fires
    Seen as we go;
They are that city's shining spires
    We travel to.
    A swordlike gleam
    Kept man, for sin,
    First out; this beam
    Will guide him in.

HENRY VAUGHAN

Through such souls alone
God stooping shows sufficient of His light
For us i' the dark to rise by . . .

ROBERT BROWNING

Those . . . canonised as saints must have revealed four essential traits: they must have been loyal to the faith; they must have been heroic when tests came to them; they must have shown the power to do what seemed impossible; they must have been radiant in the midst of the strain and stress of life.

FRIEDRICH VON HÜGEL

The dear Lord's best interpreters
    Are humble human souls;
The Gospel of a life like theirs
    Is more than books or scrolls.
From scheme and creed the light goes out;
    The saintly fact survives;
The blessed Master none can doubt
    Revealed in holy lives.

ANONYMOUS

Christians showed themselves at that time to all the heathen in the most brilliant light; for the Christians were the only people who, in the midst of so much and so great tribulation, proved by deeds their sympathy and love of their kind.

EUSEBIUS, THIRD AND FOURTH CENTURIES

All the great mystics have been energetic and influential, and their business capacity has been specially noted in a curiously large number of cases. Plotinus was often in request as guardian and trustee; St. Bernard showed great gifts as an organiser; St. Teresa as an administrator; St. Juan of the Cross displayed the same qualities; John Smith was an excellent bursar of his college; Fénelon ruled his diocese extremely well; and Madame Guyon surprised by her great aptitude for affairs; Henry More was offered posts of high responsibility.

WILLIAM R. INGE

[My work brings me] into fellowship with men and women so great in spiritual stature that I must almost stand on tiptoe, as it were, to reach their insights and their dreams.

REUBEN NELSON

> Give thanks, O heart, for the high souls
> That point us to the deathless goals . . .
> The company of souls supreme,
> The conscripts of the Mighty Dream . . .
> Brave souls, that took the perilous trail
> And felt the vision could not fail.

EDWIN MARKHAM

[Of youthful enthusiasts]: Some who thus take fire burn to the day of their death, and set light to many others, leaving a trail of radiance to generations to come.

ELLIS PETERS

SALVATION

"Men, what must I do to be saved?" . . . "Believe in the Lord Jesus, and you will be saved."

ACTS 16:30–31

> There is no expeditious road
> To pack and label men for God,
> And save them by the barrel-load.
> Some may perchance, with strange surprise,
> Have blundered into Paradise . . .

They fondly thought to err from God . . .
Lo! they were standing by His side!

FRANCIS THOMPSON

The central concern of religion is salvation . . . wholeness, deliverance from all that injures, mutilates or hinders the growth of personality. It means fulness of life, well-being, strength of character, power of purpose, richness, blessedness, happiness, righteousness, and all else that makes for the enhancement of life in peace and joy. In every respect, salvation is a *positive* experience.

ANONYMOUS

A chastened piety is not the Christian faith . . . Our only hope is to be rooted in repentance, grounded in forgiveness, established in redemption, and quickened in a real regeneration.

P. T. FORSYTH

In true contrition and humiliation, the hope of pardon hath its birth; there the troubled conscience is set at rest; the grace that was lost is found again; man is delivered from the wrath to come; and God and the penitent soul meet together with a holy kiss . . . A broken and a contrite heart the Lord never did or ever will despise.

THOMAS À KEMPIS

It is accomplished!—sacrifice complete,
Redemption purchased, and my sin forgiven;
Peace is assured, and a communion sweet,
Power to work and live, and after, hope of heaven.
Yet much remains, to rid my soul of sin,
For still I stumble, oft I miss His way:
His work *for* me is finished; that *within*
He labours still to perfect, till that Day.

ANONYMOUS

How much more wonderful the work of redemption is, in comparison with creation. It is more marvellous that God was made man than that He created the angels; that He wailed in a stable than that He reigns in the heavens. The creation of the world was a work of power, but the redemption of the world was a work of mercy.

ERASMUS

"He saves the sheep, the goats He doth not save!"
So spake the fierce Tertullian. But she sighed,
The infant church! Of love she felt the tide
Stream on her from her Lord's yet recent grave.
And then she smiled; and in the Catacombs,
With eye suffused, but heart inspirèd true,
On those walls subterranean, where she hid
Her head midst ignominy, death and tombs,
She her Good Shepherd's hasty image drew—
And on His shoulders, not a lamb, a kid.

MATTHEW ARNOLD

The apostolic experience of salvation, so rich and manysided, required a whole series of metaphors to express what Christians felt and thought. What Christ had done for sinful men was,

in priestly terms, to offer an atoning sacrifice on their behalf;

in commercial terms, to cancel ("forgive") their indebtedness to God by offering his own perfect obedience in their name;

in terms of the slave-market, to purchase ("redeem") the enslaved into freedom, at the cost of his own life;

in military terms, to break the force of evil, and lead His own in triumph;

in domestic terms, to act the (suffering) servant, washing their feet from defilement, ministering to every need;

in medical terms, to cure the various afflictions (possession, blindness, deafness, dumbness, paralysis) which sin caused;

in legal terms, as their advocate to plead for acquittal before God's throne ("justification"), despite their unquestioned guilt;

in family terms, to restore the unity of the scattered children of God, bringing his banished home again;

in political terms, through his own mediation and death to make peace ("reconciliation") between God and man, and man and man;

in terms of revelation, to manifest to men the inner nature of God as unexhausted love, despite man's ill-deserving;

in terms of life, to mediate to men a dynamic life that begins in new birth and "ends" in immortality.

In all these ways, Christ's presence in history, his life and passion, embodied God's own initiative to save. The descriptive language is unavoidably human, the analogies imperfect; the work itself was and is unarguably divine.

ANONYMOUS

A man may be damned for despairing to be saved.

JEREMY TAYLOR

By the expulsive power of a great passion for Christ, by the subduing power of an unpayable debt to Christ, by the illuminating power of a faith centred upon Christ, by the kindling power of the Christ-ideal, harmony is re-established in believing hearts, and life finds its focus, its foundation, its framework, and its final goal. Personality becomes integrated, the heart united, and Jesus can say to us, too, "Thy faith hath made thee *whole.*"

AFTER ROBERT MENZIES

SEASONS OF THE SOUL

[Elijah] went a day's journey into the wilderness, and came and sat down under a broom tree; and he asked that he might die, saying, . . . "I am no better than my fathers."

1 KINGS 19:4

Ask the saintliest men and women, and they will tell you how, in every life, there are weary flats to tread, with the heavens out of sight, no sun, no moon, and not a tint of light upon the path below; when the only guidance is the faith of brighter hours.

JAMES MARTINEAU

He had, I think, a Slough of Despond in his mind.

JOHN BUNYAN—
MR. GREATHEART, OF MR. FEARING

> Abide in me; there have been moments blest
>   When I have heard Thy voice and felt Thy power;
> Then evil lost its grasp, and passion, hushed,
>   Owned the divine enchantment of the hour.
>
> These were but seasons, beautiful and rare:
>   Abide in me, and they shall ever be;

Fulfil at once Thy precept and my prayer—
Come and abide in me, and I in Thee.

HARRIET BEECHER STOWE

We cannot kindle when we will
The fire that in the heart resides;
The spirit gloweth, and is still,
In mystery our soul abides:
But tasks in hours of insight will'd
Can be through hours of gloom fulfilled.

MATTHEW ARNOLD

The tide turns at low water as well as at high.

H. HAVELOCK ELLIS

Do you want to grow in virtue, to serve God, to love Christ? Well, you will grow, and attain to these things if you will make them a slow and sure, plodding, mountain ascent; if you are willing to have to camp for weeks or months in spiritual desolation, darkness, and emptiness at different stages in your march and growth. All demand for constant light, all attempt at eliminating the cross and trial, is so much soft folly and puerile trifling.

FRIEDRICH VON HÜGEL

Vicissitude of day and night in the spiritual life is neither new nor unexpected to those that are acquainted with the ways of God; for the ancient prophets and most eminent saints have all experienced an alternation of visitation and desertion . . . If this interchange of light and darkness, joy and sorrow, was the common state of the greater saints, surely such poor and infirm creatures as we ought not to despair, when we are sometimes elevated by fervour and sometimes depressed by coldness.

THOMAS À KEMPIS

In such times of darkness there is one crucial point—to form no conclusions, to take no decisions, to change nothing during such crises.

FRIEDRICH VON HÜGEL

"The Lord will happiness divine
On contrite hearts bestow":

Then tell me, gracious Lord, is mine
    A contrite heart, or no?

I sometimes think myself inclined
    To love Thee if I could;
But often feel another mind,
    Averse to all that's good.

Thy saints are comforted, I know,
    And love Thy house of prayer;
I therefore go where others go
    But find no comfort there.

Oh, make this heart rejoice, or ache;
    Decide this doubt for me;
And if it be *not* broken, break,
    And heal it, if it be.

WILLIAM COWPER

Ah, with what freedom could I once have prayed,
And, drenched in tears, my supplications made . . .
    But now of late methinks I feel
    Myself transforming into steel . . .
Ah, with what ardour could I once have heard,
How hath this heart of mine been sweetly stirred . . .
    But now, alas, those days are done,
    There is more life in stocks or stone . . .
Ah, when the beams of light on me did shine,
How did I gaze on heaven and think it mine . . .
    But ah! how those white hours are fled
    That earth then spurned now fills my head . . .

O thence dispatch a word, speak till I hear:
"Henceforth be this your posture: *as you were!*"

NATHANIEL WANLEY

The clouds may veil the sun, and tears my eyes,
Still reigns my Lord beyond those curtained skies.

UNKNOWN

Not always fall of leaf, nor ever Spring,
    No endless night, yet not eternal day;
The saddest birds a reason find to sing,
    The roughest storm a calm may soon allay.

Thus with succeeding turns God tempereth all,
That man may hope to rise, yet fear to fall.

ROBERT SOUTHWELL

When you have received the spirit of ardour, it is a good plan to think
what it will be like when the light goes away; and when that happens, to
remind yourself that the light can return . . . It often does you more good
to be tested like this than to have things always going the way you want
them to.

THOMAS À KEMPIS

When at Thy word the tempests form,
    When at Thy breath the mists o'ershroud,
Provide Thy still voice for the storm,
    Provide Thy rainbow for the cloud.

I may not bid the shadows flee—
    They are the shadows of Thy wing;
Give but the eye more power to see
    The love behind their gathering.

GEORGE MATHESON

O soul, canst thou not understand
Thou art not left alone,
As a dog to howl and moan
His master's absence? Thou art as a book
Left in a room that He forsook,
But returns to by and by,
A book of His dear choice—
    That quiet waiteth for His hand,
    That quiet waiteth for His eye,
    That quiet waiteth for His voice.

MICHAEL FIELD

If I stoop
Into a dark tremendous sea of cloud,
It is but for a time; I press God's lamp
Close to my breast; its splendour, soon or late,
Will pierce the gloom: I shall emerge one day.

ROBERT BROWNING

Sometimes a light surprises
The Christian while he sings;
It is the Lord who rises
With healing in His wings:
When comforts are declining
He grants the soul again
A season of clear shining
To cheer it after rain.

WILLIAM COWPER

Prudence: Can you remember by what means you find your annoyances, at times, as if they were vanquished?
Christian: Yes, when I think what I saw at the cross, that will do it; and when I look upon my broidered coat, that will do it; also when I look into the roll that I carry in my bosom, that will do it; and when my thoughts wax warm about whither I am going, that will do it.

JOHN BUNYAN

Birds sing on a bare bough:
O believer, canst not thou?

CHARLES H. SPURGEON

As torrents in summer, half dried in their channels,
Suddenly rise, though the sky is still cloudless,
For rain has been falling far off at their fountains;
So hearts that are fainting grow full to o'erflowing,
And they that behold it marvel, and know not
That God at their fountains far off has been raining.

HENRY WADSWORTH LONGFELLOW

All occasions invite His mercies, and all times are His seasons.

GEORGE HERBERT

SELF

Take heed to yourself (PAUL: 1 TIMOTHY 4:16); "You shall love . . . your neighbour *as yourself*" (JESUS: LUKE 10:27, EMPHASIS ADDED).

A man may be shrewd and the teacher of many, and yet be unprofitable to himself (SIRACH 37:19); Few are fit to be entrusted with themselves (THOMAS FULLER).

> Self-reverence, self-knowledge, self-control,
> These three alone lead life to sovereign power.
>> ALFRED TENNYSON

Self-knowledge, self-reverence, self-control are prerequisites of *altruism*, just as a true self-assessment, and even a controlled self-assertion, are inseparable from the carrying of responsibility and the wielding of influence. Self-respect is the beginning of self-discipline; self-contempt is the end of all morality.
>> AFTER JOSEPH BUTLER

Self-control

I count him braver that overcomes his desires than him who conquers his enemies (ARISTOTLE); The same people who can deny others everything are famous for refusing themselves nothing (LEIGH HUNT).

Alone, man holds an inward talk with himself, which it behoves him to regulate well.
>> BLAISE PASCAL

Self-sacrifice which denies common sense is not a virtue; it's a spiritual dissipation (MARGARET DELAND); A living sacrifice . . . (PAUL: ROMANS 12:1); The awful beauty of self-sacrifice (JOHN GREENLEAF WHITTIER).

Self-knowledge

> Know thyself.
>> ATTRIBUTED TO THALES,
>> SIXTH CENTURY B.C.

The kingdom of heaven is within you, and whosoever knoweth himself shall find it.
>> JESUS(?): EXTRA-CANONICAL SAYING

> Just stand aside and watch yourself go by;
> Think of yourself as "he" instead of "I."
>> STRICKLAND GILLILAN

There is a great deal of unmapped country within us.

GEORGE ELIOT

Someone is slighting the Saviour of men:
Lord, is it I?
Someone is spurning His love once again:
Lord, is it I?
Someone is living in selfish delight:
Lord, is it I?
Someone is turning his face from the light:
Lord, is it I?

Someone's betraying his Master today:
Lord, is it I?
Someone is walking a perilous way—
Lord, is it I?

J. R. CLEMENTS

Go to your bosom
Knock there, and ask your heart
What it doth know.

WILLIAM SHAKESPEARE

Show me myself, O holy Lord;
Help me to look within;
I will not turn me from the sight
Of all my sin.

Not mine the life I thought to live
When first I took His name:
Mine but the right to weep and grieve
Over my shame . . .

And if Thy love will not disown
So frail a heart as mine,
Chasten and cleanse it as Thou wilt—
But keep it Thine.

ANONYMOUS, *PLYMOUTH HYMNAL*

Let not soft slumber close your eyes
Before you've recollected thrice
The train of action through the day!

Where did my feet choose out their way?
What have I learned, where'er I've been,
From all I've heard, from all I've seen?
What have I more that's worth the knowing?
What have I done that's worth the doing?
What have I sought that I should shun?
What duty have I left undone,
Or into what new follies run?
These self-enquiries are the road
That lead to virtue and to God.

ISAAC WATTS

Sum up at night what thou hast done by day;
    And in the morning, what thou hast to do.
Dress and undress thy soul; mark the decay
And growth of it; if, with thy watch, that too
Be down, then wind up both; since we shall be
Most surely judged, make thy accounts agree.

GEORGE HERBERT

Self-reverence

Oft times nothing profits more than self-esteem grounded on just and right
(JOHN MILTON); The reverence of a man's self is, next religion, the chiefest
bridle of all vices (FRANCIS BACON); Self-respect is the noblest garment with
which a man may clothe himself (SAMUEL SMILES).

Not on the outer world
For inward joy depend;
Enjoy the luxury of thought,
Make thine own self friend;
Not with the restless throng
In search of solace roam,
But with an independent zeal
Be intimate at home.

LYDIA H. SIGOURNEY

I have to live with myself, and so
I want to be fit for myself to know;
I want to be able as days go by
Always to look myself straight in the eye.

EDGAR A. GUEST

It deserves to be considered whether men are more at liberty, in point of morals, to make themselves miserable without reason than to make others so . . . It should seem that a due concern about our own interest or happiness, and a reasonable endeavour to secure it, is virtue, and the contrary behaviour faulty and blameable.

JOSEPH BUTLER

Self-righteousness

The greatest of faults, I should say, is to be conscious of none.

THOMAS CARLYLE

Be always displeased at what thou art, if thou desire to attain to what thou art not; for where thou hast pleased thyself, there thou abidest.

FRANCIS QUARLES

That poor man is very foolish who, when he knows his garment is soiled, looks on others and reflects on the appearance of their clothes, instead of washing his own.

ST. HILDEGAARD OF BINGEN

SELFISHNESS

He who falls in love with himself will have no rivals (BENJAMIN FRANKLIN); A selfish, private, narrow soul brings little honour to the cause of God (RICHARD BAXTER); Every living creature loves itself (CICERO); The golden calf of self-love (THOMAS CARLYLE); Suicidal selfishness that blights the fairest feelings of the opening heart (PERCY BYSSHE SHELLEY); Nothing in Nature, much less conscious being, was e'er created solely for itself (EDWARD YOUNG).

O doom beyond the saddest guess:
As the long years of God unroll,

To make thy dreary selfishness
The prison of a soul!

JOHN GREENLEAF WHITTIER

Self-love but serves the virtuous mind to wake,
As the small pebble stirs the peaceful lake.
The centre moved, a circle straight succeeds,
Another still, and still another spreads;
Friends, parent, neighbour, first it will embrace;
His country next, and next all human race.

ALEXANDER POPE

The least pain in our little finger gives us more concern and uneasiness than the destruction of millions of our fellow-beings.

WILLIAM HAZLITT

SERVICE

"As you did it to one of the least of these my brethren, you did it to me."

JESUS: MATTHEW 25:40

The noblest service comes from nameless hands (OLIVER WENDELL HOLMES); We should do a service to a friend to bind him closer; to an enemy, to make a friend of him (CLEOBULUS SIXTH CENTURY B.C.); A useless life is an early death (GOETHE); Men are immortal till their work is done (X); The most acceptable service to God is doing good to man (BENJAMIN FRANKLIN).

O brother man! fold to thy heart thy brother;
    Where pity dwells, the peace of God is there;
To worship rightly is to love each other,
    Each smile a hymn, each kindly deed a prayer.

Follow with reverent steps the great example
    Of Him whose holy work was "doing good";
So shall the wide earth seem our Father's temple,
    Each loving life a psalm of gratitude.

JOHN GREENLEAF WHITTIER

We choose to be poor for love of God. In the service of the poorest of the poor, we are feeding the hungry Christ, clothing the naked

Christ, taking care of the sick Christ, and giving shelter to the homeless Christ.

MOTHER TERESA OF CALCUTTA:
MATTHEW 25:35–40

Give me the eye to see
    Each chance to serve.
Then send me strength to rise
    With steady nerve,
And leap at once, with kind and helpful deed,
To the sure succour of a soul in need.

W. J. MATHAMS

I am glad to think
I am not bound to make the world go right,
But only to discover and to do with cheerful heart
    The work that God appoints.

JEAN INGELOW

You find people ready enough to do the Samaritan, without the oil and the twopence.

SYDNEY SMITH

'Tis not enough to help the feeble up.
But to support him after.

WILLIAM SHAKESPEARE

Oh, it is hard to work for God,
    To rise and take His part
Upon this battlefield of earth
    And not, sometimes, lose heart!

He hides Himself so wondrously,
    As though there were no God;
He is least seen when all the powers
    Of ill are most abroad.

Thrice blest is he to whom is given
    The instinct that can tell
That God is on the field when He
    Is most invisible.

FREDERICK W. FABER

The first of the quarrymen, asked what they were doing, replied that they were hewing stone; the second retorted that he was earning five dollars a day; the third said he was helping to build a cathedral.

X

SILENCE

Even a fool, when he holdeth his peace, is counted wise.

PROVERBS 17:28, AV/KJV

He had occasional flashes of silence that made his conversation perfectly delightful (SYDNEY SMITH OF THOMAS MACAULAY); Silence is one great art of conversation (WILLIAM HAZLITT); True silence is the rest of the mind (WILLIAM PENN).

Silence is not an end in itself, but a means to a higher experience (SOCIETY OF FRIENDS *BOOK OF DISCIPLINE*); What most impresses me is the deep *silence* of the Universe, coupled with its unimaginable activity (L. P. JACKS); Silence is the element in which great things fashion themselves (THOMAS CARLYLE); In silence God brings all to pass (MENANDER).

> If for a tranquil mind you seek
>   These things observe with care:
> Of whom you speak, to whom you speak,
>   And how, and when, and where.

UNKNOWN

The word, even the contradictory word, preserves contact: it is silence which isolates.

THOMAS MANN

SIMPLICITY

The testimony of the LORD is sure, making wise the simple.

PSALM 19:7

Blissful are the simple, for they shall have much peace (THOMAS À KEMPIS); Simplicity of character is no hindrance to subtlety of intellect (JOHN MORLEY);

The greatest truths are the simplest, and so are the greatest men (J. C. AND A. W. HARE); Seek simplicity and distrust it (ALFRED NORTH WHITEHEAD).

> After all, God is very simple.
>
> OVERHEARD

SIN

All have sinned and fall short of the glory of God.

> PAUL: ROMANS 3:23

The chains of habit are generally too small to be felt until they are too strong to be broken.

> DWIGHT L. MOODY

Sin is anything in my life which keeps me from God or from other people (A. J. RUSSELL); Sin has many tools, but a lie is the handle that fits them all (OLIVER WENDELL HOLMES); The ever-recurring tendency for man's choices to be wrong (JOHN FOSTER); None are so lost as they who do not know it (X); Sin we have explained away: unluckily the sinners stay (WILLIAM ALLINGHAM); Some sin with safety, none with peace (SENECA); Cain really slew not his brother but himself (PHILO).

We are punished by our sins, not for them.

> ELBERT HUBBARD

> Think, and be careful what thou art within;
> For there is sin in the desire of sin.
> Think, and be thankful, in a different case:
> For there is grace in the desire of grace.
>
> JOHN BYROM

> An evil thought, an evil eye;
> An evil eye, an evil tongue;
> An evil tongue, an evil act;
> One evil act, an evil throng;

Till, from the heart beginning,
     That evil thought
     Hath well-nigh wrought
Necessity of sinning.

          UNKNOWN

We have not to *feel* sorry for our sins but to *be* sorry for them; and the being sorry is a matter not of emotion but of intellect and will.

          CUTHBERT BUTLER

As the distance of the sun, which man cannot reach, was first measured by a shadow cast on the desert sand, so man's true greatness is revealed in part by the magnitude of his failure to attain the good he can conceive, admire, set his heart upon, but not achieve.

          ANONYMOUS

The Slough of Despond: This miry slough is such a place as cannot be mended; it is the descent whither the scum and filth that attends conviction for sin doth continually run . . . Twenty thousand cartloads of wholesome instructions have been brought to repair it, but it remains. True, there are good and substantial steps . . . but men step aside.

          JOHN BUNYAN

Neither custom, nor example, nor vast numbers
Of such as do offend, make less the sin.

          PHILIP MASSINGER

Our outward act is prompted from within
And from the sinner's mind proceeds the sin.

          MATTHEW PRIOR

"He is a sinner" you are pleased to say.
Then love him for the sake of Christ, I pray.
If on His gracious words you place your trust
Second His call; which if you will not do
You'll be the greater sinner of the two.

          JOHN BYROM

SINCERITY

The aim of our charge is love that issues from a pure heart and a good conscience and sincere faith.

PAUL: 1 TIMOTHY 1:5

Be what thou seemest (HORATIUS BONAR); Be not ashamed to say what you are not ashamed to think (MICHEL DE MONTAIGNE); We drank the pure daylight of honest speech (GEORGE MEREDITH).

> Gracious to all, to none subservient,
> Without offence he spake the word he meant.
> THOMAS BAILEY ALDRICH

The sincere alone can recognise sincerity.

THOMAS CARLYLE

SOLITUDE

Jacob was left alone; and a man wrestled with him until the breaking of the day . . . Jacob said, "I will not let you go, unless you bless me."

GENESIS 32:24, 26

It is God's will for us that we should possess an Interior Castle (FRANCIS UNDERHILL); Genius is formed in solitude, character in the stream of human life (GOETHE); Solitude is bearable only with God (ANDRÉ GIDE); . . . is the audience-chamber of God (W. S. LANDOR); . . . is needful for the imagination as society is wholesome for the character (JAMES RUSSELL LOWELL) . . . the best nurse of wisdom (LAURENCE STERNE); . . . the playfield of Satan (VLADIMIR NABOKOV); . . . the mother of anxieties (PUBLILIUS SYRUS); . . . vivifies, isolation kills (JOSEPH ROUX); Woe unto him who is never alone, and cannot bear to be alone (P. G. HAMERTON).

> The noblest deeds in silence are thought out,
> And plans are born while only stars look on.
> MARIANNE FARNINGHAM

Solitude is dangerous to reason, without being favourable to virtue . . . the solitary mortal is probably superstitious, and possibly mad.

SAMUEL JOHNSON

Converse with men makes sharp the glittering wit,
But God to man doth speak in solitude.

J. S. BLACKIE

By all means use sometimes to be alone;
    Salute thyself; see what thy soul doth wear;
Dare to look in thy chest, for 'tis thine own,
    And tumble up and down what thou find'st there.

GEORGE HERBERT

Solitude affects some people like wine: they must not take too much of it,
for it flies to the head.

MARY COLERIDGE

Yes! in the sea of life enisled
With echoing straits between us thrown,
Dotting the shoreless watery wild,
We mortal millions live *alone*.

MATTHEW ARNOLD

SORROW

"Is it nothing to you, all you who pass by?
Look and see
if there is any sorrow like my sorrow.

LAMENTATIONS 1:12

The only cure for grief is action (G. H. LEWES); How easy it is to speak
brave words in another's grief (OVID); There is a solemn luxury in grief
(WILLIAM MASON); 'Tis held that sorrow makes us wise (ALFRED TENNYSON);
There is no wisdom in useless and hopeless sorrow (SAMUEL JOHNSON);
Where there is sorrow there is holy ground (OSCAR WILDE); Earth hath no
sorrow that heaven cannot heal (THOMAS MOORE); Sorrow makes us all
children again (RALPH WALDO EMERSON).

The soul would have no rainbow
Had the eyes no tears.

JOHN V. CHENEY

Joy is a partnership, grief weeps alone;
Many guests had Cana, Gethsemane but one.

FREDERIC L. KNOWLES

O brothers, let us leave the shame and sin
Of taking vainly, in a plaintive mood,
The holy name of Grief!—holy herein,
That by the grief of One came all our good.

ELIZABETH BARRETT BROWNING

I walked a mile with Pleasure,
And ne'er a word said she;
But oh, the things I learned from her
When Sorrow walked with me.

ROBERT BROWNING HAMILTON

Nor indolence, nor pleasure, nor the fret
Of restless passions that would not be stilled,
But sorrow, and a care that almost killed,
Kept me from what I may accomplish yet.

HENRY WADSWORTH LONGFELLOW

Grief drives men into habits of serious reflection, sharpens the
understanding, and softens the heart.

THOMAS JEFFERSON

SOUL

"What good will it be for a man if he gains the whole world, yet forfeits
his soul? Or what can a man give in exchange for his soul?"

JESUS: MATTHEW 16:26, NIV

Whether or not the philosophers care to admit that we have a soul, it
seems obvious that we are equipped with something or other which
generates dreams and ideals and which sets up values.

JOHN ERSKINE

A soul—a spark of never-dying flame that separates man from all the other beings of earth (JAMES FENIMORE COOPER); The one thing in the world of value is the active soul (RALPH WALDO EMERSON); I will hew great windows for my soul (ANGELA MORGAN); Keep a tidy soul (MARK TWAIN); Lack of wealth is easily repaired: poverty of soul is irreparable (MICHEL DE MONTAIGNE).

> Spontaneously to God should tend the soul,
> Like the magnetic needle to the Pole.
>
> THOMAS HOOD

Do you ask where the Supreme Good dwells? In the soul. And unless the soul be pure and holy, there is no room in it for God.

> SENECA

> God gave thy soul brave wings; put not those feathers
> Into a bed, to sleep out all ill weathers.
>
> GEORGE HERBERT

> I played with fire, did counsel spurn . . .
> But never thought that fire would burn,
> Or that a soul could ache.
>
> HENRY VAUGHAN

> The lark soars up in the air;
> The toad sits tight in his hole;
> And I would I were certain which of the pair
> Were the truer type of my soul!
>
> F. ANSTEY

> "Two things," the wise man said, "fill me with awe;
> The starry heavens and the moral law."
> Nay, add another wonder to thy roll:
> The living marvel of the human soul.
>
> HENRY VAN DYKE

> Out of the night that covers me,
> Black as the Pit from pole to pole,
> I thank whatever gods may be
> For my unconquerable soul.
>
> WILLIAM ERNEST HENLEY

Out of the light that dazzles me,
Bright as the sun from pole to pole,
I thank the God I know to be
For Christ, the Conqueror of my soul.

DOROTHEA DAY

STRENGTH

He gives power to the faint,
and to him who has no might he increases strength.
    Even youths shall faint and be weary,
and young men shall fall exhausted;
    but they who wait for the LORD shall renew their strength,
they shall mount up with wings like eagles,
    they shall run and not be weary,
they shall walk and not faint.

ISAIAH 40:29–31

But noble souls, through dust and heat,
Rise from disaster and defeat
The stronger.

HENRY WADSWORTH LONGFELLOW

We acquire the strength we have overcome (RALPH WALDO EMERSON); What
is strength without a double share of wisdom? (JOHN MILTON); As your
days, so shall your strength be (DEUTERONOMY 33:25); "My power is made
perfect in weakness" (2 CORINTHIANS 12:9).

Stand up! stand up for Jesus!
    Stand in His strength alone;
The arm of flesh will fail you,
    Ye dare not trust your own:
Put on the gospel armour,
    Each piece put on with prayer;
Where duty calls, or danger,
    Be never wanting there.

GEORGE DUFFIELD

Soldiers of Christ, arise
And put your armour on,
Strong in the strength which God supplies
Through His eternal Son.

Strong in the Lord of Hosts,
And in His mighty power;
Who in the strength of Jesus trusts
Is more than conqueror.

Stand, then, in His great might,
With all His strength endued;
And take, to arm you for the fight,
The panoply of God.

CHARLES WESLEY

STUDY

The sayings of the wise are like goads . . . My son, beware of anything beyond these. Of making many books there is no end, and much study is a weariness of the flesh.

ECCLESIASTES 12:11–12

To spend too much time in studies is sloth; to use them too much for ornament is affectation; to make judgement wholly by their rules is the humour of a scholar.

FRANCIS BACON

It is the vice of scholars to suppose that there is no knowledge in the world but that of books.

WILLIAM HAZLITT

Timothy was so learned he could name a horse in nine languages, and bought a cow to ride on.

BENJAMIN FRANKLIN

When nature exceeds culture, we have the rustic; when culture exceeds nature, we have the pedant (CONFUCIUS); Some despise study because they think they know everything; some, because they think they know enough; some because they do not want their cherished thoughts disturbed by information, contradiction, or enlightenment; most, because they do not wish to think (ANONYMOUS).

Grant me, I beseech Thee, O merciful God, prudently to study, rightly to understand, and perfectly to fulfil that which is pleasing to Thee, to the praise and glory of Thy name.

THOMAS AQUINAS, "ANGELIC DOCTOR"

SUFFERING

You have all heard how Job stood firm, and you have seen how the Lord treated him in the end. For the Lord is full of pity and compassion.

JAMES: JAMES 5:11, NEB

Without the experience of suffering a man's nature remains shallow. Pain that has been lived through gives to character a depth that seldom comes from the experience of happiness.

ABBÉ HUVELIN

I may not cast Thy cross away,
Thou gavest me Thy yoke to share;
Give but the arm new nerve each day.
Give but the heart fresh love to bear—
Until my thorn become my flower,
Till death itself in life shall rise;
And human sorrow's midnight hour
Ring the first chimes of Paradise.

GEORGE MATHESON

When I am feeble as a child, and flesh and heart give way,
Then on Thy everlasting strength with passive trust I stay,
And the rough wind becomes a song, the darkness shines as day.

ANNA WARING

"There is no God," the foolish saith,
But none "There is no sorrow";
And nature oft the cry of faith
In bitter need will borrow:
Eyes, which the preacher could not school
By wayside graves are raisèd;
And lips say, "God be pitiful,"
Who ne'er said "God be praisèd."

ELIZABETH BARRETT BROWNING

A great illness has often made a great soul, and even a great singer (X); Although the world is full of suffering, it is full also of the overcoming of it (HELEN KELLER).

Can I see another's woe
And not be in sorrow too?
Can I see another's grief
And not seek for kind relief?

Can a mother sit and hear
An infant groan, an infant fear?
No, no never can it be,
Never, never can it be.

And can He who smiles on all
Hear the wren with sorrows small,
Hear the small bird's grief and care
Hear the woes that infants bear,

And not sit beside the nest
Pouring pity in their breast,
And not sit the cradle near
Weeping tear on infant's tear? . . .

Think not thou canst sigh a sigh
And thy Maker is not by;
Think not thou canst weep a tear
And thy Maker is not near.

O! He gives to us His joy
That our grief He may destroy;
Till our grief is fled and gone
He doth sit by us and moan.

WILLIAM BLAKE

SUICIDE

Throwing down the pieces of silver in the temple, [Judas] departed; and he went and hanged himself.

MATTHEW 27:5

The man who kills himself kills all men; so far as he is concerned he wipes out the world . . . There is not a tiny creature in the cosmos at whom his death is not a sneer. When a man hangs himself on a tree, the leaves might fall off in anger and the birds fly away in fury: for each has received a personal affront.

G. K. CHESTERTON

> . . . the dread of something after death,
> The undiscovered country from whose bourn
> No traveller returns, puzzles the will
> And makes us rather bear those ills we have
> Than fly to others that we know not of . . .
> WILLIAM SHAKESPEARE

The question is, whether suicide is the way out or the way in.

RALPH WALDO EMERSON

> Whatever crazy sorrow saith,
> No life that breathes with human breath
> Has ever truly longed for death.
> ALFRED TENNYSON

SUNDAY

"The sabbath was made for man, not man for the sabbath; so the Son of man is lord even of the sabbath."

MARK 2:27–28

If Israel only kept one Sabbath according to the Commandment, Messiah would immediately come.

TALMUD

The rules concerning the sabbath are like mountains which hang upon a hair, for there is little scripture to support them.

RABBINIC COMMENT

The beneficent law of rest, so full of sympathy with struggling people, was translated into a series of regulations of peddling detail and incredible childishness.

JOHN WATSON

Sunday—the poor man's day (JAMES GRAHAME); . . . a day of mirth (GEORGE HERBERT); . . . Day of the Lord, as all our days should be (HENRY WADSWORTH LONGFELLOW).

> On thee, at the creation,
> The light first had its birth;
> On thee, for our salvation,
> Christ rose from depths of earth;
> On thee, our Lord victorious
> The Spirit sent from heaven:
> And thus on thee most glorious
> A triple light was given.

CHRISTOPHER WORDSWORTH

> Bright shadows of true rest! some shoots of bliss;
> Heaven once a week;
> The next world's gladness prepossessed in this;
> A day to seek
> Eternity in time; the steps by which
> We climb above all ages; lamps that light
> Man through his heap of days: and the rich
> And full redemption of the whole week's flight.

HENRY VAUGHAN

> We thank Thee that Thy church unsleeping,
> While earth rolls onward into light,
> Through all the world her watch is keeping,
> And rests not now by day or night.

As o'er each continent and island
The dawn leads on another day,
The voice of prayer is never silent,
Nor dies the strain of praise away.

JOHN ELLERTON

SUPERSTITION

[Hezekiah] suppressed the hill-shrines, smashed the sacred pillars, cut down every sacred pole and broke up the bronze serpent that Moses had made; for up to that time the Israelites had been burning sacrifices to it; they called it Nehushtan.

2 KINGS 18:4, NEB

Yet, if he would, man cannot live all to this world. If not religious, he will be superstitious.

THEODORE PARKER

In all superstition wise men follow fools (FRANCIS BACON); All people have their blind side, their superstitions (CHARLES LAMB); A superstitious soul hath no rest (ROBERT BURTON); Superstition is the religion of feeble minds (EDMUND BURKE); . . . the only religion of which base souls are capable (JOSEPH JOUBERT); . . . groundless religion (JOSEPH HALL).

Ignorance and superstition ever bear a close, even a mathematical relation to each other.

JAMES FENIMORE COOPER

TEMPTATION

No temptation has overtaken you that is not common to man. God is faithful, and he will not let you be tempted beyond your strength, but with the temptation will also provide the way of escape, that you may be able to endure it.

PAUL: 1 CORINTHIANS 10:13

One man has by nature stronger propensities to this sin, another to that: but temptation to sin is not sin—it serves rather for the exercise of virtue in him who victoriously sustains the contest.

PIERRE ABÉLARD

> Why comes temptation but for man to meet
> And master and make crouch beneath his foot,
> And so be pedestaled in triumph?

ROBERT BROWNING

There is no temptation for which Christ did not furnish a remedy (ERASMUS); What boots it at one gate to make defence, and at another to let in the foe? (JOHN MILTON); What's done we partly may compute, but know not what's resisted (ROBERT BURNS).

> Who will not judge him worthy to be robbed
> That sets his doors wide open to a thief,
> And shows the felon where his treasure lies?

BEN JONSON

> How much, preventing God, how much I owe
> To the defences Thou hast round me set;
> Example, custom, fear, occasion slow—
> These scornèd bondmen were my parapet.
> I dare not peep over this parapet

To gauge with glance the roaring gulf below,
The depths of sin to which I had descended,
Had not these me against myself defended.

RALPH WALDO EMERSON

THOUGHT

We destroy arguments and every proud obstacle to the knowledge of God, and take every thought captive to obey Christ.

PAUL: 2 CORINTHIANS 10:5

Half of our mistakes in life arise from feeling where we ought to think and thinking where we ought to feel.

JOHN CHURTON COLLINS

Beware when the great God lets loose a thinker on this planet (RALPH WALDO EMERSON); Nay, in every epoch of the world, the great event, parent of all others—is it not the arrival of a thinker in the world? (THOMAS CARLYLE); I think, therefore I am (RENÉ DESCARTES); Every thought which genius and piety throw into the world alters the world (RALPH WALDO EMERSON).

The highest possible stage in moral culture is when we recognise that we ought to control our thoughts (CHARLES DARWIN); He that will not control his thoughts will soon lose control of his actions (THOMAS WILSON).

There is no expedient to which a man will not go to avoid the real labour of thinking (THOMAS A. EDISON); He thinks too much—such men are dangerous (WILLIAM SHAKESPEARE); Nothing is too sacred to be thought about (ERNEST H. CROSBY); One can resist the invasion of armies, but not of ideas (VICTOR HUGO); Thought hath good legs (ENGLISH PROVERB); Thoughts rule the world (RALPH WALDO EMERSON); There is nothing either good or bad but thinking makes it so (WILLIAM SHAKESPEARE).

The extra calories needed for one hour of intense mental effort would be completely met by the eating of one oyster cracker, or one half of a salted peanut.

FRANCIS G. BENEDICT

We think so because other people all think so,
Or because—or because—after all, we do think so,
Or because we were told so, and think we must think so,
Or because we once thought so, and think we still think so,
Or because having thought so, we think we *will* think so.

HENRY SIDGWICK

TIME

Do not ignore this one fact, beloved, that with the Lord one day is as a thousand years, and a thousand years as one day.

2 PETER 3:8

The divine moment is the present moment (CATHERINE OF GENOA); *Now* is the watchword of the wise (CHARLES H. SPURGEON).

Time—that which man is always trying to kill, but which ends in killing him (HERBERT SPENCER); As if you could kill time without injuring eternity (HENRY DAVID THOREAU); Time is a parenthesis in eternity (ANONYMOUS); . . . eternity begun (JAMES MONTGOMERY); Devouring time (WILLIAM SHAKESPEARE).

To things immortal, Time can do no wrong,
And that which never is to die forever must be young.

ABRAHAM COWLEY

Truth is the daughter of time (ENGLISH PROVERB); Counsel to which time hath not been called, time will not ratify (FRANCIS BACON); Time brings everything to light (THALES); Time trieth truth (ENGLISH PROVERB); Time's glory is . . . to unmask falsehood and bring truth to light (WILLIAM SHAKESPEARE).

Time is the inexplicable raw material of everything (ARNOLD BENNETT); . . . the grand instructor (EDMUND BURKE); . . . a noiseless file (GEORGE HERBERT); . . . teacher of all things (AESCHYLUS); . . . a taming hand (JOHN HENRY NEWMAN); . . . the wisest counsellor of all (OVID); . . . the great physician (BENJAMIN DISRAELI); Time ripens all things—no man is born wise (MIGUEL DE CERVANTES).

He said, "What's time? leave Now for dogs and apes!
Man has forever."

ROBERT BROWNING

I dimly guess what Time in mists confounds;
Yet ever and anon a trumpet sounds
From the hid battlements of eternity;
Those shaken mists a space unsettle, then
    Round the half-glimpsed turrets wash again.

FRANCIS THOMPSON

It were good that men in their innovations would follow the example of
time itself, which indeed innovateth greatly, but quietly, and by degrees
scarce to be perceived.

FRANCIS BACON

"God," said Man, "God, is it true
A hundred thousand million years for you
Is like nothing in the way our time is reckoned?"
"True," said God.
"And God," said Man, "God, is it true
A hundred thousand million dollars, too—
They're like something handy when the waiter's beckoned?"
"True," said God.
"Then, God, slip me a dollar through,
One little dollar can't mean anything to you."
"True," said God,
"Do you mind waiting for a second?"

UNKNOWN

That great mystery, the illimitable, never-resting thing called time, rolling,
rushing on, swift, silent, this is forever very literally a miracle, a thing to
strike us dumb; for we have no word to speak about it.

THOMAS CARLYLE

But at my back I always hear
Time's wingèd chariot hurrying near.

ANDREW MARVELL

I saw Eternity the other night,
  Like a great ring of pure and endless light,
    All calm, as it was bright;

And round beneath it, Time in hours, days, years,
    Driven by the spheres
Like a vast shadow moved; in which the world
    And all her train were hurled.

HENRY VAUGHAN

What reason and endeavour
Cannot bring about, often time will.

THOMAS FULLER

Dost thou love life? Then do not squander time, for that's the stuff life's made of.

BENJAMIN FRANKLIN

For everything there is a season, and a time for every matter under heaven: a time to be born, and to die; to plant, and to pluck up; to kill, and to heal; to break down, and to build up; to weep, and to laugh; to mourn, and to dance; to cast away stones, and to gather stones together; to embrace, and to refrain; to seek, and to lose; to keep, and to cast away; to rend, and to sew; to keep silence, and to speak; to love, and to hate; a time for war, and a time for peace.

ECCLESIASTES 3:1–8, CONDENSED

Build a little fence of trust
    Around today;
Fill the space with loving work,
    And therein stay.
Look not through the sheltering bars
    Upon tomorrow;
God will help thee bear what comes
    Of joy or sorrow.

MARY F. BUTTS

TOLERANCE

Let not him who eats despise him who abstains, and let not him who abstains pass judgement on him who eats; for God has welcomed him.

PAUL: ROMANS 14:3

Though all the winds of doctrine were let loose to play upon the earth, so Truth be in the field . . . let her and falsehood grapple: who ever knew Truth put to the worse in a free and open encounter? (JOHN MILTON); Error of opinion may be tolerated where reason is left free to combat it (THOMAS JEFFERSON).

I have found in a long trial of such matters that there be some truth on all sides. I have found gospel holiness where you would little think it to be, and so likewise truth. And I have learned this principle . . . to acknowledge every truth and every goodness wherever I find it.

THOMAS GOODWIN

Whom the heart of man shuts out, sometimes the heart of God takes in (JAMES RUSSELL LOWELL); I have seen gross intolerance shown in support of toleration (SAMUEL TAYLOR COLERIDGE); The highest result of education is tolerance (HELEN KELLER); If we cannot end our differences, at least we can make the world safe for diversity (JOHN F. KENNEDY).

If all mankind minus one were of one opinion . . . mankind would be no more justified in silencing the one person than he, if he had the power, would be justified in silencing mankind.

JOHN STUART MILL

And when religious sects are mad,
   He held, in spite of all his learning,
That if a man's belief is bad
   It will not be improved by burning.

WINTHROP MACKWORTH PRAED

Where there is much desire to learn, there of necessity will be much arguing, much writing, many opinions; for opinion in good men is but knowledge in the making.

JOHN MILTON

And differing judgements serve but to declare
That truth lies somewhere, if we know but where.

WILLIAM COWPER

There is, however, a limit at which forbearance ceases to be a virtue (EDMUND BURKE); More and more people care about religious tolerance as fewer and fewer care about religion (ALEXANDER CHASE); This Laodicean cant of tolerance (MARY AUGUSTA WARD).

> I tried to save my brother's soul
> Believing I knew truth alone;
> But in my blind intolerance
> I lost my own.

NORMAN E. LAMBLY

Saith the evil, Let us lie in wait for the righteous man, because . . . he is clean contrary to our doings: he . . . objecteth to our infamy. He professeth to have the knowledge of God and he calleth himself the child of the Lord. He was made to reprove our thoughts. He is grievous unto us even to behold: for his life is not like other mens', his ways are of another fashion.

WISDOM OF SOLOMON 2:12–14 AV/KJV

TRADITION

So then, brethren, stand firm and hold to the traditions which you were taught by us, either by word of mouth or by letter.

PAUL: 2 THESSALONIANS 2:15

We know now that the apostolic *paradosis* (tradition) of practice, like the apostolic *paradosis* of doctrine, is something which actually ante-dates the writing of the New Testament documents themselves by some two or three decades (GREGORY DIX); Scripture is the tradition as committed to writing by the apostles or those closely associated with them (STEPHEN WINWARD).

A precedent embalms a principle (BENJAMIN DISRAELI); Continuity does not rule out fresh approaches to fresh situations (DEAN RUSK); Remove not the ancient landmark which your fathers have set (PROVERBS 22:28).

A love for tradition has never weakened a nation, indeed it has strengthened nations in their hour of peril. But the new view must come, the world must roll forward.

WINSTON SPENCER CHURCHILL

Protestants have nearly always rejected tradition in principle, while necessarily allowing it to reappear in practice in some other form . . . Preaching is in fact the chief Protestant form of perpetuating tradition, that is, authoritative interpretations and applications of the Word.

J. VAN ENGEN

TRIFLES

"It is precept upon precept, precept upon precept,
    line upon line, line upon line,
    here a little, there a little."

ISAIAH 28:10

He who despises small things will fail little by little.

SIRACH 19:1

Somebody turns our spy glass round . . .
We find great things are made of little things
And little things go lessening, till at last
Comes God behind them. Talk of mountains now?
We talk of mould that heaps the mountains, mites
That throng the mould, and God that makes the mites.

ROBERT BROWNING

Trifles console us, as trifles distress us (BLAISE PASCAL); Beneath the daisy's disk lies hid the pebble for the fatal sling (HELEN JACKSON); No rock so hard but that a little wave may beat admission in a thousand years (ALFRED TENNYSON); The dangerous bar in the harbour's mouth is only grains of sand (MARTIN F. TUPPER); One man's gnat is another man's camel (SAMUEL BUTLER II, HERBERT CLARKE).

One dark cloud can hide the sunlight;
    Loose one string, the pearls are scattered;
Think one thought, a soul may perish;
    Say one word, a heart may break.

ADELAIDE A. PROCTER

Don't make tragedies of trifles,
Don't shoot butterflies with rifles,
Laugh it off.

UNKNOWN

TRUST

Trust in the Lord, and do good;
so you will dwell in the land, and enjoy security.

PSALM 37:3

In One, no object of our sight,
Immutable, and infinite,
Who can't be cruel or unjust,
Calm, and resigned, I fix my trust.

MATTHEW GREEN

Leave God to order all thy ways,
And hope in Him, whate'er betide;
Thou'lt find Him in the evil days
Thine all-sufficient strength and guide:
Who trusts in God's unchanging love
Builds on the rock that naught can move.

GEORG NEUMARK

If you trust before you try you may repent before you die (ENGLISH PROVERB); It is equally an error to trust all men or no man (SENECA); He who mistrusts most should be trusted least (THEOGNIS); Trusting often makes fidelity (THOMAS FULLER).

Better trust all, and be deceived,
And weep that trust and that deceiving,
Than doubt one heart that, if believed,
Had blessed one's life with true believing.

FRANCES A. KEMBLE

I see the wrong that round me lies,
I feel the guilt within;
I hear, with groan and travail-cries,

The world confess its sin.
Yet in the maddening maze of things,
And tossed by storm and flood,
To one fixed trust my spirit clings:
I know that God is good.

JOHN GREENLEAF WHITTIER

Put your trust in God, my boys, and keep your powder dry.

OLIVER CROMWELL

TRUTH

We cannot do anything against the truth, but only for the truth.

PAUL: 2 CORINTHIANS 13:8

Great as is the power of falsehood to captivate and mislead, the convincing power of truth is always, in the end, "greater." This "greater" is the Christian's sheet-anchor of hope when he contemplates the power of falsehood in the world.

ROBERT LAW ON 1 JOHN 4:4

True ideas never die, they only go into hiding (AFTER WILLIAM R. INGE); Resistance to intellectual error is as clear a duty as resistance to wickedness (CHARLES GORE); It is confidence in the power of truth to win through that makes faith resilient (X); Truth, like a torch, the more it's shaken the more it shines (WILLIAM HAMILTON); Truth, by whomsoever it is spoken, is from God (LATIN MOTTO); Truth never hurts the teller (ROBERT BROWNING); If you shut up truth, and bury it underground, it will but grow (ÉMILE ZOLA); "The truth will make you free" (JESUS: JOHN 8:32).

Is truth ever barren? (FRANCIS BACON); I believe that in the end the truth will conquer (JOHN WYCLIFFE); Truth is tough: it will not break (OLIVER WENDELL HOLMES); It is not enough to possess a truth: it is essential that the truth also possess us (MAURICE MAETERLINCK); Truths may clash, without contradicting each other (ANTOINE DE SAINT-EXUPÉRY); Truth hath a quiet breast (WILLIAM SHAKESPEARE); Truth is open to everyone, and claims aren't all staked yet (SENECA); Why with old truth need new truth disagree? (ROBERT BROWNING); Truth is often eclipsed, but never extinguished (LIVY); The truth is always the strongest argument (SOPHOCLES); They must upward still, and onward, who would keep abreast of truth (JAMES RUSSELL LOWELL); At times, truth may not seem probable (NICOLAS BOILEAU); Truth is great, and it prevails (1 ESDRAS 4:41, VULGATE).

> We fight for truth? We fight for God?
> Poor slaves of lies and sin!
> He who would fight for Thee on earth
> Must first be true within.
>
> Then, God of truth, for whom we long,
> Thou who wilt hear our prayer—
> Do Thine own battle in our hearts,
> And slay the falsehood there.
>
> THOMAS HUGHES

> Servant of God, well done! well hast thou fought
> The better fight, who singly hast maintained
> Against revolted multitudes the cause
> Of truth, in word mightier than they in arms.
>
> JOHN MILTON

Man can certainly keep on lying (and does so), but he cannot make truth falsehood.

KARL BARTH, OBITUARY

Truth is one: falsehood has ten thousand bye-paths (CLEMENT OF ALEXANDRIA); Nature admits no lie (THOMAS CARLYLE); A lie faces God and shrinks from man (FRANCIS BACON); Every violation of truth is a stab at the health of human society (RALPH WALDO EMERSON); Repetition does not transform a lie into a truth (FRANKLIN DELANO ROOSEVELT); The cruellest lies are often told in silence (ROBERT LOUIS STEVENSON); Truth is: lies are invented (GEORGES BRAQUE); One falsehood treads on the heels of another (TERENCE); A lie travels round the world while truth is putting on her boots (CHARLES H. SPURGEON); The first of all the gospels is, that no lie lives for ever (THOMAS CARLYLE).

A wise incredulity is not superfluous at any time. The tendency to yield a facile homage to whatever is characterised by violent emotions . . . to regard anything extraordinary and sensational as possessing the credentials of truth, has borne much evil fruit in the religious world. Enthusiasm is no guarantee of truth!

ROBERT LAW

Truth is too simple for us: we do not like those who unmask our illusions.

RALPH WALDO EMERSON

It is a necessity of the human mind to theorise about truth; it is a calamity to substitute theories for truth.

JOHN WATSON

The world is a very mixed place, we say. In every man, in every current opinion, good and evil, truth and falsehood, are mingled. We will make the best of every tendency, and hope that nothing is really bad or utterly false. This is called charity, tolerance, broadmindedness. It eats at the roots of decision, makes us acquiesce, paralyses moral action . . . [because], St. John would tell us, it is *false*.

CHARLES GORE

It takes two to speak the truth: one to speak and another to hear.

HENRY DAVID THOREAU

All truth is God's: but only the free mind sees it, only the honest mind reverences it, only the courageous mind holds it firmly and follows it fearlessly; to these qualities the truth will progressively disclose itself.

X

Habit with him was all the test of truth:
"It must be right, I've done it from my youth!"

GEORGE CRABBE

Truth forever on the scaffold, Wrong forever on the throne . . .
  Behind the dim unknown,
Standeth God within the shadows keeping watch above His own.

JAMES RUSSELL LOWELL

Pushing any truth out very far, you are met by a counter-truth.

HENRY WARD BEECHER

A truth that's told with bad intent
Beats all the lies you can invent.

WILLIAM BLAKE

God offers to every mind its choice between truth and repose. Take which you please—you can never have both.

RALPH WALDO EMERSON

To myself I seem to have been only like a boy playing on the seashore and diverting myself in now and then finding a smooth pebble or a prettier shell than ordinary, whilst the great ocean of truth lay all undiscovered before me.

ISAAC NEWTON

The truths of life are not discovered by us. At moments unforeseen, some gracious influence descends upon the soul, touching it to an emotion which, we know not how, the mind transmutes into thought.

GEORGE GISSING

It is morally as bad not to care whether a thing is true, so long as it makes you feel good, as it is not to care how you got your money, so long as you have got it.

EDWIN W. TEALE

Heaven knows what seeming nonsense may not tomorrow be demonstrated truth!

ALFRED NORTH WHITEHEAD

Dare to be true; nothing can need a lie;
A fault which needs it most grows two thereby.

GEORGE HERBERT

'Tis not antiquity, nor author, that makes truth truth, although time's daughter (SAMUEL BUTLER I); The longest sword, the strongest lungs, the most voices, are false measures of truth (BENJAMIN WHICHCOTE); He who sees the truth, let him proclaim it, without asking who is for it or who is against it (HENRY GEORGE); The greatest friend of truth is time, her greatest enemy prejudice, her constant companion humility (C. C. COLTON); Truth often suffers more by the heat of its defenders than from the arguments of its opponents (WILLIAM PENN); We always weaken whatever we exaggerate (J. F. DE LA HARPE).

That a lie which is all a lie may be met and fought with outright;
But a lie which is part a truth is a harder matter to fight.

ALFRED TENNYSON

Think truly, and thy thoughts
    Shall the world's famine feed;
Speak truly, and each word of thine
    Shall be a fruitful seed;
Love truly, and thy life shall be
    A great and noble creed.

HORATIUS BONAR

Live according to the truth ("doing the truth")—Truth is not in us—Know the truth—Love . . . in truth—We are of the truth—The spirit of truth—The Spirit is the truth—him who is true . . . Jesus . . . the true God.

1 JOHN 1:6, 8; 2:21; 3:18–19; 4:6; 5:7, 20

UNITY

There is one body and one Spirit ... one hope ... one Lord, one faith, one baptism, one God and Father of us all.

PAUL: EPHESIANS 4:4–6

Truth is the medium of Christian fellowship ... as every stream of water makes for the sea, every rill of truth makes for fellowship of souls.

ROBERT LAW

As grain, once scattered on the hillsides,
    Was in the broken bread made one.
So from all lands Thy church be gathered
    Into Thy kingdom by Thy Son.

DIDACHE, SECOND CENTURY(?); TRANS.,
F. BLAND TUCKER

It is becoming impossible for those who mix at all with their fellowmen to believe that the grace of God is distributed denominationally.

WILLIAM R. INGE

We would be one in hatred of all wrong,
    One in our love of all things sweet and fair;
One with the joy that breaketh into song,
    One with the grief that trembles into prayer;
One in the power that makes Thy children free
To follow truth, and thus to follow Thee.

JOHN WHITE CHADWICK

This unfortunate idea—that the basis of spiritual unity must stand in uniformity of doctrine—has been the poisoned spring of all the dissensions that have torn Christ's body.

JOHN WATSON

Do not call yourselves Lutherans, call yourselves Christians. Has Luther been crucified for the world?

MARTIN LUTHER

Nothing doth so much keep men out of the church, and drive men out of the church, as breach of unity.

FRANCIS BACON, C.1600

If all pulled in one direction the world would keel over (YIDDISH PROVERB); When spider webs unite they can tie up a lion (ETHIOPIAN PROVERB); Against one, two are an army (UNKNOWN); When all men think alike, they are not thinking at all (A. CLUTTON BROCK).

To forego truth for the sake of unity is in the end to surrender unity also; for all Christian unity is grounded in the gospel.

X

UNIVERSE

Praise the Lord from the heavens . . . in the heights above . . . all his angels . . . all his heavenly hosts . . . sun and moon . . . all you shining stars . . . you highest heavens . . . you waters above the skies . . . from the earth . . . all ocean depths.

PSALM 148:1–4, 7, NIV

The wonders in the nebula of Andromeda—that faint mist of light in the depths of the firmament which the naked eye can sometimes detect—magnitudes so vast, forces so stupendous, operations so immense, and yet so minute, that thought simply staggers . . . "The stars above us and the graves beneath us"—great God, what a Universe!

L. P. JACKS

All the grim puzzles of the Universe
Compassed me round, all Nature's endless fight;
But I shall see a blessing, not a curse,
   If Jesus Christ was right.

H. C. BRADBY

"I accept the Universe," said the philosopher;
The scientist replied, "By gad, sir, you'd better!"

ANONYMOUS

The Universe can best be pictured as consisting of pure thought, the thought of what for want of a better word we must describe as a mathematical thinker.

JAMES JEANS

The universe is a thought of God.

J. C. FRIEDRICH VON SCHILLER

V

VICE

In my inner being I delight in God's law; but I see another law at work in the members of my body, waging war against the law of my mind and making me a prisoner of the law of sin at work within my members.

PAUL: ROMANS 7:22–23, NIV

The martyrs to vice far exceed the martyrs to virtue, both in endurance and in number.

C. C. COLTON

Vices are their own punishment.

AESOP

We make a ladder of our vices, if we trample those same vices underfoot.

AUGUSTINE

When our vices leave us, we flatter ourselves with the credit of having left them.

LA ROCHEFOUCAULD

VICTORY

Thanks be to God, who always leads us in triumphal procession in Christ and through us spreads everywhere the fragrance of the knowledge of him.

PAUL: 2 CORINTHIANS 2:14, NIV

[The Christian ideal] gently insinuated itself into the minds of men, grew up in silence and obscurity, derived new vigour from opposition, and finally erected the triumphant banner of the cross on the ruins of the Capitol.

GIBBON

Great is the facile conqueror;
Yet haply he, who, wounded sore,
Breathless, unhorsed, all covered o'er
    With blood and sweat,
Sinks foiled, but fighting evermore,
    Is greater yet.

WILLIAM WATSON

In many a war it has been the vanquished, not the victor, who has
carried off the finest spoils.

H. HAVELOCK ELLIS

Speak, History! who are Life's victors? Unroll thy long annals
        and say
Are they those whom the world called the victors—who won the
        success of a day?
The martyrs, or Nero? the Spartans who fell at Thermopylae's
        tryst
Or the Persians and Xerxes? His judges, or Socrates? Pilate,
        or Christ?

WILLIAM W. STORY

To whom God will, there be the victory.

WILLIAM SHAKESPEARE

VIRTUE

All that is true . . . noble . . . just . . . pure . . . lovable . . . gracious
. . . whatever is excellent and admirable—fill all your thoughts with these
things.

PAUL: PHILIPPIANS 4:8, NEB

Virtue is more clearly shown in the performance of fine actions than in the
non-performance of base ones.

ARISTOTLE

If there's a power above us,
(And that there is all Nature cries aloud
Through all her works) He must delight in virtue.

JOSEPH ADDISON

Virtue is not hereditary (THOMAS PAINE); That virtue which requires to be ever guarded is scarce worth the sentinel (OLIVER GOLDSMITH); Wisdom is knowing what to do next: virtue is doing it (D. S. JORDAN); Virtue rises above all laws (X).

Supplement your faith with virtue, and virtue with knowledge.

2 PETER 1:5

VOCATION

Each one should retain the place in life that the Lord assigned to him.

PAUL: 1 CORINTHIANS 7:17, NIV

Every man has his own vocation: the talent is the call.

RALPH WALDO EMERSON

Thou dost the strength to workman's arm impart;
From Thee the skilled musician's mystic art,
The grace of poet's pen or painter's hand,
To teach the loveliness of sea and land.

E. E. DUGMORE

The test of a vocation is the love of the drudgery it involves (LOGAN PEARSALL SMITH); Vocations which we wanted to pursue but didn't, bleed (HONORÉ DE BALZAC).

Thine is the loom, the forge, the mart,
The wealth of land and sea;
The worlds of science and of art
Revealed and ruled by Thee.
Then let us prove our heavenly birth
In all we do and know;
And claim the kingdom of the earth
For Thee, and not Thy foe.

JOHN ELLERTON

WAR

What causes wars, and what causes fightings among you? Is it not your passions . . . ? You covet and cannot obtain; so you fight and wage war.

JAMES: JAMES 4:1−2

With what audacity do you call upon the common Father while thrusting your sword into your brother's vitals! . . . I do not condemn every war; yet it cannot be denied that when war breaks out there is crime on one side or the other, if not on both.

ERASMUS

The just war must be fought only for defence, as a last resort, being first declared with adequate warning, not for conquest or power but for a just peace; prisoners, and all who surrender must be spared; only soldiers may be involved (AFTER CICERO); Ambrose's theory of the just war is but a Christian version, step by step, of Cicero's (X); Righteous wars may be defined as wars to avenge wrongs, when a State has to be attacked for neglecting to make reparation for misdeeds committed by its citizens, or to restore what has been wrongfully seized (AUGUSTINE); The intention must be to secure peace, not to kill, conquer, or gain honour (THOMAS AQUINAS); The object of a just war is always peace (MARTIN LUTHER); Western wars have always distinguished means which are permissible and those prohibited and criminal; belief in a just divine government of the world made it possible to dispense with unchristian practices (AFTER DIETRICH BONHOEFFER); War remained a kind of appeal to the arbitration of God (DIETRICH BONHOEFFER).

Waste of muscle, waste of brain,
Waste of patience, waste of pain,
Waste of manhood, waste of health,
Waste of beauty, waste of wealth,
Waste of blood and waste of tears,
Waste of youth's most precious years,

Waste of ways the saints have trod
Waste of glory, waste of God—
War!

STUDDERT KENNEDY

The use of force alone is but temporary. It may subdue for a moment; but it does not remove the necessity of subduing again: and a nation is not governed which is to be perpetually conquered.

EDMUND BURKE

What passing-bells for these who die as cattle?
Only the monstrous anger of the guns;
Only the stuttering rifles' rapid rattle
Can patter out their hasty orisons.

WILFRED OWEN

A man may build himself a throne of bayonets but he cannot sit on it.

WILLIAM R. INGE

For heathen heart that puts her trust
In reeking tube and iron shard,
All valiant dust that builds on dust,
And, guarding, calls not Thee to guard,
For frantic boast and foolish word
Thy mercy on Thy people, Lord.

RUDYARD KIPLING

O shame of men! Devil with devil damned
Firm concord holds; men only disagree
Of creatures rational, though under hope
Of heavenly grace, and, God proclaiming peace,
Yet live in hatred, enmity, and strife
Among themselves, and levy cruel wars,
Wasting the earth, each other to destroy,
As if (which might induce us to accord)
Man had not hellish foes enow besides,
That day and night for his destruction wait.

JOHN MILTON

One of Christ's essential commands was: Passivity at any price! Suffer dishonour and disgrace, but never resort to arms. Be bullied, be outraged, be killed; but do not kill . . . Christ is literally in no-man's land. There men often hear His voice: *Greater love hath no man than this, that a man lay down his life for a friend.* Is it spoken in English only, and French? I do not believe so. Thus you see how pure Christianity will not fit in with pure patriotism.

WILFRED OWEN

Onward Christian soldiers,
Each to war resigned,
With the cross of Jesus
Vaguely kept in mind.

PAUL DEHN

The most disadvantageous peace is better than the most just war (ERASMUS); They make a desert and they call it peace (TACITUS. C. 80 A.D.).

WEALTH

The love of money is the root of all evils; it is through this craving that some have wandered away from the faith and pierced their hearts with many pangs.

1 TIMOTHY 6:10

He who holds possessions as the gifts of God, and ministers from them to the God who gives them; who knows that he possesses them more for the sake of the brethren than for his own; who is superior to the possession of them, not their slave, does not carry them about in his soul, nor blind and circumscribe his life with them; and who is able with cheerful mind to bear their removal: this is he called *poor in spirit, heir of the kingdom*; and not one who could not live rich.

CLEMENT OF ALEXANDRIA

Mammon led them on,
Mammon, the least erected spirit that fell
From heaven; for ev'n in heaven his looks and thoughts
Were always downward bent, admiring more
The riches of heaven's pavement, trodden gold,

Than aught divine or holy else enjoyed
In vision beatific.

JOHN MILTON

I once brought odium on myself because I broke up the sacred vessels to redeem captives. Who can be so hard, cruel, iron-hearted, as to be displeased because a man is redeemed from death, or a woman from barbaric impurity, or boys and girls and infants from the pollution of idols. Far better to preserve souls than gold for the Lord . . . living vessels than golden ones.

AMBROSE OF MILAN

It is not wrong to have money. It only becomes wrong when money is loved as an end instead of looked on as a means.

ERASMUS

I cannot afford to waste my time making money (JEAN LOUIS AGASSIZ); Property is theft (PIERRE J. PROUDHON); A man is rich in proportion to the number of things he can afford to let alone (HENRY DAVID THOREAU); A monk should own nothing but his harp (FRANCISCAN SAYING); Believe not much them that seem to despise riches: they despise them that despair of them (FRANCIS BACON); Better to have fewer wants than greater riches to supply increasing wants (AUGUSTINE); He is rich who hath enough to be charitable (THOMAS BROWNE); The ass loaded with gold still eats thistles (GERMAN PROVERB); To be content . . . is the greatest wealth of all (CICERO); He is rich enough who does not want bread (JEROME); . . . that needeth not to flatter, nor to borrow (THOMAS FULLER); Surplus wealth is a sacred trust (ANDREW CARNEGIE).

Poverty—mother of crime (CASSIODORUS); . . . of manhood (LUCAN); . . . of temperance (PALLADAS); . . . of miseries (ROBERT SOUTHEY); Poverty is very good in poems, very bad in a house (HENRY WARD BEECHER); The poor man's wisdom is despised, and his words are not heeded (ECCLESIASTES 9:16).

Seek not proud riches, but such as thou mayest get justly, use soberly, distribute cheerfully, and leave contentedly.

FRANCIS BACON

I cannot call riches better than the "baggage" of virtue . . . The Roman word is better, *impedimenta*—it cannot be spared, nor left behind, but it hinders the march; and the care of it sometimes loses or hinders the victory.

FRANCIS BACON

Covetousness has such a blinding power that all the arguments in the world will not convince a man that he is covetous.

THOMAS WILSON

It is rather a strong check to one's self-complacency to find how much of one's right doing depends on not being in want of money.

GEORGE ELIOT

Get all you can, honestly; save all you can, thriftily; give all you can, generously.

AFTER JOHN WESLEY

There has always been a slight tendency in Christianity to regard community of goods as the ideal, but the only serious attempt to carry it into effect was in the monasteries . . . Communism is possible only under two conditions—a religious basis, and celibacy.

WILLIAM R. INGE

To be clever enough to get all that money one must be stupid enough to want it.

G. K. CHESTERTON

> Train up thy mind to feel content;
>   What matters then how low thy store?
> What we enjoy, though not possess,
>   Makes rich or poor.

W. H. DAVIES

WILL

"Father, if thou art willing, remove this cup from me; nevertheless not my will, but thine, be done."

JESUS: LUKE 22:42

Where your will is ready, your feet are light.

GEORGE HERBERT

> In idle wishes fools supinely stay;
> Be there a will, and wisdom finds a way.

GEORGE CRABBE

To deny the freedom of the will is to make morality impossible (JAMES A. FROUDE); All theory is against the freedom of the will, all experience for it (SAMUEL JOHNSON); The only way of setting the will free is to deliver it from wilfulness (J. C. AND A. W. HARE); Will will have [its] will though will woe win (ENGLISH PROVERB); The will cannot be compelled (LATIN PROVERB).

> Though with judgement we on things reflect,
> Our will determines, not our intellect.

EDMUND WALLER

Many men have too much will-power; it's wont-power that they lack.

J. A. SHEDD

> Our wills are ours, we know not how;
> Our wills are ours, to make them Thine.

ALFRED TENNYSON

WISDOM

If any of you lacks wisdom, let him ask God, who gives to all men generously and without reproaching, and it will be given him.

JAMES: JAMES 1:5

I will light in your heart the lamp of understanding, which shall not be put out (2 ESDRAS 14:25); The fear of the LORD is the beginning of wisdom (PSALM 111:10).

Who with the wise consorts will wise become (MENANDER); Some folks are wise, some otherwise (TOBIAS G. SMOLLETT); He is not wise to me who is wise in words only, but he who is wise in deeds (GREGORY THE GREAT); That curious and almost stunning shrewdness which the unworldly can sometimes wield like a club of stone (G. K. CHESTERTON); Nine-tenths of wisdom is being wise in time (THEODORE ROOSEVELT); Wisdom is ofttimes nearer when we stoop than when we soar (WILLIAM WORDSWORTH); We are sure to judge wrong if we do not feel right (WILLIAM HAZLITT); It is not wise to be wiser than necessary (PHILIPPE QUINAULT); He that has grown to wisdom hurries not (G. GUINICELLI).

No man is wise enough by himself (PLAUTUS); . . . at all times (PLINY THE ELDER); . . . in everything (MICHEL DE MONTAIGNE); . . . by chance (SENECA).

> The generous Christian must as well improve
> In the quality of the serpent, as the dove;
> He must be innocent; afraid to do
> A wrong; and crafty to prevent it too.
> They must be mixed, and tempered with true love:
> An ounce of serpent serves a pound of dove.
>
> FRANCIS QUARLES

> Wisdom cries, "I know not anything";
> And only faith beholds that all is well.
>
> SYDNEY LYSAGHT

Foresight confers distinction on every effort; it elevates economy into providence, broadens business into enterprise; politics become statesmanship, and literature prophecy; life gains perspective—its spies return to brace and cheer the soul; it becomes the mother of all strenuous virtues.

JOHN WATSON

Not only is there but one way of doing things rightly, but there is only one way of seeing them, and that is, seeing the whole of them.

JOHN RUSKIN

Raphael paints wisdom, Handel sings it, Phidias carves it, Shakespeare writes it, Wren builds it, Columbus sails it, Luther preaches it, Washington arms it, Watt mechanizes it.

RALPH WALDO EMERSON

Common sense suits itself to the ways of the world; wisdom tries to conform to the ways of heaven.

JOSEPH JOUBERT

O World, thou choosest not the better part!
It is not wisdom to be only wise,
And on the inward vision close the eyes;
But it is wisdom to believe the heart.

GEORGE SANTAYANA

WITNESS

"You shall receive power . . . and you shall be my witnesses."

JESUS: ACTS 1:8

What the soul is to the body, that we Christians are in the world . . . the preservers of the world.

TO DIOGNETUS, SECOND-THIRD CENTURY

Heaven doth with us as we with torches do,
Not light them for themselves; for if our virtues
Did not go forth of us, 'Twere all alike
As if we had them not.

WILLIAM SHAKESPEARE

Thou art Fire and Light,
(Give *us* hearts of flame!)
Make us to burn like beacons
In defiance of ancient Night.
Make us braziers in the cold streets of the cities;
Make us lamps in Thy sanctuaries;
Make us candles . . .
The World is lost, and is looking for the Way.

M. FARROW

No man boasted of himself, none told the secrets of the soul. But the Glen took notice of its saints, and did them silent reverence, which they themselves never knew.

JOHN WATSON

WOMEN

"Behold, I am the handmaid of the Lord; let it be to me according to your word."

MARY OF NAZARETH: LUKE 1:38

Female and male God made the man; His image is the whole, not half.

COVENTRY PATMORE (GENESIS 1:27)

The woman was made of a rib out of the side of Adam; not out of his feet to be trampled upon by him, but out of his side to be equal with him, under his arm to be protected, and near his heart to be loved.

MATTHEW HENRY

The weaker sex, to piety more prone (WILLIAM ALEXANDER); The eternal feminine draws us upward (GOETHE); The woman is so hard upon the woman (ALFRED TENNYSON); I'm not denyin' the women are foolish: God Almighty made 'em to match the men (GEORGE ELIOT); Heavens! what women you Christians have! (LIBANIUS, OF ANTHUSA, MOTHER OF CHRYSOSTOM).

> "Women are door-mats, and have been":
> The years those mats applaud—
> They keep their men from going in
> With muddy feet to God.

MARY C. DAVIES

Men have been very wise . . . to keep women within doors tending the babies. If they ever get out, God help us. A woman lawyer, for instance, would outwit Satan.

NORAH LOFTS

When the Saviour was come, women rejoiced in Him before either man or angel. I read not that ever any man did give unto Christ so much as one groat; but the women . . . ministered to Him of their substance. It was a woman that washed His feet with tears, and women that anointed His body to the burial. They were women that wept when He was going to the cross, and women that followed Him from the cross and sat by His sepulchre . . . They were women that were first with Him at His resurrection-morn, and women that brought tidings first to His disciples that

He was risen from the dead . . . Women, therefore, are highly favoured, sharers in the grace of life.

JOHN BUNYAN, PURITAN, 1678

Perhaps it is no wonder that women were first at the cradle and last at the cross. They had never known a man like this Man . . . A prophet and teacher who never nagged at them, never flattered, coaxed, patronised, never made arch jokes about them, never treated them as "The women, God help us!" or "The ladies, God bless them!"; who praised without condescension; who never mapped out their sphere, never urged them to be feminine . . . who had no axe to grind, no uneasy male dignity to defend. Nobody could possibly guess from the words and deeds of Jesus that there was anything "funny" about woman's nature.

DOROTHY SAYERS (ABBREVIATED)

> Not she with trait'rous kiss her Saviour stung;
> Not she denied Him with unholy tongue;
> She, while apostles shrank, could dangers brave:
> Last at the cross, and earliest at the grave.

EATON S. BARRETT

When you educate a man, you educate an individual; when you educate a woman, you educate a whole family.

C. D. McIVER

WORDS

We all make many mistakes, and if any one makes no mistakes in what he says he is a perfect man, able to bridle the whole body also.

JAMES: JAMES 3:2

Jesus said, It is always well that those who possess by nature the capacity for hearing and interpreting human speech should pay diligent attention to what is, from time to time, being uttered in public discourse—or, in His rapier words, "He that hath ears to hear, let him hear."

ANONYMOUS

A fool and his words are soon parted (WILLIAM SHENSTONE); Kind words are benedictions (FREDERICK SAUNDERS); Good words cool more than cold water (ENGLISH PROVERB); A word is the skin of a living thought (OLIVER WENDELL HOLMES); An acute word cuts deeper than a sharp weapon (THOMAS FULLER); Well done is better than well said (BENJAMIN FRANKLIN); Words may be deeds (AESOP); You can stroke people with words (F. SCOTT FITZGERALD); It is not as far from the heart to the mouth as it is from the mouth to the hand (JOSEPH ROUX).

Putting all his words together,
'Tis three blue beans in one blue bladder.
MATTHEW PRIOR

Words are things: imagination hurls them like thunderbolts, sharpens them like knives, polishes them like silver, sets them like gems, builds great arguments with them like solid stones, caresses them like lover's hands.
ANONYMOUS

How vile a thing is the abstract noun; it wraps a man's thought round like cotton wool.

A. T. QUILLER-COUCH

The similarity of words lays traps for the unwary:
capable means *equipped* to be able;
curable means *able* to be cured;
vulnerable means *liable* to be wounded;
admirable means *worthy* to be admired;
returnable means *under obligation* to be returned;
negotiable means *permitted* to be negotiated;
laughable means *deserving* to be laughed at;
debatable means *needing* to be debated.
ANONYMOUS

A word fitly spoken is like a boss of gold set in a filigree of silver (PROVERBS 25:11, LITERALLY); To make an apt answer is a joy to a man, and a word in season, how good it is (PROVERBS 15:23); "How forceful are honest words" (JOB 6:25); Whatever you do, in word or deed, do everything in the name of the Lord Jesus (PAUL: COLOSSIANS 3:17); "On the day of judgment men will render account for every careless word they utter; for by your words you will be justified, and by your words you will be condemned (JESUS: MATTHEW 12:36–37).

We should have a great many fewer disputes in the world if words were taken for what they are, the signs of our ideas only, and not for things themselves.

JOHN LOCKE

WORK

We gave you this rule: "If a man will not work, he shall not eat."

PAUL: 2 THESSALONIANS 3:10, NIV

All these rely upon their hands,
    and each is skillful in his own work.
Without them a city cannot be established . . .
    Yet they are not sought out for the council . . .
nor do they attain eminence . . .
    But they keep stable the fabric of the world,
and their prayer is in the practice of their trade.

SIRACH 38:31–34

Father, I scarcely dare to pray,
So clear I see, now it is done,
How I have wasted half my day,
And left my work but just begun.

HELEN H. JACKSON

Everything considered, work is less boring than amusing oneself (CHARLES BAUDELAIRE); Idle folk have the least leisure (CHARLES H. SPURGEON); Work expands to fill the time available for its completion (C. N. PARKINSON); Slave of the wheel of labour—what to him are Plato and the swing of Pleiades? (EDWIN MARKHAM); Give us this day our daily work (ELBERT HUBBARD).

No race can prosper until it learns there is as much dignity in tilling a field as in writing a poem.

BOOKER T. WASHINGTON

God is living, working still,
All things work and move;

Work, or lose the power to will;
Lose the power to love.

JOHN S. DWIGHT

To work is to pray (BENEDICT); He who has been stealing must steal no longer, but must work, doing something useful with his own hands, that he may have something to share with those in need (PAUL: EPHESIANS 4:28, NIV).

WORLD

The world and all that is in it is mine (GOD: PSALM 50:12); Do not love the world or the things in the world (JOHN: 1 JOHN 2:15).

Long time before
I in my mother's womb was born,
A God preparing did this glorious store,
The world, for me adorn;
Into this Eden so divine and fair
So wide and bright, I come, his son and heir.

A stranger here
Strange things doth meet, strange glories see,
Strange treasures lodged in this fair world appear;
Strange all, and new, to me:
But that they mine should be, who nothing was,
That strangest is of all; yet brought to pass.

THOMAS TRAHERNE

The world, which took but six days to make, is like to take six thousand to make out.

THOMAS BROWNE

The most incomprehensible thing about the world is that it is comprehensible.

ALBERT EINSTEIN

The world has narrowed to a neighbourhood before it has broadened to a brotherhood.

LYNDON B. JOHNSON

The world—A small parenthesis in eternity (THOMAS BROWNE); . . . a great factory of power, with its rotating constellations, times, and tides (RALPH WALDO EMERSON); . . . a beautiful book (CARLO GOLDONI); . . . a nettle: grasp it firmly, it stings not (OWEN MEREDITH); . . . a looking-glass (WILLIAM MAKEPEACE THACKERAY); . . . a net to snare the soul (GEORGE WHETSTONE); . . . a prophecy of worlds to come (EDWARD YOUNG); . . . made for me, not me for the world (TOBIAS G. SMOLLETT); . . . a bubble (FRANCIS BACON).

> Give us wills of steel
> And be our magnetic pole.
> Draw us unwavering through the wastes
> Whence the signs of salvation are vanishing.
> Thou art our journey's end . . .
> The world has forgotten its home,
> And the things that belong to its peace.
> If our compass fail
> Our footsteps stagger and reel.
> And our marchings nothing avail
> But to bring us back on ourselves in circles,
> In dizzying, nightmare, maniac rings
> From whence is no release.
> Draw us home . . .
> The world is lost, and is looking for the way.
> M. FARROW

> This world is full of beauty, as other worlds above;
> And if we did our duty it might be full of love.
> GERALD MASSEY

It is not an accident that wherever we point the telescope we find beauty; that wherever we look with the microscope, there we find beauty. It beats in through every nook and cranny of the mighty world.
RUFUS M. JONES

Call the world, if you please, "the vale of soul-making."
JOHN KEATS

The Father's World
> The world's no blot for us,
> Nor blank; it means intensely, and means good;
> To find its meaning is my meat and drink.
> ROBERT BROWNING

You never enjoy the world aright till the sea itself floweth in your veins,
till you are clothed with the heavens and crowned with the stars: and
perceive yourself to be the sole heir of the whole world, and more than
so, because men are in it who are every one sole heirs as well as you.
Till you can sing and rejoice and delight in God as misers do in gold,
and kings in sceptres, you never enjoy the world.

THOMAS TRAHERNE

We are not to think that God is interested only in Christians, and has left
the world to its own devices.

MARTIN LUTHER

"What do I love, when I love you O God? Not a beautiful body, nor a
fine climate, nor the clear light which—just look!—is so dear to these
eyes, not the lively tunes of songs and ditties, nor the sweet smells of
flowers and perfumes and spices, nor manna, nor honey, nor limbs it is
agreeable to take in close embrace." The music of [Augustine's] words
conveys the thrill of his emotions in face of these earthly joys, so
appealing to the frail heart of man.

H. I. MARROU

It becomes man seriously to employ his eyes considering the works of
God, since a place has been assigned to him in this most glorious theatre
. . . Sculpture and painting are gifts of God . . . manual and liberal arts
. . . intelligence. In reading profane authors, the admirable light of truth
displayed should remind us that the human mind is still adorned and
invested with admirable gifts. In despising the gifts we insult the Giver. Nor
can we shun things which seem more subservient to delight than to
necessity . . . [In creating] food, we shall find God consulted not only our
necessity but also our enjoyment . . . [so with] clothing, comeliness,
honour, herbs, fruits, gracefulness of appearance, sweetness of smell.

Has the Lord adorned flowers with all the beauty which spontaneously
presents itself to the eye, and the sweet odour which delights the sense of
smell, and shall it be unlawful for us to enjoy that beauty and this odour
. . . ? [So with colours, gold, silver, ivory, marble]. Has God not given
many things value without necessary use? Have done then with that
inhuman philosophy which . . . cannot be realised without depriving man
of all his sense.

JOHN CALVIN (abbreviated)

The world's a stage where God's omnipotence,
His justice, knowledge, love, and providence,
Do act the parts.

G. S. DU BARTAS

WORLDLINESS

In a world which is Christ's, "worldliness" is the Christian way. To regard
Christianity as a religion of salvation *from* this world is a cardinal error;
this world must not be prematurely written off.

AFTER DIETRICH BONHOEFFER

Be wisely worldly: be not worldly wise.

FRANCIS QUARLES

Unworldliness based on knowledge of the world is the finest thing on
earth; but unworldliness based on ignorance of the world is less admirable.

WILLIAM R. INGE

Such is the world. Understand it, despise it, love it; cheerfully hold on thy
way through it, with thine eye on the highest loadstar.

THOMAS CARLYLE

The church is not in the world to save itself, but to save the world.
Either the church must pour a steady stream of saving power into the
community, or it will receive a steady stream of poisonous influence from
the community.

WASHINGTON GLADDEN

The world is under a believer's feet ... He travelleth through it to his
home, nor doth he make any great matter whether his usage in it be kind
or unkind ... indifferent whether for so short a time he be rich or poor
... further than as tendeth to his Master's service.

RICHARD BAXTER

Let not the cooings of the world allure thee;
Which of her lovers ever found her true?

EDWARD YOUNG

When a man begins to doubt whether it is lawful to use linen sheets, shirts, napkins, handkerchiefs, he will not long be secure as to hemp, and will at last have doubts as to tow. Should he deem a daintier food unlawful, he will afterward feel uneasy for using loaf bread. If he hesitates as to a more genial wine . . . at last he will not dare to touch water if more than usually sweet and pure.

JOHN CALVIN, ABBREVIATED

The world is too much with us; late and soon,
Getting and spending, we lay waste our powers:
Little we see in Nature that is ours;
We have given our hearts away, a sordid boon!

WILLIAM WORDSWORTH

I fear that Christians who stand with only one leg upon earth also stand with only one leg in heaven.

DIETRICH BONHOEFFER

The world will, in the end, follow only those who have despised as well as served it (SAMUEL BUTLER II); The world is possessed by those who are not possessed by it (WILLIAM R. INGE); Thoroughly worldly people never understand even the world (G. K. CHESTERTON).

The world was to be outwitted . . . You could not threaten to starve a man who was ever striving to fast. You could not ruin him and reduce him to beggary, for he was already a beggar . . . You could not put his head in a halter without the risk of putting it in a halo.

G. K. CHESTERTON, ON FRANCIS OF ASSISI

The world is a house . . . I am outside the house, on the roof, not yet in heaven, but also not in the world. I have the world beneath me and the heavens above: I am suspended in faith between life in the world and eternal life.

MARTIN LUTHER

A man crossing a river on a tight-rope ought not to be curious about wearing silver slippers, nor will he be much concerned with the colour of the waves.

WILLIAM LAW

One of the greatest wonders that history has to show is how ordinary Christians *out-lived, out-died,* and *out-thought* the powerful pagan world.

AFTER T. R. GLOVER

WORSHIP

"You shall worship the Lord your God
and him only shall you serve."

JESUS: MATTHEW 4:10

To worship is to quicken the conscience by the holiness of God, to feed the mind with the truth of God, to purge the imagination by the beauty of God, to open the heart to the love of God, to devote the will to the purpose of God.

WILLIAM TEMPLE

Not what I would, O Lord, I offer Thee,
     Alas! but what I can . . .
     Four things, which are in Thy treasury,
I lay before Thee, Lord, with this petition:
My nothingness, my wants, my sin, and my contrition.

ROBERT SOUTHEY

Wonder is involuntary praise (EDWARD YOUNG); When a soul holds on to God in trust—this is the highest worship (JULIAN OF NORWICH); Wonder is the basis of worship (THOMAS CARLYLE); . . . the seed of our science (RALPH WALDO EMERSON); What greater calamity can fall upon a nation than the loss of worship (RALPH WALDO EMERSON); The worship of God is not a rule of safety; it is an adventure of the spirit, a flight after the unattainable (ALFRED NORTH WHITEHEAD).

Worship—*to behold* the beauty of the LORD, and *to inquire* in his temple (PSALM 27:4); Worship—the only gift we can bring to God that he himself has not first given to us (ISOBEL RALSTON); In worship we meet the power of God and stand in its strengthening (NELS F. S. FERRÈ).

> With antique pillars massy proof
> And storied windows richly dight,
> Casting a dim religious light:
> There let the pealing organ blow
> To the full-voiced choir below
> In service high, and anthems clear,
> As may, with sweetness, through mine ear
> Dissolve me into ecstasies
> And bring all Heaven before mine eyes.

JOHN MILTON

The worldly religious have contrived for themselves a worship that calls for no humiliation before God, and no complete surrender of heart and will to Him.

MARCUS DODS

YOUTH

Rejoice, O young man, in your youth.

ECCLESIASTES 11:9

Only the young have a full life to give: how good it is to close with Christ betimes.

OLIVER CROMWELL

When I survey the wondrous cross
    Where the young Prince of glory died,
My richest gain I count but loss,
    And pour contempt on all my pride.

ISAAC WATTS (original version)

O choose me in my golden time,
    In my dear joys have part;
For Thee the glory of my prime,
    The fullness of my heart.

I cannot, Lord, too early take
    The covenant divine:
Oh, ne'er the happy heart may break
    Whose earliest love was Thine.

THOMAS H. GILL

Those who love the young best stay young longest (EDGAR FRIEDENBERG); I go to school to youth to learn the future (ROBERT FROST); Youth is not a time of life, it is a state of mind (SAMUEL ULLMAN); Don't keep us young too long (GEORGE LAWTON); Keep the young generations in hail, and bequeath to them no tumbled house (GEORGE MEREDITH); It's all the young can do for the old, to shock them and keep them up to date (GEORGE BERNARD SHAW); We are none of us infallible—not even the youngest of us (W. H. THOMPSON); I felt so young, so strong, so sure of God (ELIZABETH BARRETT BROWNING); Jesus looking upon him loved him (MARK 10:21).

Heaven lies about us in our infancy!
Shades of the prison-house begin to close
    Upon the growing Boy,
But he beholds the light, and whence it flows,
    He sees it in his joy;
The Youth, who daily farther from the east
    Must travel, still is Nature's Priest,
    And by the vision splendid
    Is on his way attended;
At length the Man perceives it die away,
And fade into the light of common day.

WILLIAM WORDSWORTH

To be young is glorious; but our cynicism, sophistries, and sins, have made the modern world a fearfully difficult place in which to be young, good, and happy.

ANONYMOUS

Z

ZEAL

I bear them witness that they have a zeal for God, but it is not enlightened.

Zeal without knowledge is a runaway horse (ENGLISH PROVERB); . . . fire without light (ENGLISH PROVERB); . . . the sister of folly (JOHN DAVIES).

Nothing great was ever achieved without enthusiasm (RALPH WALDO EMERSON); . . . truth accomplishes no victories without it (EDWARD BULWER-LYTTON); Knowledge without zeal is mere ornament; skill without enthusiasm, talent without labour, vision without valour, purpose without perseverance, are all idle dreaming, wasting precious assets (ANONYMOUS).

Whenever we find ourselves more ready to persecute than to persuade, we may then be certain that our zeal has more of pride in it than of charity.

CHARLES C. COLTON

Fanaticism consists in redoubling your effort when you have forgotten your aim (GEORGE SANTAYANA); A fanatic is a man who consciously overcompensates a secret doubt (ALDOUS HUXLEY); We are often moved with passion and think it to be zeal (THOMAS À KEMPIS); Zeal that is not zeal for keeping God's commandments is but egotism subtly disguised (ROBERT LAW).

It is unfortunate, considering that enthusiasm moves the world, that so few enthusiasts can be trusted to speak the truth.

ARTHUR JAMES BALFOUR

Jesus could have neither part nor lot with men destitute of enthusiasm.

J. R. SEELEY

LIST OF SOURCES

Abélard, Pierre (1079?–1144) *Breton theologian*
Abercrombie, Lascelles (1881–1938) *English poet*
Acton, Lord John E. E. (1834–1902) *English historian*
Adams, Henry (1838–1918) *American historian, author*
Addison, Joseph (1672–1719) *English essayist*
Addleshaw, G. W. O. (twentieth century) *English church historian*
Aeschylus (525–456 B.C.) *Greek playwright*
Aesop (620–560 B.C.) *Greek fabulist*
Agassiz, Jean Louis (1807–1873) *Swiss-American naturalist*
Agathon (445–400 B.C.) *Greek poet*
Aggrey, James E. (1875–1927) *African-American missionary*
Albery, J. (1838–1889) *English dramatist*
Alcott, Amos B. (1799–1888) *American philosopher*
Aldington, Richard (1892–1962) *English poet, author*
Aldrich, Thomas Bailey (1836–1907) *American poet, playwright*
Alexander, William (1567–1640) *Scottish poet*
Allingham, William (1824–1889) *Irish poet*
Ambrose, St. (c. 339–397) *bishop of Milan*
Amiel, Henri F. (1821–1881) *Swiss philosopher, poet*
Anaximander (610–c. 547 B.C.) *Greek philosopher*
Angela of Foligno (1248–1309) *Italian mystic*
Aquinas, Thomas (1225–1274) *Italian theologian*
Aristotle (384–322 B.C.) *Greek philosopher*
Armstrong, John (1709–1779) *English poet, essayist*
Arnold, Matthew (1822–1888) *English essayist*
Ascham, Roger (1515–1568) *English classical scholar*
Athanasius, St. (c. 293–373) *Alexandrian theologian*
Atkinson, Brooks (twentieth century) *American essayist*
Atkinson, J. (twentieth century) *English church historian*
Attlee, Clement (1883–1967) *British prime minister*
Attwater, Donald (twentieth century) *English hagiologist*
Auden, W. H. (1907–1973) *English-American poet*
Augustine, St. (354–430) *North African theologian*
Ault, Norman (1880–1950) *English poet*

Aurelius, Marcus (121–180) *Roman emperor, philosopher*
Austin, Alfred (1835–1913) *English poet*
Bacon, Francis (1561–1626) *English statesman, philosopher*
Bailey, P. J. (1816–1902) *English poet*
Baillie, Joanna (1762–1851) *Scottish poet*
Baillie, John (1886–1960) *Scottish theologian*
Bainton, Roland H. (twentieth century) *English church historian*
Balfour, Arthur James (1848–1930) *Scottish statesman, philosopher*
Balzac, Honoré de (1799–1850) *French novelist*
Banks, G. L. (1821–1881) *English author*
Barbauld, Anna L. (1743–1825) *English poet*
Barclay, William (1907–1978) *Scottish biblical scholar*
Barrett, Eaton S. (1786–1820) *English author*
Barrett, G. S. (twentieth century) *English biblical commentator*
Barth, Karl (1886–1968) *Swiss theologian*
Baudelaire, Charles (1821–1867) *French poet*
Bax, Clifford (1886–1926) *English hymnist*
Baxter, Richard (1615–1691) *English divine*
Beard, Charles A. (1874–1948) *American historian*
Beaumont, Francis (1584–1616) *English playwright*
Beaumont, Joseph (1616–1699) *English poet*
Becket, Thomas à (1118–1170) *English archbishop*
Beecher, Henry Ward (1813–1887) *American divine*
Belloc, Hilaire (1870–1953) *English author*
Benedict, Francis G. (1870–1957) *American chemist*
Benedict, St. (480–547) *Italian monastic reformer*
Bengel, Johann Albrecht (1687–1752) *German Lutheran scholar*
Benham, W. G. (1859–1944) *English compiler*
Bennett, Arnold (1867–1931) *English novelist*
Berdyaev, Nicolas (1874–1948) *Russian philosopher*
Bernanos, Georges (1888–1948) *French novelist*
Bernard of Clairvaux, St. (1090–1153) *French theologian*
Berry, John (twentieth century) *American author*
Bickersteth, Edward H. (1825–1906) *English hymnist*
Bierce, Ambrose (1842–?1914) *American author*
Birrell, Augustine (1850–1933) *English biographer*
Blackie, J. S. (1809–1895) *Scottish scholar*
Blair, Robert (1699–1746) *Scottish poet*
Blake, William (1757–1827) *English poet*
Bode, John E. (1816–1874) *English poet*
Bodenham, John (fl. 1600) *English writer*
Boileau, Nicolas (1636–1711) *French poet*

Bolt, Robert (twentieth century) *English playwright*
Bonar, Horatius (1808–1889) *Scottish divine*
Bonhoeffer, Dietrich (1906–1945) *German theologian*
Book of Common Prayer (sixteenth century, etc.) *Church of England*
Borchert, Otto (twentieth century) *German theologian*
Bradby, H. C. (1868–1947) *English poet*
Brainard, J. G. (1796–1828) *American poet*
Brainard, Mary G. (fl. 1860) *American poet*
Braithwaite, William C. (1862–1922) *English Quaker poet*
Braque, Georges (1882–1963) *French painter*
Brock, A. Clutton (1868–1924) *English essayist, critic*
Brontë, Anne (1820–1849) *English novelist*
Brontë, Emily (1818–1848) *English novelist*
Brooks, Phillips (1835–1893) *American divine*
Broome, William (1689–1745) *English poet*
Brown, Mary E. (1842–1917) *American hymnist*
Brown, Thomas (1663–1704) *English satirist*
Browne, Thomas (1605–1682) *English author*
Browning, Elizabeth Barrett (1806–1861) *English poet*
Browning, Robert (1812–1889) *English poet*
Bryant, William Cullen (1794–1878) *American poet*
Buber, Martin (1878–1965) *Jewish philosopher*
Buchan, John (1875–1940) *Scottish biographer, novelist*
Bulwer-Lytton, Edward G. E. (1803–1873) *English novelist*
Bunyan, John (1628–1688) *English Puritan writer*
Burke, Edmund (1729–1797) *English statesman, philosopher*
Burleigh, W. H. (1812–1871) *American author*
Burne-Jones, Edward (1833–1898) *English artist*
Burns, Robert (1759–1796) *Scottish poet*
Burton, Robert (1577–1640) *English divine*
Butler, Cuthbert (1858–1934) *English Roman Catholic abbot*
Butler, Joseph (1692–1752) *English philosopher, bishop*
Butler I, Samuel (1612–1680) *English poet, satirist*
Butler II, Samuel (1835–1902) *English philosophical writer*
Butterfield, Herbert (1901–1979) *English historian*
Buttrick, George Arthur (twentieth century) *English author*
Butts, Mary F. (1836–1902) *American poet*
Byrom, John (1692–1763) *English hymnist*
Cadoc, St. (sixth century) *Welsh fabulist*
Caird, G. B. (twentieth century) *English biblical scholar*
Calvin, John (1509–1564) *French theologian*
Camden, William (1551–1623) *English historian*

Campbell, Thomas (1777–1844) *Scottish poet*
Canning, Victor (twentieth century) *English novelist*
Canton, W. (1845–1926) *English poet*
Carey, William (1761–1834) *English missionary*
Carlyle, Thomas (1795–1881) *Scottish historian, critic*
Carnegie, Andrew (1835–1919) *Scottish industrialist, philanthropist*
Carr, J. Dickson (twentieth century) *American novelist*
Carruth, W. H. (1859–1924) *American poet*
Case, Lizzie York (1840–1911) *American poet*
Cassiodorus (c. 490–c. 585) *Roman author*
Catherine of Genoa, St. (1447–1510) *Italian mystic*
Cecil, G. W.—W. A. Lawrence (twentieth century) *American
    copywriter*
Cervantes, Miguel de (1547–1616) *Spanish author*
Chadwick, John White (1840–1904) *American author*
Chadwick, Samuel (1860–1932) *English evangelist*
Chardin, Teilhard de (1881–1955) *French scientist, theologian*
Chase, Alexander (twentieth century) *American journalist*
Chaucer, Geoffrey (c. 1342–1400) *English poet*
Cheney, John V. (1848–1922) *American poet*
Chesterton, G. K. (1874–1936) *English apologist, essayist, novelist*
Chillingworth, William (1602–1644) *English divine*
Cholmondeley, Hester H. (nineteenth century) *English writer*
"Agatha Christie"—Lady Mallowen (1890–1976) *English novelist*
Chrysostom, St. John (c 347–407) *Syrian biblical expositor*
Churchill, Charles (1731–1764) *English satirist*
Churchill, Winston Spencer (1874–1965) *English prime minister*
Cicero, Marcus T (106–43 B.C.) *Roman statesman, moralist*
Clarke, Herbert (nineteenth/twentieth century) *English poet*
Clarke, John (fl. 1639) *English compiler*
Claudian (c. 395–404) *Roman poet*
Cleghorn, Sarah N. (1876–1959) *American poet*
Clement of Alexandria, St. (150–215) *Greek theologian*
Clements, J. R. (untraced)
Clemo, Jack (twentieth century) *English poet*
Cleobulus (633–564 B.C.) *Greek poet*
Clifford, John (1836–1923) *English divine*
Clough, Arthur H. (1819–1861) *English poet*
Coffin, Henry Sloane (1877–1954) *American divine*
Coke, Edward (1552–1634) *English jurist*
Coleridge, Hartley (1796–1849) *English poet*
Coleridge, Mary Elizabeth (1861–1907) *English poet*

Coleridge, Samuel Taylor (1772–1834) *English poet*
Collins, John Churton (1848–1908) *English critic*
Collins, Mortimer (1827–1876) *English author*
Colton, Charles C. (c. 1780–1832) *English aphorist*
Confucius (551–479 B.C.) *Chinese philosopher*
Conkling, R. (1829–1888) *American politician*
Cooper, James Fenimore (1789–1851) *American novelist*
Cooke, Alistair (twentieth century) *English international correspondent*
Cowley, Abraham (1618–1667) *English poet*
Cowper, William (1731–1800) *English poet*
Cox, Coleman (twentieth century) *American humorist*
Crabbe, George (1754–1832) *English poet*
Cranmer, Thomas (1489–1556) *English archbishop*
Crashaw, Richard (c. 1613–1649) *English poet*
Craster, Mrs. Edmund (d. 1874) *American writer*
Crockett, David (1786–1836) *American congressman, soldier*
Cromwell, Oliver (1599–1658) *English Puritan "protector"*
Crosby, Ernest H. (1856–1907) *American publicist*
Cullen, Countée (1903–1946) *American black poet*
Curran, John Philpot (1750–1817) *Irish jurist*
Cyprian, St. (martyred 258) *North African bishop*
Daniel, Samuel (1562–1619) *English poet*
Dante (1265–1321) *Italian poet*
Darwin, Charles (1809–1882) *English naturalist*
Davies, John (1565–1618) *English poet*
Davies, Mary C. (twentieth century) *American poet*
Davies, W. H. (1870–1940) *English poet*
Day, Dorothea (twentieth century) *American author*
De Burgh, William G. (1866–1943) *American philosopher*
Dehn, Paul (twentieth century) *English poet*
Dekker, Thomas (c. 1570–1641) *English dramatist*
De La Mare, Walter (1873–1956) *English poet*
Deland, Margaret (1857–1945) *American author*
De Morgan, William F. (1839–1917) *English novelist*
Denney, James (1856–1917) *Scottish theologian*
Descartes, René (1596–1650) *French philosopher*
Dewey, John (1859–1952) *American philosopher*
Dibelius, Martin (1883–1947) *German biblical scholar*
Dickens, A. G. (twentieth century) *English church historian*
Dickens, Charles (1812–1870) *English novelist*
Dickinson, Charles M. (1842–1924) *American author*
Dickinson, Emily (1830–1886) *American poet*

Didache, The ("Teaching of the Twelve Apostles," first/second century) *author unknown*

Diogenes Laertius (fl. 211–235) *Greek biographer*

"Diognetus" (anonymous epistle to, second/third century)

Disraeli, Benjamin (1804–1881) *English statesman, author*

Dix, Dom Gregory (1901–1952) *English monk and liturgiologist*

Dodd, C. H. (1884–1973) *English biblical scholar*

Doddridge, Philip (1702–1751) *English divine*

Dods, Marcus (1834–1909) *Scottish theologian*

Dole, C. F. (1845–1927) *American divine*

Donne, John (1573–1631) *English poet*

Dostoyevsky, Fyodor (1821–1881) *Russian novelist*

Dowden, Edward (1843–1913) *English critic*

Drinkwater, John (1882–1937) *English poet*

Drummond, Henry (1851–1897) *Scottish theologian*

Drummond, William (1585–1649) *Scottish poet*

Dryden, John (1631–1700) *English poet*

Du Bartas, G. S. (1544–1590) *French poet*

Duffield, George (1818–1888) *American divine*

Dugmore, E. E. (1843–1925) *English divine*

Dunbar, William (1465–1529) *Scottish poet*

Dunning, T. G. (twentieth century) *English divine*

Dwight, John S. (1813–1893) *American critic*

Dyke, Henry Van: see Van Dyke

East, James T. (1860–1937) *English divine*

Eaton, Nathaniel (1609–1674) *English poet*

Eckhart, Meister (c 1260–1327) *German mystic*

Eco, Umberto (twentieth century) *Italian novelist, historian, philosopher*

Edwards, Jonathan (1703–1758) *American theologian*

Edison, Thomas A. (1847–1931) *American inventor*

Einstein, Albert (1879–1955) *German-Swiss physicist*

"George Eliot"—Mary Ann Evans/Cross (1819–1880) *English novelist*

Eliot, John (1604–1690) *English missionary to American Indians*

Eliot, T. S. (1888-1965) *American/English poet*

Ellerton, John (1826–1893) *English hymnist*

Elliott, Charlotte (1789–1871) *English hymnist*

Ellis, H. Havelock (1859–1939) *English psychologist*

Emerson, Ralph Waldo (1803–1882) *American poet, essayist*

Empedocles (fifth century B.C.) *Greek philosopher*

Epictetus (c. 50–130) *Greek philosopher*

Epitaph, in Cambridgeshire, England
Erasmus, Desiderius (c. 1466–1536) *Dutch Christian humanist*
"Ernest Bramah,"—E. Bramah Smith (1867–1942) *English author*
Erskine, John (1879–1951) *American educator, novelist*
Eucken, R. C. (1846–1926) *German philosopher*
Euripides (c. 480–405 B.C.) *Greek playwright*
Eusebius (c. 260–340, born in Palestine) *church historian*
"Sister Eva"—Eva Tiele-Winckler (1886–1930) *German social
   pioneer*
"F. Anstey"—T. A. Guthrie (1856–1934) *English humorist*
Faber, Frederick W. (1814–1863) *English poet*
Fairbairn, A. M. (1838–1912) *Scottish theologian*
"Michael Fairless"—Margaret Fairless Barber (1869–1901) *English
   nature-writer, mysticist*
"Marianne Farningham"—Marianne Hearn (1834–1909) *English
   poet*
Farrar, Frederic W. (1831–1903) *English divine*
Farrow, M. (untraced)
"Father Andrew"—Henry E. Hardy (1869–1946) *English poet,
   social worker*
Fénelon, François (1651–1715) *French divine*
Ferré, Nels F. S. (twentieth century) *theologian*
"Michael Field"—Katherine Bradley (1846–1914) and Edith
   Cooper (1862–1913: joint-poets
Findlay, G. G. (1849–1919) *English biblical scholar*
Findlay, J. A. (twentieth century) *Scottish theologian*
Finney, Charles G. (1792–1875) *American evangelist*
Fisher, St. John (1469–1525) *English divine*
Fitzgerald, Edward (1809–1883) *English poet*
Fitzgerald, F. Scott (1896–1940) *American novelist*
Flavel, John (1630?–1691) *English divine*
Fletcher, Giles, Jr. (1588?–1623) *English poet*
Fletcher, John (1579–1625) *English playwright*
Fletcher, Phinehas (1582–1650) *English poet*
Flexner, Abraham (1866–1946) *American educator*
Ford, John (1586–1639?) *English playwright*
Forsyth, P. T. (1848–1921) *English theologian*
Fosdick, Harry Emerson (1878–1969) *American divine*
Foster, John (twentieth century) *English church historian*
Francis of Assisi, St. (1181/2–1226) *Italian monastic reformer*
Frankfurter, Felix (1882–1965) *American jurist*
Franklin, Benjamin (1706–1790) *American philosopher, diplomat*

Freeman, Robert (1878–1940) *American divine*
Freud, Sigmund (1856–1939) *Austrian psychoanalyst*
Friedenberg, Edgar (twentieth century) *American sociologist*
Friends' Book of Discipline
Fromm, Erich (twentieth century) *German-American psychoanalyst*
Frost, Robert (1874–1963) *American poet*
Froude, James A (1818–1894) *English historian*
Fry, Elizabeth (1780–1845) *English prison reformer*
Fuller, Thomas (1608–1661) *English divine*
Fullerton, W. Y. (1857–1932) *Irish divine*
Gandhi, Mahatma (1869–1948) *Indian independence leader*
Garfield, James A. (1831–1881) *American president*
Garnett, Richard (1835–1906) *English author*
Garrison, William Lloyd (1805–1879) *American emancipationist*
Gary, Romain (1914–1980) *Russian-born French novelist, diplomat*
Gay, John (1685–1732) *English poet*
George, David Lloyd (1863–1945) *Welsh statesman*
George, Henry (1839–1897) *American economist*
Gibbon, Edward (1737–1794) *English historian*
Gibbons, James (1834–1921) *American Roman Catholic cardinal*
Gibbs, Philip (1877–1962) *English novelist*
Gibran, Kahlil (1883–1931) *Syrian-American poet*
Gide, André (1869–1951) *French author*
Gill, F. C. (twentieth century) *English divine*
Gill, Thomas H. (1819–1906) *English divine, hymnist*
Gillilan, Strickland (1869–1954) *American poet*
Gillman, F. J. (twentieth century) *English author*
Ginsberg, Louis (twentieth century) *American poet*
Gissing, George (1857–1903) *English author*
Gladden, Washington (1836–1918) *American divine*
Gladstone, William E. (1809–1898) *English statesman*
Glover, T. R. (1869–1943) *English classical scholar*
Goethe, Johann Wolfgang von (1749–1832) *German dramatist*
Goldoni, Carlo (1707–1793) *Venetian dramatist*
Goldsmith, Oliver (1728–1774) *English author*
Goodwin, Thomas (1600–1680) *English divine*
Gore, Charles (1853–1932) *English theologian, bishop*
Gracian, Baltasar (1601–1658) *Spanish philosopher*
Grahame, James (1765–1811) *Scottish poet*
Green, Matthew (1696–1737) *English poet*
Gregory, St.–the Great (540–604) *Roman ecclesiastic*
Grenfell, Wilfrid (1865–1940) *English missionary doctor*

Grote, Harriet (1792–1878) *English biographer*

"Anastasius Grün"—A. A. Auersperg (1806–1876) *Austrian poet*

Guedella, Philip (1889–1944) *English historian*

Guest, Edgar A. (1881–1959) *English-American poet*

Guinizelli, G. (c. 1240–1276) *Italian poet*

Guiterman, Arthur (1871–1943) *American poet*

H., G. (untraced)

Hagger, J. O. (twentieth century) *English divine*

Hall, Charles A. (1872–1965) *English divine*

Hall, Joseph (1574–1656) *English divine*

Halliday, W. Fearon (twentieth century) *English author*

Hamerton, P. G. (1834–1894) *English critic*

"Gail Hamilton"—Mary Abigail Dodge (1836–1896) *American essayist*

Hamilton, Robert Browning (b. 1880, untraced)

Hamilton, William (1788–1856) *English metaphysician*

Hammarskjöld, Dag (1905–1961) *Swedish secretary general of United Nations*

Hammond, J. L. (1872–1949) *English editor, author*

Hankey, Donald (1884–1916) *English soldier, essayist*

Hannington, James (1847–1885) *English missionary to Africa*

Hare, J. C. and A. W. (1795–1855, 1792–1834) *English divines*

Harnack, Adolf (1851–1930) *German theologian*

Harrison, Benjamin (1833–1901) *American president*

Harvey, F. W. (1888–1957) *English poet*

Hasler, J. Ireland (twentieth century) *English missionary*

Havergal, Frances Ridley (1836–1879) *English hymnist*

Hawkins, G. (twentieth century) *English of prison service staff training college*

Haydon, A. E. (1880–?) *American musicologist*

Hazlitt, William (1778–1830) *English essayist*

Heber, Reginald (1783–1826) *English missionary bishop*

Heiler, Friedrich (1892–1967) *German theologian*

Heine, Heinrich (1797–1856) *German-Jewish poet*

"R. A. Heinlein"—Anson MacDonald (twentieth century) *American novelist*

Helps, Arthur (1813–1875) *English author*

Helwys, Thomas (c. 1550–1616) *English divine*

Henley, William Ernest (1849–1903) *English poet, critic, playwright*

Henry, Matthew (1662–1714) *English Bible commentator*

Heraclitus (c. 500 B.C.) *Greek philosopher*
Herbert, George (1593–1633) *English divine, poet*
Herrick, Robert (1591–1674) *English poet*
Heywood, Thomas (1574?–1641) *English dramatist*
Higham, F. (twentieth century) *Scottish divine*
Hildegaard of Bingen, St. (1098–1179) *German mystic*
Hillerman, Tony (twentieth century) *American novelist*
Hilton, Walter (?–1396) *English mystic*
Hodge, Charles (1797–1878) *American theologian*
Hodgson, Leonard (1889–1969) *English theologian*
Höffding, Harald (1843–1931) *Danish philosopher*
Hoffer, Eric (twentieth century) *American philosopher*
Holland, Josiah G. (1819–1881) *American novelist, poet*
Holmes, John H. (1879–1964) *American divine*
Holmes, Oliver Wendell (1809–1894) *American novelist, poet*
Holtby, Winifred (1898–1935) *English novelist*
Hood, Thomas (1799–1845) *English poet*
Horace, Quintus H. F. (65–8 B.C.) *Roman poet and satirist*
Horne, C. Silvester (1865–1914) *English divine*
Horne, Richard H. (1803–1884) *English poet*
Hosmer, Frederick L. (1840–1929) *American hymnist*
Houghton, Frank (1894–1972) *English bishop, missionary leader*
How, William W. (1823–1897) *English divine*
Howard, Elizabeth F. (twentieth century) *English poet*
Howe, Julia Ward (1819–1910) *American poet*
Hsi, Pastor (?–1896) *Chinese, Confucian scholar*
Hubbard, Elbert (1859–1915) *American essayist*
Hudson, W. Cadwalader (1843–1915) *American publicist*
Hügel, Baron Friedrich von (1852–1925) *Austrian theologian*
Hughes, Thomas (1822–1896) *English biographer, novelist*
Hugo, Victor (1802–1885) *French novelist*
Hunt, Leigh (1784–1859) *English poet, essayist*
Hunter, A. M. (twentieth century) *English biblical scholar*
Huvelin, Abbé (nineteenth century) *French scholar, divine*
Huxley, Aldous (1894–1963) *English novelist*
Huxley, Julian (1887–1975) *English polymath*
Huxley, Thomas H. (1825–1895) *English biologist*
Ibn Omar: see Omar
Ignatius, St. (c. 35–107) *Syrian bishop*
Inge, William R. (1860–1954) *English divine*
Ingelow, Jean (1820–1897) *English poet*
Ingersoll, Robert G. (1833–1899) *American lawyer*

Irenaeus, St. (c. 130–200) *of Smyrna, theologian*
Jacks, L. P. (1860–1955) *English divine*
Jackson, Helen H. (1831–1885) *American novelist, poet*
James, Alice (nineteenth century) *American diarist*
James, P. D. (twentieth century) *English novelist*
James, William (1842–1910) *American psychologist*
Jeans, James (1877–1946) *English astronomer*
Jefferson, Thomas (1743–1826) *American president*
Jerome, St. (c. 342–420) *Italian Bible scholar and translator*
Jerrold, Douglas (1803–1857) *English dramatist*
Jesus (i: New Testament; ii: extra-canonical sayings)
John, St. *apostle, evangelist*
Johnson, Lyndon B. (1908–1973) *American president*
Johnson, Robert Underwood (1853–1937) *American editor, poet*
Johnson, Samuel (1709–1784) *English lexicographer, critic*
Jones, Rufus M. (1863–1948) *American Quaker leader*
Jones, T. S. (1882–1933) *American poet*
Jonson, Ben (1573?–1637) *English poet*
Jordan, D. S. (1851–1931) *American naturalist*
Joubert, Joseph (1754–1824) *French novelist*
Jowett, John Henry (1864–1923) *Scottish divine*
Julian of Norwich, Dame (c. 1343–1413) *English mystic*
Jung, Carl G. (1875–1961) *Swiss psychiatrist*
Justin Martyr, St. (c. 100–165) *Samaritan apologist*
Kant, Immanuel (1724–1804) *German philosopher*
Keats, John (1795–1821) *English poet*
Keble, John (1792–1866) *English poet*
Keller, Helen (1880–1968) *American lecturer*
Kemble, Frances A. (1809–1893) *English actress, poet*
Kemp, Harry (1883–1960) *American poet, playwright*
Ken, Thomas (1637–1711) *English bishop, poet*
Kennedy, John F. (1917–1963) *American president*
Kennedy, Studdert (1883–1929) *Irish/English poet*
Kierkegaard, Søren (1813–1855) *Danish philosopher*
Kipling, Rudyard (1865–1936) *English poet*
Knowles, Frederic L. (1869–1905) *American poet*
Knox, John (c. 1513–1572) *Scottish divine*
Knox, Ronald A. (1888–1957) *English divine*
Koran, The (7th century) *sacred book of Islam*
Krummacher, Cornelius (1824–1884) *German divine*
Krutch, Joseph Wood (1893–1970) *American critic, essayist*
Lamb, Charles (1775–1834) *English essayist*

Lambly, Norman E. (? dates) *American poet*
Landor, W. S. (1775–1864) *English poet, essayist*
Langer, Susanne K. (twentieth century) *American philosopher*
Langhorne, John (1735–1779) *English poet*
Langland, William (c. 1330–1400) *English poet*
La Harpe, J. F. de (1739–1803) *French poet*
Lanier, Sidney (1842–1881) *American poet, naturalist*
Lao Tse (c. 604–531 B.C.) *Chinese philosopher*
Larcom, Lucy (1824–1893) *American poet*
La Rochefoucauld, see Rochefoucauld
Latimer, Hugh (1485?–1555) *English divine*
Law, Robert (1860–1919) *Scottish theologian*
Law, William (1686–1761) *English divine*
Lawrence, St. (martyred 258) *Spanish church treasurer at Rome*
Lawton, George (untraced)
Lec, Stanislaw (twentieth century) *Polish poet*
Lerner, Max (twentieth century) *Russian-American author*
Lewes, G. H. (1817–1878) *English writer*
Lewis, H. D. (twentieth century) *English philosopher*
Lewisohn, Ludwig (1883–1955) *German-American novelist, critic*
Libanius (314–393) *Syrian pagan lecturer*
Lichtenberg, Georg C. (1742–1799) *German physicist*
Lincoln, Abraham (1809–1865) *American president*
Livy, Titus L. (59 B.C.–17 A.D.) *Roman historian*
Locke, John (1632–1704) *English philosopher*
Lofts, Norah (twentieth century) *English novelist*
London Review (1859)
Longfellow, Henry Wadsworth (1807–1882) *American poet*
Lowell, James Russell (1819–1891) *American poet*
Loyola, Ignatius (1491–1556) *founder of the Society of Jesus*
Lucan, Marcus A. (39–65) *Roman poet*
Luther, Martin (1483–1546) *German theologian, reformer*
Lyly, John (1554?–1606) *English dramatist*
Lynch, Thomas T. (1818–1871) *English hymnist*
Lynd, Robert (1879–1949) *Irish essayist*
Lysaght, Sydney (1874–1941) *Irish writer*
Lyte, Henry Francis (1793–1847) *English hymnist*
Macdonald, George (1824–1905) *Scottish divine, novelist, poet*
Mackintosh, Hugh Ross (1870–1936) *Scottish theologian*
"Ian Maclaren"—John Watson (1850–1907) *Scottish divine*
MacNicoll, Nicol (1870–1952) *Scottish translator*
Maeterlinck, Maurice (1862–1949) *Belgian poet, essayist*

Magna Carta (English "Charter of Personal and Political Liberty," 1215)

Malloch, Douglas (1877–1938) *American poet, author*

Malone, Walter (1866–1915) *American jurist, poet*

Maltby, W. R. (1866–1951) *English divine*

Mann, Thomas (1875–1955) *German novelist, essayist*

Manning, Bernard L. (1892–1941) *English hymnologist*

Maritain, Jacques (1882–1973) *French theologian*

Markham, Edwin (1852–1940) *American poet*

Marquis, Don (1878–1937) *American author*

Marrou, H. I. (twentieth century) *French church historian*

Marsh, Ngaio (twentieth century) *New Zealander novelist*

Martineau, James (1805–1900) *English theologian*

Marvell, Andrew (1621–1678) *English poet*

Mary of Nazareth

Mason, William (1725–1797) *English divine, poet*

Massey, Gerald (1828–1907) *English poet, mystic*

Massieu, Jean Baptiste (1742–1818) *French divine*

Massinger, Philip (1583–1640) *English playwright*

Mathams, W. J. (1853–1931) *English divine*

Matheson, George (1842–1906) *Scottish divine*

Maugham, W. Somerset (1874–1965) *English novelist*

Maurice, F. D. (1805–1872) *English theologian*

May, G. Lacey (twentieth century) *English poetry anthologist*

Mazzini, Giuseppe (1805–1872) *Italian patriot, writer*

McComiskey, T. E. (twentieth century) *American biblical scholar*

McFadyen, J. E. (1870–1933) *Scottish divine*

McGinley, Phyllis (twentieth century) *American essayist, poet*

McIver, C. D. (1860–1906) *American educator*

McMullen, Mary (twentieth century) *American novelist*

Medea, in Greek mythology, wife of Jason

Meir, Golda (1898–1978) *Jewish prime minister of Israel*

Melanchthon, Philipp (1497–1560) *German theologian*

Melville, Andrew (1545–c. 1622) *Scottish theologian*

Melville, Herman (1819–1891) *American novelist, poet*

Menander (c. 342–292 B.C.) *Greek playwright*

Menzies, Robert (twentieth century) *Scottish divine*

Meredith, George (1828–1909) *English novelist, poet*

"Owen Meredith"—E. Robert Bulwer Lytton (1831–1891) *English poet, novelist*

Meynell, Alice (1847–1922) *English poet, essayist*

Michelangelo (1475–1564) *Italian artist, poet*

Midlane, Albert (1825–1909) *English hymnist*
Mill, John Stuart (1806–1873) *English philosopher, economist*
Milton, John (1608–1674) *English poet*
Mizner, Addison (1872–1933) *American writer*
Monsell, John S. B. (1811–1875) *English hymnist*
Montague, C. E. (1867–1928) *English editor, novelist*
Montaigne, Michel de (1533–1592) *French essayist*
Montesquieu, Charles-Louis de S. (1689–1755) *French philosopher*
Montgomery, James (1771–1854) *Scottish poet*
Moody, Dwight L. (1837–1899) *American evangelist*
Moore, Thomas (1779–1852) *Irish poet*
More, Hannah (1745–1833) *English writer*
Moreland, J. R. (1880–1947) *American poet*
Morgan, Angela (twentieth century) *American poet*
Morgan, _____ (twentieth century) *Scottish theologian*
Morley, Christopher (1890–1957) *American novelist, essayist*
Morley, John (1838–1923) *English statesman, author*
Morris, C. H. (twentieth century) *English hymnist*
Moule, Handley G. C. (1841–1920) *English divine*
Mullins, E. Y. (1860–1928) *American divine*
Murrow, Edward R. (1908–1965) *American news commentator*
Murry, John Middleton (1889–1956) *English author*
Myers, Frederic W. H. (1843–1901) *English poet, essayist*
Nabokov, Vladimir (1899–1977) *Russian poet, novelist*
Napoléon I (1769–1821) *Emperor of France*
Neander, Joachim (1650–1680) *German historian, hymnist*
Neaves, Lord Charles (1800–1876) *English jurist*
Neill, Stephen (twentieth century) *English biblical scholar*
Nelson, Reuben (twentieth century) *American divine*
Neumark, Georg (1621–1681) *German poet*
Newman, John Henry (1801–1890) *English divine*
Newton, Isaac (1642–1727) *English scientist*
Newton, John (1725–1807) *English hymnist*
Nimitz, Chester W. (1885–1966) *American admiral*
Noel, R. B. W. (1834–1894) *English divine*
Norden, Eduard (twentieth century) *German classical scholar*
Norris, W. E. (1847–1925) *English novelist*
Oldham, J. H. (1874–1969) *Scottish divine*
Omar, Ibn Al-Khattab (c. 581–644) *second caliph of Islam*
Orchard, W. E. (1877–1955) *English divine*
O'Reilly, J. B. (1844–1890) *Irish-American poet*
O'Shaughnessy, Arthur (1844–1881) *English poet*

Ostrogorski, M. Y. (1854–1919) *Russian sociologist*
Ottley, R. L. (1856–1933) *English theologian*
Ovid, Publius (43 B.C.–17 A.D.) *Roman poet*
Owen, John (1616–1683) *English theologian*
Owen, Wilfred (1893–1918) *English poet*
Paget, Francis (1851–1911) *English divine*
Paine, Thomas (1737–1809) *English-American political theorist*
Palgrave, Francis T. (1824–1897) *English poet, anthologist*
Palladas (fl. 400) *Greek epigrammatist*
"Panchatantra" (fifth century?) *Sanskrit folklore*
Parker, Joseph (1830–1902) *English divine*
Parker, Theodore (1810–1860) *American divine*
Parkhurst, C. H. (1842–1933) *American divine*
Parkinson, C. N. (twentieth century) *English writer*
Parnell, Thomas (1679–1718) *Irish poet*
Pascal, Blaise (1623–1662) *French moralist*
Patmore, Coventry (1823–1896) *English poet*
Paul, St. *apostle and martyr*
"Acts of Paul and Thecla": Abstract from "Acts of Paul," apocryphal
    book of mid-second century
Peacock, Thomas L. (1785–1866) *English novelist, poet*
Penn, William (1644–1718) *English-American Quaker leader*
Peter, St. *apostle and martyr*
"Ellis Peters"—Edith Pargeter (twentieth century) *English novelist*
Petrarch, F. (1304–1374) *Italian poet, biographer*
Phillips, Stephen (1864–1915) *English poet, dramatist*
Philo Judaeus (c. 20 B.C.–c. 40 A.D.) *Jewish philosopher*
Piggott, W. Charter (1872–1943) *English divine*
Plato (428–347 B.C.) *Greek philosopher*
Plautus, T. M. (fl. 254–184 B.C.) *Roman dramatist, poet*
Pliny, the Elder (23–79 A.D.) *Italian historian, encyclopaedist*
Plumptre, Edward H. (1821–1891) *English divine*
Plunkett, J. M. (1887–1916) *Irish poet*
Plutarch (fl. 66) *Greek moralist, biographer*
Plymouth Hymnal (1893?) *American*
Pollock, Robert (1798–1827) *Scottish poet*
Polycarp, St. (c. 69–155) *of Smyrna, "Apostolic Father," martyr*
Pope, Alexander (1688–1744) *English poet*
Pott, Francis (1832–1909) *English hymnist*
Praed, Winthrop Mackworth (1802–1839) *English poet*
Preston, Keith (1884–1927) *American poet*
Prior, Matthew (1664–1721) *English poet, diplomat*

Proctor, Adelaide A. (1825–1864) *English poet*
Protagoras (c. 485–415 B.C.) *Greek philosopher*
Proudhon, Pierre J. (1809–1865) *French political theorist*
Publilius Syrus (fl. 43 B.C.) *Latin epigrammatist*
Pullen, Alice M. (1889–?) *English hymnist*
Pusey, E. B. (1800–1882) *English theologian*
Quarles, Francis (1592–1644) *English poet*
Quiller-Couch, A. T. (1863–1944) *English professor of literature, novelist*
Quinault, Philippe (1635–1688) *French poet, dramatist*
Quintilian, Marcus F. (c. 35–99) *Roman rhetorician*
Raleigh, Sir Walter (1554–1618) *English courtier, author*
Raleigh, Walter A. (1861–1922) *English literary scholar*
Ralston, Isobel (twentieth century) *Scottish teacher*
Ramsey, Arthur Michael (1904–) *English, Archbishop of Canterbury*
Ramsey, Paul (twentieth century) *English moralist*
Rashdall, Hastings (1858–1924) *English theologian*
Rathbone Family (Six generations) *English philanthropists*
Rauschenbusch, Walter (1861–1918) *American divine*
Rawson, George (1807–1889) *English hymnist*
Ray, John (1627–1705) *English naturalist*
Reade, Charles (1814–1884) *English novelist*
Remond, C. Lenox (1810–1873) *American abolitionist, orator*
Renan, J. Ernest (1823–1892) *French literary scholar*
Richter, Jean Paul Friedrich (1763–1825) *German novelist, humorist*
Ridley, Nicholas (c. 1500–1555) *English ecclesiastic, martyr*
Ritschl, Albrecht (1822–1889) *German theologian*
Roberts, Richard (1879–1945) *English divine*
Robinson, Forbes (1867–1904) *English university chaplain*
Robinson, G. Wade (1838–1877) *Irish hymnist*
Robinson, N. H. G. (twentieth century) *English theologian*
Rochefoucauld, François Duc de La (1613–1680) *French epigrammatist*
Rogers, Will (1879–1935) *American actor, humorist*
Roosevelt, Franklin Delano (1882–1945) *American president*
Roosevelt, Theodore (1858–1919) *American president*
Rossetti, Christina (1830–1894) *English poet*
Rossetti, Dante Gabriel (1828–1882) *English poet*
Roux, Joseph (1834–1905) *French divine*
Royce, Josiah (1855–1916) *American philosopher*
Rusk, Dean (twentieth century) *American statesman*

Ruskin, John (1819–1900) *English art critic*
Russell, A. J. (twentieth century) *English author*
Russell, Bertrand (1872–1970) *English philosopher*
Rutherford, Samuel (c. 1600–1661) *Scottish divine*
Ruysbroeck, Johannes (1293–1381) *Flemish mystic*
Sa'di-Shaiki-a-Din (c. 1258) *Persian poet*
Saint-Exupéry, Antoine de (1900–1944) *French author*
Saintsbury, George E. B. (1845–1933) *English critic*
Sandburg, Carl (1878–1967) *American poet*
Santayana, George (1863–1952) *Spanish-American philosopher*
Sarah, wife of Abraham
Sargant, W. A. (twentieth century) *English medical psychologist*
Sartre, Jean-Paul (1905–1980) *French philosopher, playwright*
Saunders, Frederick (1807–1902) *American essayist*
Savile, George (1633–1695) *English pamphleteer*
Sayers, Dorothy (1893–1957) *English novelist, essayist*
Schiller, J. C. Friedrich von (1759–1805) *German poet, dramatist*
Schweitzer, Albert (1875–1965) *Alsatian theologian, missionary*
Scott, E. F. (1868–1954) *Scottish New Testament scholar*
Scott, Sir Walter (1771–1832) *Scottish novelist, poet*
Scupoli, Lorenzo (sixteenth century) *Italian inspirational writer*
Seeley, J. R. (1834–1895) *English historian*
Selden, John (1584–1654) *English jurist, scholar*
Selwyn, E. G. (1885–1959) *English divine*
Selwyn, G. A. (1809–1878) *English bishop in New Zealand*
Seneca, L. A. (B.C. 4–65 A.D.) *Roman educationist, moralist*
Shakespeare, William (1564–1616) *English poet, dramatist*
"William Sharp"—Fiona Macleod (1855–1905) *English poet*
Shaw, George Bernard (1856–1950) *Irish dramatist, author*
Shedd, J. A. (1859–?) *American educator, epigrammatist*
Shelley, Percy Bysshe (1792–1822) *English poet*
Shenstone, William (1714–1763) *English poet*
Sheppard, H. R. L. (1880–1937) *English divine*
Sherwood, Robert E. (1896–1955) *American playwright, author*
Shillito, Edward (1872–1948) *English divine, poet*
Sidgwick, Henry (1838–1900) *English moralist*
Sigourney, Lydia H. (1791–1865) *American poet*
Smart, Christopher (1722–1771) *English poet*
Smiles, Samuel (1812–1904) *Scottish inspirational writer*
Smith, Adam (1723–1790) *Scottish economist*
Smith, David (1866–1932) *Scottish New Testament scholar*
Smith, Elizabeth Oakes (1806–1893) *American writer*

Smith, Logan Pearsall (1865–1946) *American critic, essayist*
Smith, Sydney (1771–1845) *English divine*
Smollett, Tobias G. (1721–1771) *Scottish novelist*
Smyth, John (c. 1554–1612) *English divine*
Snowden, Rita (twentieth century) *English inspirational writer*
Sockman, Ralph W. (1889–1970) *American divine*
Sophocles (495–406 B.C.) *Greek poet, dramatist*
Sorley, Charles H. (1895–1915) *Scottish poet*
Southey, Caroline (1786–1854) *English poet*
Southey, Robert (1774–1843) *English poet*
Southwell, Robert (c. 1561–1595) *English poet, martyr*
Spencer, Herbert (1820–1903) *English philosopher*
Spenser, Edmund (1552–1599) *English poet*
Spinoza, Baruch (1632–1677) *Dutch-Jewish philosopher*
Spranger, _____ (nineteenth century) *German inspirational writer*
Spurgeon, Charles H. (1834–1892) *English divine*
Staël, Madame Anne-Louise-Germaine de (1766–1817) *French author*
Stalker, James (1848–1927) *Scottish divine*
Stanley, Arthur Penrhyn (1815–1881) *English divine*
Stansfield, J. S. (1854–1939) *English missioner*
Steele, Richard (1672–1729) *English essayist, dramatist*
Sterne, Laurence (1713–1768) *English novelist*
Stevenson, Adlai (1900–1965) *American lawyer, statesman*
Stevenson, Robert Louis (1850–1894) *Scottish poet, novelist*
Stewart, James S. (twentieth century) *Scottish divine*
Storr, Graham (untraced)
Story, William W. (1819–1895) *American sculptor, poet*
Stowe, Harriet Beecher (1811–1896) *American novelist*
Streeter, B. H. (1874–1937) *English biblical scholar*
Swift, Jonathan (1667–1745) *Irish-English satirist*
Symonds, J. Addington (1840–1893) *English historian, critic*
Tabb, John Bannister (1845–1909) *American poet*
Tacitus, Cornelius (c. 56–120) *Roman lawyer, historian*
Tagore, Rabindranath (1861–1941) *Indian poet, philosopher*
Talmud (fourth century?) *collected Jewish traditions, reflections*
Taylor, Jeremy (1613–1667) *English divine*
Taylor, Vincent (twentieth century) *English New Testament scholar*
Teale, Edwin W. (1899–1980) *American educator, naturalist*
Te Deum Laudamus (fourth century?) *Latin hymn*
Temple, William (1881–1944) *English archbishop*
Tennyson, Lord Alfred (1809–1892) *English poet*

Terence, Publius T. (second century B.C.) *Roman poet, playwright*
Teresa, Mother (twentieth century) *Yugoslav nun, social worker*
Tersteegen, Gerhard (1697–1796) *German mystic, poet*
Tertullian, Quintus S. F. (c. 150–230) *Carthaginian theologian*
Thackeray, William Makepeace (1811–1863) *English novelist*
Thales (c. 624–546 B.C.) *Greek philosopher*
Theognis (sixth century B.C.) *Greek poet*
Thérèse of Lisieux (1873–1897) *French Carmelite nun*
Thomas à Kempis (1379–1471) *German mystic*
Thomas à Becket: see Becket
Thomas, Dylan (1914–1953) *Welsh poet*
Thomas, Edith M. (1854–1925) *American poet*
Thompson, Francis (1859–1907) *English poet*
Thompson, W. H. (1810–1886) *English scholar*
Thomson, James (1700–1748) *Scottish poet*
Thoreau, Henry David (1817–1862) *American essayist, poet*
Thornely, Thomas (1855–1949) *English historian, writer of
    limericks*
Thurber, James (1894–1961) *American journalist, humorist*
Tilak, Narayan Vaman (1862–1919) *Indian teacher, social worker*
Tolstoi, Leo N. (1828–1910) *Russian philosopher, mystic*
Traherne, Thomas (1634?–1704) *English poet*
Trench, Richard C. (1807–1886) *Irish divine, poet*
Trollope, Anthony (1815–1882) *English novelist*
Trowbridge, J. T. (1827–1916) *American novelist, poet*
Tucker, F. Bland (twentieth century) *American divine*
Tung, Father John (martyred c. 1946) *Chinese Christian leader*
Tupper, Martin F. (1810–1889) *English moralist, poet*
Tuttiett, Lawrence (1825–1897) *English divine*
"Mark Twain"—Samuel Langhorne Clemens (1835–1910)
    American author
Twells, Henry (1823–1900) *English divine*
Ullmann, Samuel (untraced)
Unamuno, Miguel de (1864–1936) *Spanish philosopher, poet*
Underhill, Evelyn (1875–1941) *English writer on mysticism*
Underhill, Francis (twentieth century) *English divine*
UNESCO Constitution, 1945
Ussher, Howard (untraced)
Ustinov, Peter (twentieth century) *English actor, playwright*
Vahanian, Gabriel (twentieth century) *American educator*
Van Dyke, Henry (1852–1933) *American divine, poet*
Van Engen, J. (twentieth century) *American historian*

Vasari, Giorgio (1511–1574) *Italian art historian*
Vaughan, Henry (1622–1695) *Welsh poet*
Vauvenargues, Marquis (1715–1747) *French moralist*
Vedder, David (1790–1854) *Scottish poet*
Vere, Aubrey de (1814–1902) *Irish dramatist, poet*
Vere, D. W. (twentieth century) *English medical practitioner*
Vine, A. H. (1845–1917) *English divine, poet*
Von Hügel see Hügel
Walker, William (1623–1684) *English schoolmaster*
Waller, Edmund (1606–1687) *English poet*
Walter, Howard A. (1883–1918) *American divine*
Walton, Izaak (1593–1683) *English biographer, essayist*
Wanley, Nathaniel (1634–1680) *English divine, poet*
Ward, (Mrs. Humphrey Mary Augusta (1851–1920) *English
    novelist, biographer, social worker*
Waring, Anna L. (1823–1910) *English hymnist*
Warren, Earl (twentieth century) *American jurist*
Washbourne, Thomas (1608–1687) *English poet*
Washington, Booker T. (1856–1915) *American educator, author*
Washington, George (1732–1799) *American president*
Watson, William (1858–1935) *English poet*
Watt, Lauchlan Maclean (1867–1957) *Scottish divine*
Wattles, Willard A. (1880–1950) *American educator, poet*
Watts, Isaac (1674–1748) *English theologian, hymnist*
Weatherhead, Leslie (1893–1976) *English divine, author*
Webb, Mary (1881–1927) *English novelist*
Webster, Daniel (1782–1852) *American statesman, orator*
Weeks, Edward (twentieth century) *American lecturer, essayist*
Weiss, Johan (1818–1879) *American divine, critic*
Wells, H. G. (1866–1946) *English novelist, social analyst*
Wesley, Charles (1707–1788) *English hymnist*
Wesley, John (1703–1791) *English divine*
Whale, J. S. (twentieth century) *English divine*
Whetstone, George (1551?–1587) *English writer*
Whichcote, Benjamin (1606–1683) *English philosopher, divine*
Whitcomb, Selden L. (1866–1930) *American educator*
White, Glenda A. (twentieth century) *English educationist*
Whitefield, George (1714–1770) *English divine, evangelist*
Whitehead, Alfred North (1861–1947) *English philosopher*
Whitman, Walt (1819–1892) *American poet, essayist*
Whittier, John Greenleaf (1807–1892) *American poet*
Whittle, David W. (1840–1901) *American soldier, evangelist*

Wilde, Oscar (1856–1900) *Irish poet, playwright*
Wiley, Hiram O. (1831–1873) *American lawyer*
Willis, L. Maria (1824–1908) *American hymnist*
Wilson, Edward (1872–1912) *English Antarctic explorer*
Wilson, Thomas (1663–1755) *English divine*
Wilton, Richard (1827–1903) *English poet*
Winter, William (1836–1917) *American poet, critic*
Winward, Stephen (twentieth century) *English divine, inspirational writer*
Wodehouse, Helen (1880–1964) *English author*
Wolfenden, John (twentieth century) *English educator*
Wood, H. G. (1879–1963) *English historian, theologian*
Woodberry, George E. (1855–1930) *American poet, critic*
Wordsworth, Christopher (1774–1846) *English divine, educator*
Wordsworth, William (1770–1850) *English poet*
Wycliffe, John (c. 1329–1384) *English divine*
Wyon, Olive (twentieth century) *English author, translator*
Xavier, Francis (1506–1552) *Spanish missionary*
Xenophon (c. 431–c. 352 B.C.) *Greek historian, essayist*
Young, Edward (1683–1765) *English poet*
Zola, Émile (1840–1902) *French novelist*

SCRIPTURE INDEX